58-13221   Ordered   4/28/59

NATIONS OF THE MODERN WORLD

SCOTLAND   Sir Robert Rait, C.B.E., M.A.,
                  LL.D., and George S. Pryde, M.A.,
                  Ph.D.
                  Revised by G. S. Pryde
                  Reader in Scottish History and
                  Literature, Glasgow

AUSTRALIA   J. C. Horsfall
                  First editor of the AUSTRALIAN FINAN-
                  CIAL REVIEW

EGYPT   Tom Little
                  Arab News Agency, Beirut

FRANCE   P. E. Charvet
                  Fellow of Corpus Christi College
                  and University lecturer in French,
                  Cambridge

MODERN INDIA   Sir Percival Griffiths, C.I.E., I.C.S.
                  (Ret.)
                  Honorary adviser to India, Pakistan
                  and Burma Association

IRAQ   Brig. S. H. Longrigg, O.B.E., D.Litt.
                  Formerly of the Government of Iraq, and
                  the Iraq Petroleum Company
                  and
                  Frank Stoakes
                  Director of Middle Eastern Studies,
                  St. Antony's College, Oxford

A

ISRAEL	Norman Bentwich, O.B.E., M.C., LL.D. (Hon.) *Professor of International Relations, Hebrew University of Jerusalem*
ITALY	Gerardo Zampaglione *Italian Diplomatic Corps*
PORTUGAL	J. B. Trend *Late Fellow Christ's College, and Emeritus Professor of Spanish, Cambridge*
SA'UDI ARABIA	H. St. John Philby, C.I.E., F.R.G.S. *Economic adviser to the late King Abdul-Aziz II, Ibn Sa'ud*
SOUTH AFRICA	J. H. Hofmeyr, B.A., B.Sc. *Revised by* J. P. Cope *Editor-in-chief of* THE FORUM
THE SUDAN	Sir Harold MacMichael, K.C.M.G., D.S.O. *One time Civil Secretary to Sudan Government, and Governor-General*
SYRIA AND LEBANON	Nicola A. Ziadeh, B.A. (Hons.), Ph.D. *Associate Professor of Modern History, American University, Beirut*
TURKEY	Geoffrey Lewis, M.A., D.Phil. (Oxon.) *Senior lecturer in Islamic Studies, Oxford*

IRAQ

IRAQ

By

STEPHEN HEMSLEY LONGRIGG

and

FRANK STOAKES

FREDERICK A. PRAEGER
NEW YORK

BOOKS THAT MATTER

Published in the United States of America
in 1958 by Frederick A. Praeger, Inc.,
Publishers, 15 West 47th Street,
New York 36, N.Y.

*This book is part of the NATIONS OF THE
MODERN WORLD series*

Library of Congress Catalog Card Number
58—13221

PRINTED IN GREAT BRITAIN

Contents

vii

10945

Preface

THE IRAQI revolution, which occurred when this book was at the proof stage, has made parts of the second section—the analysis of the current scene—no less history than the first. The tenses in the political chapter have been altered in recognition of this fact; elsewhere they have been allowed to remain, in the belief that the revolutionary government will, as a matter of fundamental policy, proceed vigorously with the programme of national development and regeneration and that, under whatever régime, many of the essential problems are the same. The fact that these problems have been described in isolation from the rest of the world does not imply that they are peculiar to Iraq; the authors are, on the contrary, convinced that in pursuing her own path of progress and resolving her own problems Iraq is contributing to far more than her own knowledge and advancement. The main body of the book has as far as possible been brought up to the date of the revolution; a very brief account of the revolution itself is given in an epilogue.

The authors wish to acknowledge the generous help they have received from many Iraqi and British friends. Thanks are due particularly to Mr John Shearman, Mr Michael Ionides and Mr M. T. Audsley for their invaluable assistance in preparing the sixth and seventh chapters and to Mr Albert Hourani, Mr Elie Kedourie, Sir Herbert Todd and Sir John Troutbeck for their helpful suggestions throughout the second part of the book, none of whom is however responsible for the opinions expressed. A debt must also be recorded to the admirable publications of the Principal Bureau of Statistics of the Iraqi Government (which, as more specialised in character and less easily available in this country, have been omitted from the short bibliography at the end) and to the personal publications and unfailing assistance of the Director of the Bureau, Dr K. G. Fenelon.

5 *August* 1958

INTRODUCTION

Country and People

Chapter 1

Country and People

AMONG THE NATIONS

A TERRITORY with highly characteristic features, well marked and strongly felt in many fields, the Iraq of the mid-twentieth century can well excite an interest, and inspire a goodwill, out of proportion to its size, population or present material endowment. In it can be studied, with unusual advantage, not only a singular and varied physical conformation, but also the effect of geology, climate and land-surface on generations of human life. Its geographic position, which throughout history has made it part of the great Eurasian landbridge and a highway of peoples and of trade, gave it interest in modern times as a short-cut to India and the East—and as such made it a sphere of rival European diplomacies—and to-day with the advent of peaceful and warlike use of air-communication, raises it also to a place of leading strategic importance in the calculations of hemispheric war and politics, a place lately increased by Iraq's own attainment of a position in the forefront of nations of Western Asia and of the Arab world. A classic case of the age-long absorption of immigrant and intrusive peoples, the population of the territory to-day offers features of unusual interest as a racial and cultural mixture—or, in the Arab-Kurdish dichotomy and in some minor enclaves, of persisting racial distinctness. Its citizens, whether in the political, social, cultural, or economic field, have much to offer in high and sensitive intelligence and the capacity for progress. They have before them for their solution peculiar problems of government, created not least by the varying levels of public enlightenment in their own ranks, the political and social structure of their society, the strongly marked individualism of the national character, and the striking regional differences within the kingdom. The territory, beyond any of its neighbours, possesses such resources of cultivable land and beneficent waters as to assure it an important future as a food-producing country; and its oil-deposits, already under full exploitation, are upon a scale sufficient to interest not merely its own treasury and its neighbours, but the whole energy-consuming world. Based in large part upon this wealth, Iraq as a nation and a society can expect, or is already embarked upon, a rapid material development of not only domestic but considerable foreign interest. The realisation of this development must pose problems of great, and far more than local, significance in the spheres of economics, of industry, of scientific agriculture and irrigation, of rapidly expanding public services, of finance and administration, and—not the least deserving of study—of the abiding east-west dilemma of the modern Islamic world, and the unnaturally rapid evolution of a relatively backward people into the problems and temptations of full modernity.

Meanwhile, Iraq's claim to consideration as the scene of the earliest human civilisation, of the great empires of conquering dynasties at and soon after the dawn of history, with their legacy of famous names, and of a medieval Islamic pre-eminence such as to make Baghdad, for five centuries, almost or quite the leading city of the world, cannot well be contested. From earliest antiquity until the end of the middle ages Iraq's place in the world was one justly eminent in the eyes of civilised man. In no country in the world are archeological remains richer, or more keenly studied. The place of the territory to-day in the tradition of three great religions—Islam, Christianity, Judaism—is considerable, and it contains famous shrines of both the dominant branches (but most notably of the Shi'i branch) of the first-named of these.

The Iraq state, with its present area of some 172,000 square miles, has as its neighbours Persia (Iran) on the east, Turkey on the north, Syria, Jordan and Sa'udi Arabia on the west, and Kuwait and the Persian Gulf on the south. All these are Islamic and all, save Persia and Turkey, are Arab states. It possesses, as a territory, no greater natural unity or delimitation than is roughly indicated by the middle and lower Tigris-Euphrates valley, which forms about half the country: but this does not include the adjoining and similar Iraqi-type flatlands of the lower Karun, which belong politically to Persia. On the other hand, the western desertic areas of Iraq are strictly of Arabian character, the uplands of the Jazira in northern Iraq run continuously into Syria without natural frontier, and the mountain country of north-eastern Iraq (home of the Kurds) would belong with greater physical appropriateness to Turkey and Persia. At no time prior to the present century has Iraq formed a state containing all, and only, its present territory; governments with their capitals within it have possessed at times a far greater, at times a far less extent of country. Its present boundaries, which cannot claim to be 'natural' save on part of its eastern frontier, result—like those, after all, of nine states out of ten—not from geography or logic, but from longdrawn war and varied phases of diplomacy and compromise. Its unity must, therefore, be the moral creation of its own subjects. Meanwhile it differs markedly, except in its marginal areas, from any of its neighbours, and possesses its own individuality, character and atmosphere.

Though none of the territory surrounding Iraq is impassable to man or beast, nor has failed at some period (especially in earlier centuries, when movement was wheel-less) to produce its quota of invaders or infiltrators, the most-used approaches to the Iraq plains have been from central and northern Persia, from east-central and southern Anatolia, from north Syria, and (for desert-folk only) from the north and east of the Arabian peninsula. To-day, apart from its narrow but vital foothold on the Persian Gulf, Iraq's outward communications, except for local traffic and some eastward transit-movement, are mainly with the eastern Mediterranean. It is a weakness of its inland position that the latter region is cut off from it by the territory of other states—Syria, Lebanon, Israel, Jordan—whose favour alone can permit transit: that its great southernmost river-stretch, the Shatt al-'Arab, is on one bank Persian; and that its own oceanward sea-route from Basra and the Persian Gulf is narrowed and vulnerable at the Strait of Hormuz as well as at both ends of the Red Sea. It may one day prove no less a drawback that both of its two great rivers rise in Turkey, while the Euphrates passes also, for more than 200 miles of its length, through Syria. These are important hostages to fortune; but on a still wider view there is interest and probable advantage in the remarkable centralness of Iraq's position in the land-mass of the old world: it lies equidistant from West Africa and Eastern China, from Lapland and South Africa, from London and Madras.

The territory possesses a climate admittedly severe and demanding some adaptation to it, but neither unhealthy nor dangerous, though endemic diseases are widespread. Over by far the greatest area of it, the summer (May to October) is extremely hot, dry and cloudless, with prevailing northerly winds (often dust-laden), but blessed with cool nights; a distressing humidity is felt only near swamps and in the extreme south. The summer is somewhat shorter, and the nights colder, in the northern uplands. The winter months are generally mild in the south, colder or at times very cold in the north; frost can occur anywhere. Rainfall occurs only in winter months, preceded often by dusty south winds; it would be more copious if the rain clouds, moving eastwards from the Mediterranean, had not already deposited most of their moisture in Turkey and the Syrian coastal ranges. An average of over 12 inches falls (on about 60 days in the year) on the upper Tigris, 15 inches or more in the north-eastern foothills, but not much more than a third of that deposit, and on only some 20 days in the year, in the south-western and the Basra areas. Wide variation occurs in the yearly rains, resulting in a notorious and (without irrigation) incurable precariousness of agriculture. Though it is commonly believed, on the evidence of geology and land-surface, that in earlier ages a much higher rainfall produced great flood-channels and richer living conditions, it is probable that in fact the high-rainfall period, whose existence is beyond doubt, did not fall within the last half-million years, and was therefore without significance to man. Since at least the dawn of human history, Iraq has doubtless been in scene and climate the sort of country we know to-day; the disappearance of the lion and ostrich, the abandoned alignment of ancient canals, the location of ancient cities in areas now desolate, have other reasons than those of recent climatic change.

VARIETY IN UNITY

THE MAIN zones into which Iraq's land-surface falls to-day reflect faithfully the geological events of the remote past which created them. The dominant elements in its geological record have been the presence, to the west, of the hard and immobile African-Arabian 'shield', little folded and only marginally (though in places heavily) sedimented: to the north and east, towards central Asia, other resistant areas which have exercised pressure on the regions of softer formation between them and Arabia: and an intermediate area of depression—that of the great Persian Gulf geosyncline—in which occurred the long and deep sea-bed sedimentation of the ancient Tethys Ocean, and part of which was at one stage, or perhaps successive stages, uplifted by powerful and fairly symmetrical folding (partly contemporary with, but partly subsequent to, the main Alpine-Himalayan folding of Eur-Asia), to form the Zagros ranges which in our age mark the eastern and north-eastern flank of the depressed area. West and south-west of these was left a broad belt more gently and, as it stretches westward, decreasingly folded, and to-day largely covered and flattened by recent alluvial deposits. It is in the up-lifted areas (now in Persia) and in the gentler and largely con-cealed folded areas of the intermediate belt—intermediate between the Zagros system and the Arabian shield—that the vast oil resources of modern Iraq and of the Persian Gulf were allowed, by millions of years of organic deposit and favourable stratifica-tion and preservation in the vast geosyncline, to form and to survive. And it was the declivity from the uplifted north of Iraq, and of Turkey beyond that, towards the Persian Gulf depression that enforced the southward run of the Tigris and Euphrates rivers which, with the Karun descending similarly from west-central Persia, have throughout ages brought down the silt to create, out of shallow sea, the still incomplete delta area of central and southern Iraq. This, geologically speaking, rapid reclamation of the northernmost Persian Gulf, which is still proceeding to-day at a rate of one mile in every 50 years, and the formation from it of much of the best-known modern Iraqi countryside by river-borne silt, is a continuing process whose past history is generally agreed. The southward but uneven extension of the main land-mass involved also in places the land-locking of areas of water, and the conversion of these into lakes, then swamps—the 'great swamp' of the middle ages—of which the Hammar Lake to-day survives. And Iraqi history had well begun, its civilisation was already highly developed, before a large part of the territory itself had come into existence: a phenomenon, no doubt, unique in the world's experience.

Obedient to its geological history, Iraq to-day consists of well-marked if overlapping land-areas, in each of which differences of scene, soil, water and conditions are reflected in varying ways of life.

The mountainous region of north-eastern and northern Iraq—strangely unfamiliar to many who claim to 'know the country'—is a region of striking wildness and beauty; the highest peak, Halgurd, exceeds 12,000 feet. With enclosed valleys, occasional plateaux, and hundreds of seasonal water-courses as well as the upper waters of the (Iraqi) Khabur, the two Zab rivers, the 'Udhaim and the Diyala, the region consists of ranges and massifs of bare, or scrub-covered, or forest-covered mountains and hills, with a relatively heavy rainfall, much winter snow, and a cool summer. The area, pierced by a thousand mountain-tracks but roadless until the latest age, forms the southernmost territory of the Kurdish race, whose villages in their hundreds, grouped in the modern provinces of Mosul, Arbil, and Sulaimaniya, give homes to hardy cultivators in the valleys and to herdsmen in the uplands which offer summer grazing. The villages, often built on steep hillsides, are of solid stone-built houses of traditional and still primitive pattern. Cultivation, on rain and in the channelled streams, is practised in the valleys or on terrassed hillsides, and produces grain, rice, vegetables, vines, fruit and tobacco; much of the land surface is, however, uncultivable by reason of its steepness or denudation. The natural vegetation is in part Alpine. The willow, hawthorn, oak and (rarer) pine, the wild pear and almond, grow wild in scenery of varied charm; the stream-beds abound with oleander and tamarisk; the mulberry, walnut and poplar are tended near to the villages. Game birds are the black partridge, snowcock, and two types of hill-partridge. The eagle, bustard and hawk abound among a great variety of bird life. The larger wild animals are the ibex and mouflon, brown bear, snow-leopard and hyena. The ox, mule and donkey are the beasts of burden; the camel, ill at ease in a mountain setting, occasionally visits from the plains.

This mountain zone, together with the lower and more open country to which it breaks down on its southern and south-western face, occupies about one-tenth of the surface of the Iraq state. As much again is the region, that of ancient Assyria, which stretches northward from the Jabal Hamrin range of low hills and covers the modern province of Kirkuk, the flatter western half of Arbil, and that of Mosul excluding its high-mountain area but including its westward extension beyond the Tigris. In this region, lying from 750 to 1,500 feet above sea-level, Arab, Kurd and Turkoman are close neighbours though still easily distinguishable. It is a district of undulating treeless upland; its rainfall, of an average 13 to 15 inches a year, is adequate in most years to produce spring grain-crops without irrigation, and summer vegetables in the beds of drying watercourses. The cultivation in

summer of maize, millet, vetches, oil seed and vegetables is augmented by water-pumping or lifting, and some flow-irrigation,
from the rivers, and by the characteristic *kahriz* system of capturing
sub-surface water. The flora and animal life are less diverse than
in the hills, and of more desertic type: the gazelle and jerboa
appear, the camel flourishes, game is less varied but is increased
by millions of desert-breeding 'sand-grouse'. The rivers are full of
coarse but edible fish. The climate, with shorter summers, less
dust and keener winters than those of lower Iraq, is healthy and
invigorating.

This Assyrian country is extended without barrier westwards
beyond Tigris into and across the Upper Jazira (the 'island'
between Tigris and Euphrates) where, however, different conditions prevail. Except along the banks of the Two Rivers, which
are heavily cultivated by water-lift and peopled by many settlements of cultivators and small market-towns, the Upper Jazira
region is one of light marl or sand, generally flat but with
occasional rises and salty depressions, mainly uncultivable and
able to produce (except in years of generous rainfall) no more than
miserable spring-grazing for the camels of the Shammar tribesmen.
Country of similar type, and in geology as in scene a part of
Arabia rather than of the Fertile Crescent, lies over the whole
western flank of Iraq, from the confines of the Euphrates valley
to the stony or sandy, and wholly barren, uplands of northern
Arabia. This wide area, all destitute of cultivation and offering
only the scantiest pasture and infrequent waterholes, belongs to
the Iraqi provinces of Dulaim, Karbala, Diwaniya and Muntafiq;
it is the rainless, sand-strewn domain of pure Arab-tribal
nomadism, under steppe-desert conditions as remote as is well
imaginable from the cool Mountain-Zone and the lush river-
valleys alike. Two-thirds of the whole surface of Iraq consists of
this valueless, inhospitable wilderness, into the nearer fringes of
which the half-nomadic riverain tribes (or nomadic sections of
settled tribes) send their sheep and goat grazing-parties in the
spring, to enjoy its powdering of light grass and its tough camel-
thorn: and from which the pure camel-breeding desert-folk
approach (not always harmlessly) the waters and markets of the
settled areas in the season of worst heat and aridity. These are
the typical movements of desert economics and society in every
part of Arabia, in the politics and councils of which the Iraqi *badu*
have ever had their place with the rest.

Below the latitude of old Assyria and the barren Northern
Jazira, and wedged between the North-Arabian desert and the
Persian hills south of Diyala, lies the most characteristic area of
Iraq. It forms the central-Iraqi provinces of Baghdad, Diyala,
Kut, Hilla, Diwaniya, 'Amara, Muntafiq and Basra. Separated
by a clear demarcation from northern Iraq as from western, the
country is that of the true Tigris-Euphrates delta, geologically of
recent date. Characterised by extreme alluvial flatness and the
absence of all stone, it extends unbroken also south-eastward
across the modern Persian frontier into the plain and delta of the
Karun. The southernmost part of the Iraq plain offers the great
river-highway of the Shatt al-'Arab, debouching on the Gulf:
this is lined by immense well-ordered groves of date-trees, behind
which, westward, lie desert and marsh. North-west of Basra, for
some 200 miles, lower Iraq consists of stark desert, wherever
irrigation has not reached it: of vast marshes and seasonal in-
undations where flood-water is uncontrolled or survives in
permanent lakes from an earlier age: of extensive date gardens:
of rice fields, flooded every spring: and of cornfields made possible
by irrigation channels which take water at high flood, and by
works of controlled irrigation or pump-lift which secure the spring
grain-crops—the rainfall of a mere 8 to 4 inches a year being quite
inadequate—and the smaller areas of summer grains, cotton and
vegetables. The water-buffalo is the characteristic animal of the
region, fishing a source of livelihood to many. Houses of reed-
matting in the marshes—including the imposing and highly
evolved reed-palaces of the greater shaikhs—and of sun-baked
mud and date-fronds in the dry lands, are the normal dwelling,
and have changed little for many centuries.

Central Iraq—the old Turkish vilayet of Baghdad—is similar
in scene, with less area of marshland, smaller palm-groves, better
controlled waters, and narrower expanse of waterless desert
enclaves. The country is marked by many lines of ancient canals—
and, indeed, of former, now abandoned, beds of the main Rivers
themselves—and some stagnant drainage-lakes survive. Cultivation
of wheat and barley, but not of rice, is possible wherever water
can reach, and offers wide possibilities for scientific irrigation;
limited areas are devoted to cotton, to market gardening and to
fruit other than dates. Agriculture, in central as in all other
parts of Iraq, is the accepted way of life, and is pursued on its
age-long traditional lines in every varying province, except where

modern means and methods have made a local but significant appearance.

THE PEOPLE

How ALMOST universally Iraq is an agricultural country except in the towns and the marshes and among the true camel-breeding, tent-dwelling nomads of the western desert, the upper Jazira and some lesser enclave areas, has been already suggested; and it has been seen that, from the fringe of the Turkish and Persian mountains to the warm waters of the Persian Gulf, Iraqi society is grouped in settlements ranging from a few hovels in gardens or on the fringe of corn or rice-fields, to compact mud-built villages, small market towns with a growing pride in good order and amenity, the bigger provincial towns, now rapidly extending and modernising—Nasiriya, 'Amara, Kut, Hilla, Najaf, Karbala, Ba'quba, Kirkuk, Arbil—and the three great cities of Basra, Mosul and the capital Baghdad, with their spreading suburbs.

Throughout the territory, a general similarity of culture does not, it is evident, preclude considerable or even striking local differences of scene and atmosphere. Every town possesses its own distinctive characteristics derived from its history and setting, its special mixture of population, its aspect and building-style, and its place in administrative or economic or tribal life, while a world of such difference exists—has doubtless existed throughout history—between the countryside settlements and townships of the desert edge, the lush rice-lands, the trim suburban fields, the deep date-groves, the upland grain-lands, the riverain villages busy with water-lift and sailing-craft, the high and remote homes of Kurdish Aghas: all of which, however, have their place in the Iraqi scene, society and national politics of to-day.

Such strongly-marked divergencies between various areas of Iraq, which seem to exceed those normal to a politically unified country of moderate area and small population, give both charm and richness, and multiply aspects of interest; but they involve the presence, at least potentially, of endemic conflicts between (for instance) the desert and the sown, between mountain and plain, Kurd and Arab, tribe and town. They involve the risk of a regionalism destructive of unity of sentiment, and perhaps of national loyalty: the regionalism of a tribal *dira*, of a great provincial city, of a religious centre—Karbala, Najaf, Samarra—or

of northern or southern as opposed to central Iraq. They involve
the danger of imperfect comprehension between the dwellers in
different areas, with their varying orientations of mind, habit
and economies. They emphasise the widely differing stages in
cultural evolution reached by various strata, and districts, of the
population, precluding unity of conception and aspiration among
the Iraqi electorate. And the attraction of familiar trans-frontier
neighbours can distract from the politically desired centripetal
force of the Capital and its domestic loyalties: frontier-dwelling
Kurds can tend to look to Persia or Russia, Mosul Christians to
French patrons in the Levant, *badu* of western Iraq to tribal
dignitaries of Arabia.

Accepting the facts of local variation and, *prima facie*, of
imperfect internal unity, the enquirer will next ask 'Of what,
then, does the Iraqi population itself consist, and what significant
differences exist within it?' The brief answer will be that it consists
of Arabs and Kurds, with certain other small communities, to an
approximate total number (in 1957) of six and a half million;
and that the social differences it contains are characteristic and
important.

The Arab character of the mass of the Iraq people cannot be
questioned, but can with profit be more closely examined. Of such
a character or claim there was, of course, no dominance until the
seventh century of our era, though Arabia, then as now, was an
active and at times an invading or infiltrating neighbour. The
pages hereinafter to be devoted to Iraq's history will show in what
circumstances an Arab and an Islamic character was imposed
upon its aboriginal and mixed un-Arab population. Of 'pure
Arab blood' (itself a myth, since even primitive Arabia was racially
mixed) there can be no question in a land whose settled population,
composed (as will be seen) of many elements, had with essential
continuity lived and bred in its villages for millennia bfore Arabism
appeared as one further contribution. But the prevalence (save in
Kurdistan) of the Arabic language and pride in that culture, the
self-identification of the people with Arab history and tradition,
the emotional consciousness and approval of Arab claims in
modern politics, the grouping of much of the country on an
Arab-tribal basis, and even the claimed descent of many families—
or whole tribes—from an Arabian source, leave no doubt that the
claim to be 'Arab' cannot be gainsaid. This applies to town,
countryside and tribe alike, and includes such non-Islamic

elements as the Arabic-speaking Christian communities to be found in the greater cities, and in the Mosul plain. Indeed, though much might be written of the persistent connection (or at certain times and places, indeed, the near-identification) between Arabism and Islam, they must in the modern world be held distinct: neither in Iraq nor other modern Arab states has religion formed a barrier against acceptance within the Arab community, and often within its politically most militant ranks. At the same time the extent to which a self-conscious Arab sentiment influences the nomad, the townsman or the village cultivator, tribal or otherwise, can evidently vary within the widest limits both personal and environmental.

In physique and appearance the Iraqis show clearly the heterogeneity of their origins. The small-boned slightness of peninsular Arabs is far from universal, skull-forms are long, broad, or medium, bodily structure and stature show no uniformity, colour ranges from the pigments of central Africa to those of southern Europe (with the latter predominating in urban areas), facial type is no less various though normally pleasing. Traces of recent African-negro admixture are clear in individuals and families, the 'Armenian' head-shape in others, traces of 'Turkish' or Mongoloid cheekbones can be seen in the old Assyrian region, and the fineness of the central-Arabian among the western desert folk. The Kurds are distinguishable by a generally heavier or tougher build, more deliberate motions, and their different dress. The loose, convenient clothing of the Iraqi countryside and villages, with its characteristic brown flowing cloak and blue or red cotton head-dress was until recently in universal use. but *kaffiya* and *'agal* have given place in the last generation to dress of European pattern in the towns, schools, and Army.

Within the Arab community certain distinctions are to be drawn as having sometimes political, sometimes social interest, or both. Those of dialect have little of either; though each area has its peculiarities, and it is easy to tell by speech a Mosulawi from a native of 'Ana, or the lower Euphrates, or Basra, these are of little significance; the 'higher colloquial' of polite society differs little, while the style of the newspapers and public speakers is strictly uniform. In general, the Arabic of Iraq is phonetically purer than that of the Levant or Egypt, and uses a rich vocabulary, but owes to its long Turkish occupation a perceptible (perhaps now diminishing) accretion of Turkish words. The Iraqi like his

Arab brothers elsewhere, is fortunate that his native language—
an unceasing source of pride to every Arab—is equally that of a
dozen other states, from whom he need feel no barrier but every
affinity.

The deep cleavage in Islam itself, between the followers of the
Sunna (orthodox traditions of the Prophet) and the Shi'a, or
Schism, divides Iraq more conspicuously and more evenly,
perhaps, than other Arab or Islamic lands. The difference,
originally political, became centuries ago doctrinal and meta-
physical also, and has for ages in Iraq possessed a considerable
social and political significance. Northern and part of central
Iraq is Sunni; southern and part of central Iraq is Shi'i; and from
considerations of family to those of religious discipleship, from
urban to tribal groupings, and from political affinities to a greatly
differing share (in Turkish times, and not without some survival
to-day) in public life, education and appointments, the two great
communities of Islamic Iraq have for long years shown significant
distinctness and often mutual antipathy. This is to-day diminishing, by reason of closer intercommunication, the advance of
modernity—and perhaps of religious indifference—and the shared
fields of present-day endeavour in political and economic effort.
The powerful influence of the Shi'i *mujtahid* and his theocratic
conceptions, the exclusion of the Shi'i from public office, and the
mutual aversion of the two communities, are fast passing away.

The same may be largely, but will never be wholly, true of the
Muslim-Christian distinction, still perceptible in fields beyond
that merely of religion. There is normally no intermarriage;
some difference in cast of thought is perceptible, by reason of
differing community traditions, and one finds among the
Christians a greater specialisation of occupation (in trade, the
professions, and industry) and inevitably a continuing sense of
minority status within the Arab fold. The Arab-Christian communities are those of the Chaldeans (who are Nestorians converted
to Catholicism), Syrian Orthodox and Syrian Catholics (fewer),
Greek Orthodox and Greek Catholics, and a very few Protestants.
These are recognised by government as legally authorised communities. Except for the Chaldean villages around Mosul, all are
town dwellers. Their educational level is relatively high, their
participation in local politics sometimes hesitant, sometimes
enthusiastic. Other Arab-speaking but non-Arab minorities—
Armenians, Jews, Mandeans—will be referred to hereinafter.

It would have been possible, a generation ago, to speak with confidence of clear lines of distinction between a ruling or potentially ruling urban minority and the more backward folk of the tribes or countryside. And, indeed, such differences of education, awareness, evolution and aspiration are still perceptible: the western-educated intelligentsia still stands far (not least in its own estimation) from the buffalo-breeder of the marshes, or the nomad, or the still illiterate villager at his plough. But these are distinctions which, if still real and indeed striking, must become yearly less categorical with the outward spread of education, the speed and ease of inter-communication, the attractions of urban life, and wireless broadcasting. The acute observer must allow already for less heterogeneity in evolutionary levels than in former years, and for still speedier assimilation in the future.

The same is doubtless true of tribalism itself. The institution of the Arab tribe is infinitely various in its scale and degree of cohesion and subdivision, its measure of discipline, its habit of life, its mythical or factual, topographic or utilitarian nuclei of loyalty; and the limits of the tribal communities are, except in the desert, hard to assign as they merge into areas of tribeless folk, are fragmented and assimilated, or (save for individuals in their hour of need) allow tribal devotions to fade and die under stress of other interests and loyalties. Iraq, a country of famous tribes both nomadic and settled, and known as such to the world at large, is to-day a country of disintegrating tribalism, in which modern influences have for years tended to diminish, and little is likely to occur to increase, the hold of the tribe as an important background of life. Even though for two or three generations to come tribal pride may be felt, and tribal claims—to land, to immunity, to precedence—may be heard, it is likely that the fate of the Scottish clans may befall the lately tribe-conscious Iraqis of the 19th and earlier centuries. It is a form of grouping which, in settled areas and under a government of modern type, has to-day no irreplaceable functions or necessity. But meanwhile the shaikhs of important tribes, whatever their habitat and the environment of their followers, are still figures of interest, often of distinction, in Iraqi society and politics, and they include men of ability and influence.

This, in spite of certain differences between Arab and Kurdish tribes, is no less true of the latter than of the former; indeed,

Kurdish tribalism, except in the remotest areas, is increasingly threatened by education, modern communications, town-life, and rival claims to the interest and loyalty of the younger generation of Kurds. The latter race forms the greatest of non-Arab minorities in the territory, and little short of a million live within Iraq in the higher mountains and lower hills of the north-east. Both their racial group and their environment have full continuity with those of the adjoining Persian and Turkish Kurds: the race, purest Iranian and perhaps direct successor of the Medes, is thus incurably partitioned and, in spite of abortive movements and isolated champions—in spite also of a developed and sometimes a militant sense of racial pride and distinctness—has never achieved national status. These Kurds are by vast majority agriculturalists, with a minority of herdsmen still partly (but far less than half a century ago) nomadic as between summer and winter pastures. Their standard of life is low, though higher perhaps than that of the Arab countryside, and their living conditions are simple. The movement into the towns—Sulaimaniya, Arbil, Kirkuk—has been marked in recent years, and an urban Kurdish middle class is, for the first time in history, in process of formation. The Kurdish language, of which the southern or Kurmanj branch prevails in Iraq, is an Aryan tongue akin to, but not derived from, Persian; it has been written, and has acquired an infant literature, only within the last thirty years, and there are pronounced dialect differences within the Kurdish area. Many leading Kurds spoke also Turkish in the days of that Empire, and more, apart from bilingual villages and tribes close to Arab territory, speak Arabic as a second language to-day. Their religion is, with small enclaves of dissident Sufi sects, that of strict Sunnism of the Shafi'i or Qadiri schools: it is, indeed, through this circumstance that the Sunni population of Iraq, between Kurd and Arab, narrowly outnumbers the Shi'i. Of the Iraqi-Kurdish political attitude and fortunes in recent days, more will be said on later pages. The character of the people is dour, hardy, and virile, with less (but still not negligible) social and imaginative graces than the Arab, but an equal appreciation of the essential Islamic code. Between Kurd and Arab there is in popular sentiment, regrettably, a general antipathy and little mutual respect.

The lesser minorities, or non-Arab culture-groups, surviving in modern Iraq are rather interesting than significant. Nearest to the Kurds, probably, in racial origins are the Yazidis. These, of whom most live in a compact group in the Jabal Sinjar due west of Mosul, with a smaller group at their shrine of Shaikh 'Adi north of that city, form a community unusually isolated not only in habitat and language—a dialect akin to Kurdish—but in the exclusiveness of their peculiar religion. Of this, which incorporates Islamic, Christian and pagan elements, the best-known feature is their careful propitiation of the Devil, whose present outcast status they believe to be temporary: they are in consequence commonly, but inaccurately, known as devil-worshippers. Numbering, perhaps, 30 to 40 thousand souls, their society is closed to outsiders, their character reputed stern and unfriendly, their political desideratum to be left alone, and their past history one of lawlessness and suppression. They contribute nothing of value to the Iraq state of to-day. The tiny community of the Shabak, on Tigris-side south of Mosul, resembles the Yazidi in its Kurdish speech—and probably its blood—and in the profession of a religion believed to depart, up to or beyond the verge of heresy, from that of the Prophet.

Of the Assyrians, a community Nestorian (monophysite) in their variety of Christianity, Syriac in their speech, and mountain-dwelling in their habit—they live in settlements around 'Amadiya and Rowanduz—more will be said when, on later pages, we trace the unhappy fortunes which brought them to Iraq from their former homes in Turkey and Persia, and expelled again to Syria all but the present remnant. (The ancient name given to this community gives no assurance of actual descent from, or continuity with, the subjects of Sargon or Ashur-Nasir-pal). Households of Assyrians are found in Baghdad and other towns, many work in the oil industry and as servants and drivers: but the majority, still organised in their ancient clan-system and led by their rustic priesthood, are villagers and cultivators who appear at last, after long reluctance, to have accepted life in Iraq as their destiny. Their martial qualities have been admired, their occasional indiscipline deplored. A large number have served in the British forces, where they made many friends. The Assyrians in Iraq number probably between 30 and 40 thousand souls: another 12,000 are in northern Syria.

No community could differ more from these exiled and long unhappy Christians, than the next group here to be mentioned, twice or thrice as numerous—that of the Turkomans. These

sturdy town and village-dwellers of north-eastern Iraq, dispersed
along the historic high-road from the Diyala by Kirkuk to Mosul,
are a relic of early Turkish (but pre-Ottoman) invasion or infiltration into Iraq. Tribalism is unknown among them, though
they have friendships in both Kurdish and Arab tribes. Their
religion is that of Sunni Islam, with a few adherents of the extreme,
or even heretical, Shi'i sects. Physically, they retain much of a
Turkish complexion and facial type and are, even after centuries,
self-consciously non-Arab; and, with their largest concentrations
at Khanaqin, Kifri, Kirkuk and Arbil, they retain their rural
or provincial dialect of the Turkish language but are without
other Turkish cultural affiliations. Many Turkoman officials,
notably those of Kirkuk, have reached high rank. These are
quiet, virile and law-abiding people, less brilliant and less
emotional than Arabs (towards whom they are habitually
uncordial) but not unprogressive and of solid merit as officials,
cultivators, craftsmen and labourers. Gradual disappearance of
their community, by absorption into the Iraqi-Arab majority,
probably awaits them. Their present numbers are of the order
of 80 to 100 thousand.

The resident Persians, all in central and southern Iraq,
represent, except for a few hundreds of merchants, craftsmen,
and Lurish weight-lifting porters, the community attracted to
Iraq in past centuries by the presence of the great Shi'i shrines,
and the Shi'i divines who have long served and taught there with
dominant authority. The middle-Euphrates Shi'i influence or
pressure-group was, indeed, for many years led by the resident
Persian *mujtahids*, or Doctors of the religious Law, on theocratic
lines, and has been a powerful factor in Iraq politics and in Perso-
Iraqi complications. To-day the Persian community, a bulwark of
Shi'ism, is still far from negligible; but the *'ulama* of Najaf,
Karbala, Kadhimain and Samarra no longer form the disloyal
obstruction to organised government which, as we shall see, they
were capable of being as recently as the early 'twenties of the
present century. There are to-day perhaps 50,000, or slightly
more, Iraqi residents of Persian nationality; nearly all speak
Arabic as well as Persian, and an increasing proportion of their
households will no doubt accept, as in the past thousands have
accepted, full membership of the Iraq state.

A very different past, and future, belongs to the Iraqi Jews,
whose community in the territory, dwelling for long ages 'by the

waters of Babylon', was until the middle of the present century the largest, and probably the most advanced, Jewish colony in Asia. Clearly marked off by religion, observance and tradition from the Muslim majority, and largely differentiated also by their range of urban occupations, dwelling quarters and even in dress, the Jews of Iraq attained, since the middle ages, a position of comparative wealth, economic influence, representation in government, and in normal times freedom from persecution, though never without a certain stigma of inferiority in social acceptability. Baghdad in 1914 was, numerically, a greater Jewish than Arab city, and no town in the country was without its industrious, law-abiding, Arabic-speaking Jewish community. To-day, no more than some 10,000 Jews remain in Iraq.

The Iraqi Armenians had, and have, aspects of similarity to the Jews in their exceptional talent for commerce, industry and handicraft, their skill and frugality, their relatively advanced educational level, and their ready, but never complete, assimilation with the majority communities. The Armenians, who have played little or no part in modern Iraqi politics, though moving sometimes in high social circles, retain fully their loyalties to their own historic Church and long-scattered nation, and preserve their own speech in addition to Arabic: but they have no nationalist aspirations (such as proved the ruin of their much larger settlements in Turkey in past years), and are law-abiding Iraqi subjects.

These minorities, which add a richness and variety to the Iraqi scene and contribute their particular gifts to its society and economics, form nevertheless—with the single and most important exception of the Kurds—no significant part of the population, pose no problems to the Government, and detract little from the predominant Muslim-Arab character of the State and territory.

LAND AND WATER

WITH THE exception always of its phenomenal richness in petroleum (an asset realised only in the latest generation of her history), and its agricultural potential, Iraq is a country sadly deficient in natural wealth. Its hill forests are scanty, deteriorated and in need of complete replanning and re-establishment, which their high ultimate value and the hope thereby of a diminished soil-erosion will abundantly justify. Fuel, other than oil and bitumen, is limited to a single small outcrop of bituminous coal; for lack of better, the scanty desert scrub is commonly used for domestic fires and to supply the older brick-kilns, and dried dung furnishes the kitchens of the villagers. Favourable sites exist in the mountain zone for the production of hydro-electricity, but only at the cost of major works of damming and construction, and too often far from centres of consumption. Building stone, including the soft but ornamental 'Mosul marble', is confined solely to the northern area, where the materials for cement-making, and the ubiquitous burnt gypsum for use as mortar, are also available: elsewhere burnt or sun-dried bricks, dried mud and tough matting serve their purposes, with a dozen uses for the trunk, fibres, fronds and leaves of the date-tree. Salt is abundant, but no other minerals save some traces of sulphur and quartz. Wild vegetable produce which can be turned to account is found in the river-side liquorice, exportable in pressed bales on a considerable scale: gum-tragacanth from the thorny bushes of the northern mountains: and the gall-nuts of the Valonia oak.

If the mineral and vegetable raw-materials capable of contributing to local industry or to export are thus scanty, and if wild animal-life contributes little or nothing, the produce of the country's flocks and herds can do more. This has throughout history been a country of hardy sheep, whose skins and wool (though of indifferent quality), meat and 'casings' are valuable assets: of still hardier goats, whose milk and hair (the characteristic fabric in Arab tent-making), are locally used: of water-buffalo, givers of milk and leather: and of cattle, valued for their milk, for their service at the plough and in turning water-wheels and, in Kurdistan, for pack-carrying also. Stock-rearing in its various forms is widely spread throughout the territory, though even to-day on generally primitive lines: its contribution to local industry is important, and can well be more so, and the export of animal produce—wool, hair, casings, fat, leather, and live animals—is and has always been of value. Camels are bred, always in desert or desert-adjoining areas, for meat and milk and load-carrying, and above all because Bedouin life and migration is inconceivable without them; but their range and uses tend to be restricted in the present age when their monopoly of desert transport has been broken down, and other fashions have prevailed. Mules, horses and donkeys carry loads, pull ploughs, and serve for riding. The more famous strains of the Arab horse have always been highly prized, in sentiment and economics alike, and are still valued, though the export trade in them is now diminished.

On a more general and more confident view of its resources, the country is unique among the Arab states, and in Western Asia, for its combination of wide cultivable lands with abundant water: a joint gift of nature which has throughout history destined it as a territory of large-scale, as well as intensive, agriculture. A high proportion of its total surface is in fact uncultivable, by reason of its own barren substance (sand, rock, or salt-swamp), or its elevation above possible irrigation-level, or its mountain ruggedness; but, after all deductions, more still remains well capable of cultivation than even the whole flow of Two Rivers could avail to irrigate at a single time. The methods and objects of such cultivation must necessarily vary with the zone of the territory, and the mode and economics of its irrigation: but everywhere success (except for the humble objective of mere subsistence) can be assured only if agriculture is so far technically efficient as to render its produce competitive with that of rival exporters—which for ages past it has not been: if crop-types and the excellence of produce are such as to appeal to buyers in the world's markets—which they have done all too little for some centuries past: if transport, storage and packing are well and economically handled—which is no matter of course: and if the effort in industry and agriculture itself are based on an adequate social and economic (and perhaps fiscal) foundation, with a sound land-tenure system, adequate capital, and just distribution of proceeds—which are conditions notably lacking in the modern ages of Iraq, and which it would be rash to assume as fully existing even in its days of ancient fame and greatness. And apart from long-standing defects in these regards, Iraqi agriculture must always face, and has faced, the immense disadvantage of its scanty and uncertain rainfall, its frequent pests (largely immigrant from beyond its borders), its damaging winds and dust, and the high cost of irrigation-grown produce as against that of countries more fortunate in rainfall. It is indeed a complete illusion to hold that Iraq, or the Middle East in general, is ecologically a favoured region for agriculture; its conditions, on the contrary, render it barely competitive with the great food-producing regions of the world, and are chiefly responsible for the age-long poverty of its masses. With deficient rainfall, the main burden of Iraqi agriculture must fall upon the Rivers; and these, adequate in their

total discharge for the watering of wide areas, have at all ages
been, with varying scale and success, used and harnessed to this
end. But the task is no simple one, and it was solved, even in the
golden ages of Iraq's history, with a success far less, it may be,
than the glowing legends of those times depict. The beds of the
Tigris and Euphrates, after their southward emergence from the
uplands into the delta across the ancient shore-line of the glacial
ages, have by gradual earth-movement or silting been so far raised
up as to render them inadequate channels for the spring flood-
waters, with a consequent threat to the surrounding countryside
with wide-scale inundation when the floods—fed in far-off Turkey
by melting snow, and aggravated by sudden, unpredictable rain-
storms in the Kurdish mountains—may raise the water-level
suddenly by 5, or 10, or 20 feet, and turn scores or hundreds of
square miles into lake. Protection from this constantly recurring
tragedy (which has not spared the cities, and Baghdad itself, as
well as villages, gardens and farm-lands) must involve endless
vigilance, ever-repeated expenditure on flood-dykes, and, at best,
the construction of great control-works designed to divert the
excess flood water safely to neighbouring depressions, to give
assured winter irrigation, and to conserve water for the needs of
summer crops. The flood period comes at the season when the
spring grain-crops are maturing, which precludes mere permitted
Egyptian-fashion inundation; but the spring harvest has been
reaped, and the water is already back at a low level in the river
bed, when irrigation is most needed in the rainless summer, and
water for that purpose must be lifted and canalised. At the same
time the uncompromising flatness of lower Iraq, and the slope of
the country rather away from than towards the rivers, involve
great difficulties in drainage; and in default of this must occur
the ruin by salination of wide flooded or irrigated areas which
must somehow, at great cost, be reclaimed. The great but faulty
rivers of the territory, with their inadequate beds and the enormous
difference between their spring and autumn discharge, give
alternately too much, and too little—and give it at seasons ill-
suited to human needs, and to a land surface maladroitly disposed
to receive their water.

The régime of the rivers has, indeed, by its age-long sequence
created the Iraq of historic times, is still adding to it mile by mile,
and alone makes human life there possible; but their gifts carry
also disadvantages even beyond what has already been described.

One of these, of which history gives tragic examples, is the certainty of disaster which must follow any deterioration—or, still more, the destruction—of whatever arrangements or works have been devised, by the civilisation of the time, to control the river-waters; Iraqi prosperity, and even the bare safety of life, must always depend upon such control and upon the complex and costly system—of bridges, dykes, head-works, canals, channels, flood-escapes—which can ensure it. Next, the steep descent of the rivers from Anatolia to north-central Iraq gives them (in spite of the extraordinary slightness of the subsequent declivity from the latitude of Baghdad to the sea) a swift flow at all seasons of the year; this, and at the same time their changeable courses, summer shallowness and easy silting, render them navigable, by other than the various small (and in design immemorial) paddling or sailing craft, only with such difficulty and restriction that, above Basra, modern-type river transport has still, after high hopes and a century of enterprise, no important place in Iraqi economics. This contrasts, on the one hand, with lands whose rivers are highways of trade and traffic, and, on the other, with Persia, Turkey or Syria which (save for a few miles of the Karun) are wholly without navigable rivers.

The port of Basra, Iraq's sole sea-gateway, faces the same problems of silting; a deep-water channel is barely kept open off-shore of Fao by continual dredging, and from the costly inconvenience of this the future can hold no escape as long as the Two Rivers, and with them the Karun, continue to deposit on the Gulf bed, in millions of tons a year, the off-scourings of Turkish and Persian mountains. Nor is it irrelevant to add that the stone-less silt, of which all central and southern Iraq is composed, is the worst of materials for road building or the support of railways— even if these essential means of communication were not, as they are, constantly interrupted by flooding, or saved therefrom only at heavy expense. Iraq, in short, pays a grave and a various price for the curious geology and hydrology which gave it birth and give it sustenance.

B

PART ONE

The Iraq of Yesterday

Chapter 2

Early Ages

DAWN AND MORNING

JUSTIFICATION for reviewing the history of a modern nation, and more especially its early history, can be sought on various lines. It is a part of human affairs as a whole, and of the concerned region in particular, and thereby necessary for the proper evaluation of the latter. It can satisfy the curiosity of the reader who asks 'For what has this territory in fact stood for in the past? What, notably, has it done or suffered?' It can explain the pride which the modern people of the territory—Greeks, Italians, Egyptians, Iraqis—feel in the prowess and fame of their earlier centuries. It can indicate the many sources which have in past ages fed the stream of the national community now surviving, in terms of blood and race (indistinguishable as may now be such far-off contributions), and even more in terms of character, social forces and national structure; the lessons of modern psychology, that influences of earliest infancy deeply affect adult life, are doubtless applicable not less to peoples. Above all, since wise judgment of the present and expectation of the future can only be in the light of history, and such history has been conditioned by the whole complex of geographic, climatic and ecological factors, some survey of the past is needed for a just appreciation of the essentials and potentialities of the nation, in an identical setting, to-day and to-morrow.

That part of western Asia which is to-day northern and north-central Iraq was among the first regions to be occupied by man. In post-glacial, or even interglacial, times it offered to the earliest human communities, even those prior to the evolution of *homo sapiens*, a healthy, accessible area of sunshine and water, vegetation and game. What type of men, wandering from what original dispersal-centres, led their obscure lives of hunting and food-collection in the uplands and riverside plains of prehistoric Iraq, while its present south was still a desolate area of marsh and open sea, cannot be known; but not only probability, but the discovery

of paleolithic tools at far-separated points from Kurdistan to the
Shamiya desert, attest the presence of very early human life. Ages
elapsed, incomparably longer than the few centuries of recorded
history, while the skills and manners of the Old Stone Age passed
stage by stage to those of the Middle and the New: while the
migratory life of hunting gave way to that of the earliest agriculture: while the domestication of animals proceeded, and tools
and dwellings were improved: and while by natural increase and
power of self-defence, or by the influx of strange invaders, a
prevailing race or races were stabilised in the region.

To the question 'To what race belonged these earliest inhabitants?', no answer is possible. There is little satisfying content
for the historian in the speculations of the proto-ethnologist, whose
raw-material in western Asia is the wide-spread brown, small-
limbed, long-headed Mediterranean race: the round-headed,
heavily-built, hook-nosed Armenoid (a division of the Alpine)
race, with his characteristic back-head flatness; and perhaps also
a separate proto-Iranian, round-headed branch of the Alpines,
and the pervasive negro or negrito. But to determine the extent
or order to which these or others formed the 'original' Iraqis, or
even those who first emerge into history, is but a barren study.
In cranial index, hair-type, skin-colour, bodily frame and stature,
the earliest Iraqis were already a deeply mixed people produced
by millennia of movement, invasion and absorption—and, in the
large, in spite of many later additions, may have differed not very
considerably from their modern descendants.

Even of the neolithic ages of Iraqi pre-history, millennia with
the slowest of progress in mental development, in living standards
and artifacts, in adaptation to environment had passed before the
deposit, in the last centuries of the New Stone Age, of those
surviving remains wherefrom the modern archaeologist has
become directly aware of that earliest life which we can call
civilised: before, that is, the pre-metallic period, perhaps in the
sixth millennium B.C. when, as appears from debris unearthed at
the lowest levels of village-sites, well-planned houses were being
built, ornamented pottery was plentiful, serviceable domestic
implements and weapons were in use.

It is unknown how long or by whose hands this earliest discovered form of Iraqi civilisation was maintained; but its eventual
and probably gradual supersession was, some archaeologists
believe, at the hands of folk immigrant from southern Anatolia.

These, or their way of life, spread in time over most territory from the Mediterranean to the Zagros or beyond, and may have prevailed for a period of some centuries: it was marked by more elaborate houses, strong fortresses, skilfully painted pottery, well-adapted utensils. The dominance of this culture seems in turn to have yielded gradually to that of further immigrants, this time (it is believed) from the uplands of western Persia. They brought with them new pottery-types adorned with geometric designs, new forms of ornament, a priesthood and the ideas lying behind it, new skills in architecture, fishing, agriculture, weaving: and their manner of life not only prevailed in north and central Iraq but spread into regions of the south where, by perhaps 4500 or 4000 B.C., dry or drying land had thrust back the Gulf coastline to the vicinity of modern Nasiriya and 'Amara.

Archaeologists can trace, in succession to this so-called al-'Ubaid culture-period, two more phases of development. The first, known as the Uruk period, may again have been initiated by invaders from the north; it was marked by larger-scale religious and public buildings, skilful carving, the earliest use of metal (copper), the domestication of more animals (the water-buffalo), improved utensils, and the use of such markings on clay tablets as clearly foreshadowed the art of writing itself. The subsequent period, known by the site-name of Jamdat Nasir and covering perhaps the later years of the fourth millennium B.C., shows differences in pottery-styles, developed carving and statuary, an advance towards pictographic writing, more uses of metal, and the evolution of better tools and weapons. Archaeologists fail to associate the Jamdat Nasir culture with any foreign region; it may have evolved from within the territory.

The dawn of history finds Iraq, therefore, a long-settled, long-civilised country of village and urban communities, inheritors of many centuries of progress in the arts of evolved and complicated living and government, of trade and agriculture and, no doubt, already a developed and intricate irrigation, and of speculation and worship. Its civilisation, contemporary with that of the Nile Valley—but excelling this, thanks to its invention of writing— was already an achievement the more remarkable by its successful integration of foreign elements, and its adaptation to natural conditions by no means wholly favourable. Whether Sumer and Sumerian are the names of one racial element immigrant into southern Iraq, or a self-evolved name for the land and its composite people as these existed in the middle-fourth millennium, it is by this name that their kings and scribes knew themselves in the earliest inscriptions which came from, or refer to, that period. It was a race of, to us, unknown origin, of small, dark, round-headed, large-nosed physical type, and of obscure agglutinative language. Its culture prevailed, it would seem, throughout Iraq, though not without local variation in the central areas (known as Akkad) north of Sumeria proper, and in the northern plains of later Assyria; in the latter, indeed, different gods were worshipped, the racial mixture was by no means identical—was, indeed, non-Sumerian—and the prevailing language was distinct. Both in proto-Assyria (or Shubartu) and in Akkad a discernible penetration of Semitic-speaking folk, from the steppes to the west or north-west, led early to a spread of dialects (the Babylonian and the Assyrian) of that language-group. These later displaced the earlier tongue, and helped to create a regional consciousness distinct from, or even reacting from, the Sumerian; especially in the northern plains the eastward-moving Semites deeply affected the physical type, tastes and society of the pre-Assyrian population.

In the far south, from a date prior to 3000 B.C., the title of 'Lord of Sumer and Akkad' was claimed by the rulers of such of the small city-states, each with its own township, lands, army, and gods, as could for a time form a miniature empire over the others, or some of them; such were those of Kish, Erech, Ur, Lagash, Akshak, Agade, Eridu, Larsa and others, whose own jealous interrelations varied from decade to decade, century to century, and of whose heroes the inscriptions carry the titles and pretensions. Their claim to empire, other than cultural, over Shubartu in the north was one rarely made good; but their widespread foreign trade, and their raids into the Persian hills supplied the necessities and the luxuries which their country lacked; materials from Asia Minor, the Caucasus, north Syria, Persia, the Persian Gulf and Oman were found in the bazaars of Sumeria. Their cuneiform writing on clay tablets kept the records of trade and government, their wealth permitted a high standard of domestic comfort, with good woollen clothes and accoutrements, they indulged in sport and amusements, and their powerful priesthood developed elaborate religious ceremonies in the vast, raised temples of the time. Wheeled vehicles were drawn by well-kept animals, though not yet the horse. Their forces of chariots and infantry, spearmen and archers, were in constant employment.

This first recorded civilisation in Iraq was, indeed, one of extra-ordinary achievement; progressive at the calm speed of an early age, prosperous with its assured food-supply based on irrigated fields and well-adapted methods, secure within the shifting balance of power among the city-states and the occasional raids of hill- or desert-folk, it was already a world removed from the simpler and wilder lives of earlier millennia, and in outline offered already the pattern to which Iraq society for the next two millennia would conform.

THE FIRST GREAT EMPIRES

THE FIRST half of the third millennium B.C., with its increasing scale of foreign contacts, brought also a greater desire for self-assertion among the Semitic-speaking folk of Akkad, and possibly also fresh immigrations from the western home-areas of the latter. An Akkadian king, Sargon of Agade, was able about 2400 B.C. not only to impose his authority on the southern city-states, but to lead expeditions to northern Iraq and the Persian plateau, the Mediterranean coast and Asia Minor. The Akkadian conqueror became for a few years the leading figure of western Asia, was known and feared in Egypt itself; but he founded no empire, his raiding parties left no trace of an administration behind them, even in Sumer his authority had little effect on the society and prosperity of the cities, and the dominion of Agade survived Sargon's death by less than a life-time. But a precedent had been set, and an Iraqi ruler had imposed himself on a wide ring of neighbouring countries.

The 'vacuum of power' which followed the decline of Agade was brutally filled by an invasion of southern Iraq by hill-tribesmen, the Guti, of whom almost nothing is known. They could claim authority, of a sort, in Sumeria for three or four centuries, but contributed nothing to its wealth or culture; parallel dynasties of Lagash (with good King Gudea), of Erech, and of Ur continued to reign, and on the withdrawal of the Guti overlords the field was left open to a Sumerian revival led by the kings of Ur. This was in turn weakened, years later, by invaders or infiltrators in mass—Amurru (Amorites) from the west, perhaps from Jordan or southern Syria, and the proto-Iranian Elamites from south-western Persia.

But the dynamism of Akkad was not exhausted. Similar in-

B*

coming elements of the Amurru, blending with or taking command of the mid-Euphrates folk, had by 1900 B.C. made possible the formation of a promising confederation of Amorite-Akkadian cities with its capital at a hitherto small and obscure city, Babylon or Babel. A century later Babylon, with already its own distinctive culture, gods and loyalties, found an outstanding ruler and empire-builder in Hammurabi, the 'Amraphel, king of Shinar' of the Bible. His conquests of northern Iraq and the eastern and northern hill-country were less permanent than the extraordinary advances in written law, in administration and government machinery, in commercial methods and in rural economics which date from his lifetime: here, in the first Iraqi prince to stand in the full light of history, was no petty potentate or raiding chieftain, but a great man and ruler, in a setting destined to survive as the greatest of Iraqi cities for many centuries. The line of Hammurabi did not long survive, and the manner of its fall is a reminder that this period was already one of formidable empires and restless folk-movements. The Hittite empire of Asia Minor, now at the height of its power, struck southward and sacked the Iraqi capital, which struggled back into life only to meet a more persistent enemy, the hill-bred, horse-using, still uncivilised Kassites (Kassu) from the east.

If the Guti and other early invaders of Iraq from western Persia represented the ill-known, pre-Aryan inhabitants of that country, the Kassu were, it seems, a fragment of the Aryan-speaking stock which, from early in the second millennium, had been entering the Persian highlands—and, more or less contemporaneously, India and Europe—from original homes east or north of the Caspian. Vigorous and unspoilt, they came in Persia to represent the ruling clans or families imposed on the existing population, and they brought, for ultimate general adoption, their Iranian physical type, their language, religion and way of life. They formed, in the period 1700–1400 B.C., a number of states not only on the Persian plateau and the Kassu country, but also further west on the periphery of Iraq—the Khurri north of Mosul in the Hakkari mountains, and the Mitanni principality on the upper Khabur which lasted for three or four centuries, and included, for a time, most of the Mosul vilayet. The Kassites, with their vitality and the unity of a ruling caste, could maintain for five centuries their hold on most of the later Baghdad and Basra vilayets: a hold, however, which, though at times extended by war

or diplomacy over Assyria and the north, and able to stand up to
Hittite provocations, was of the lightest, and did little to diminish
the individuality, prosperity or progress of the delta cities, while
the Kassite rulers learnt civilisation from the subjects, and adopted
their ways and religion. Nothing is known in detail for a half-
millennium of the course of events in Babylonia, except for the
formation, from unknown north-Arabian or Gulf-coast invading
elements, of a new and long-persisting state of 'the Sealand' in
southernmost Iraq.

During the long Kassu dominion of Babylonia, the plains of
Shubartu to the north were witnessing the growth of a new
power within Iraq. Semitic-speaking elements had long since
prevailed athwart the upper Tigris and the two Zabs, though
much of the prevailing culture was still that of Sumer and Akkad;
and the many transfrontier dangers which threatened the region
had developed unusual warlike qualities, and martial techniques
unknown before. The tiny state of Ashur on the Tigris survived
Hittite and Mitanni raids before falling for a time under the latter;
grown more considerable, it bought off the aggression of the
Pharaoh of Egypt, dealt on equal terms with its Kassite neighbour
to the south and at least once won a campaign against him, over-
turned (or saw Hittites overturn) the Mitanni state, raided far into
the mountains of eastern Turkey, formed ambitions for empire
over all Babylonia, and organised an aggressive military power
which was too strong to be threatened even by the resurgence of
Babylon under Nebuchadnezzar I (about 1170 B.C.), after the
disappearance of the Kassites.

The Assyrian state, of whose cities Arbil and Kirkuk at least
still stand, was to be thenceforward for five centuries one of the
leading powers, and for three the dominant power, of western
Asia—that is, of the contemporary world. Admirable or execrable,
its methods, successes and ideals were strongly characterised; it
owed nothing, except the foreign treasures and revenues it could
seize, to other than Iraqi sources; and Iraq now, with centuries of
cultural achievement behind her, could for half a millennium
claim also the most formidable temporal power. The wholly
autocratic government of Assyria, with its capital placed successively at Ashur, Nimrud, Khorsabad and Nineveh, all in the
north Iraqi uplands, did little for the happiness of its subjects. It
was content uncreatively to enjoy (though in some material
respects to develop) the culture of Babylonia, worshipped its own

frightful gods, and gloried in its tradition of atrocious violence; but it imposed fear and respect upon a wide ring of countries, developed the arts of war (in part by the free use of iron weapons and horse-drawn chariots), constructed vast buildings and public works, and in its cuneiform writings and stone-carvings left, as no government before, a record of its achievements, its court and its magnificence.

In the ruling dynasty itself rebellion and usurpation were habitual, and these assisted, perhaps, in producing a line of rulers of whom few were inadequate and some outstanding. The names of Tiglath-Pileser, Ashur-Nasir-pal, Shalmaneser, Sargon, Sennacherib, Esarhaddon are even to-day unforgotten; and these were served by trained officers whose elaborated administration was military in character and subordinated all to military needs and to purposes personal to the sovereign. In Babylonia, Babel had still easy precedence, though the smaller (and older) city-states retained their status, high culture and wide-spread commerce, and the relations of the Assyrian king with these varied from near-equality to the imposition of tributary vassaldom, from open war to alliance, from ceremonial visits and assumption of the old Lordship of Sumer and Akkad to the looting and part-destruction of the southern capital: but, wholly different in conception and objectives, Babylon could survive, could occasionally strike back, retained its superiority in learning and living-standards, and was ultimately long to outlive its rival. Both the Sea-land dynasty and the neighbouring hill-power of Elam constantly threatened or repudiated the authority of Babylon, and at times defied Assyria itself. The latter meanwhile extended its power over the Khurri and Mitanni states, raided the Zagros ranges and beyond these to the Caspian, invaded Asia Minor and the Hittite power from Van to Cilicia, overran the Syrian hinterland and coast, subdued the Jewish state, and thrice entered Egypt to sack its great cities of Thebes and Memphis. The vast military effort involved by these centuries-long operations, ever repeated in face of constant secession and revolt, and the active diplomacy conducted with the not less ambitious rulers of the Hittites, the Anatolian and Syrian states and Egypt, were not directed, or knew no way, to found a stable empire; their aim was to conquer, despoil and destroy—and, by a policy which by its scale and persistence must have appreciably modified the Iraqi population itself, to move whole populations from their homes to Iraq, and vice versa.

The fall of Nineveh and the Assyrian state was induced at last by its own exhaustion and by a new grouping of its enemies: a threat by Egypt, a northward move by Babylon (now revitalised by a usurping 'Chaldean', perhaps proto-Arab, dynasty from the Sea-land under Nabopolassar), and above all by invasion from north Persia by another virile and powerful member of the Iranian race. The Medes, emerging under a strong dynasty as the dominant element in Persia, had for some years been on bad neighbourly terms with the Assyrian state: and in 612 B.C. their armies advanced into Iraq, took and sacked Nineveh, extinguished for ever the Assyrian power, and assumed empire over all its provinces save those of central and lower Iraq, which were left for the Chaldeans of New-Babylon.

The latter was to enjoy, for nearly a century, an extraordinary flowering of power and luxury. Under the great Nebuchadnezzar II her forces successfully invaded Syria and Palestine, sacked Jerusalem and carried off 40,000 Jews into captivity in Iraq, threatened but did not invade Egypt, arbitrated between Medes and Lydians, built the great 'Median Wall' across Iraq to secure the northern frontier, and made Babylon the greatest city in the world; Babylonian public works, palaces, arts and writings, wealth, science and commerce became proverbial. But within a generation from the death of Nebuchadnezzar it fell, never to regain full imperial status. A South-Persian nation under Khosrau (Cyrus) had from its home-province of Fars gained ascendancy in that country, had subdued or absorbed other Iranian groups, and had superseded the privileged Medes as the ruling caste. The army of Khosrau, after a victorious campaign in Asia Minor, swept into central Iraq in 539 B.C., brushed aside opposition, besieged and captured Babylon.

Thus closed the long period in which Iraq, repeatedly invaded but always absorbent of its invaders and their gifts and cultures, had invented, fostered and developed its own civilisation, extended its own conceptions of society and government, waged its own wars. Though a united territory as a focus of national loyalty must be unthinkable to the Iraqis of the time, and though to the peasant or townsfolk it could matter little who occupied the palaces, commanded the armies or served the gods as long as the canals flowed and routes were safe, yet in every aspect of life the country had in fact, hitherto, been self-sufficient and creative. It had throughout centuries, and throughout its masses, solved its problems of agriculture and irrigation, transport and flood-management, artisanship and trade, and ordered, civilised society; but from now onward, from the capture of Babylon by the Persians until the establishment of the 'Abbasid Caliphate, for nearly thirteen centuries of time, Iraq was to be a province of other empires, and the battle-field of others' wars.

PERSIAN AND GREEK

THE FIRST of the three great Persian empires of antiquity, that of the Achaemenid kings, was to rule Iraq for two centuries. The period (539-333 B.C.) was in general one of peace and order in each of the satrapies into which Iraq was divided; and the population, or its more enlightened citizens, could observe the working of a state whose conceptions of government—that of an immense and complex Empire stretching from India to the Mediterranean and Europe—were in efficiency and in humanity far ahead of those of Nineveh, or of Babylon itself. It is, indeed, curious to speculate upon the connection, if any, of the racial qualities of the early Iranians which accompanied their Aryan speech, and their cousin-ship with peoples, like the Greeks themselves, already established as European, with their outlook upon society and government which was so far removed from the bloodthirsty despotism of Assyria. The autocratic government of Cyrus, Cambyses, Darius, Xerxes and Artaxerxes was, indeed, strongly nationalist and proudly Persian in tone and complexion, believed in its mission to govern the world, used pure-bred Persians in most high positions, maintained Persian troops and Persian-officered mercenaries at key points and vigilant royal officials within each satrapy, and emphasised the supremacy of its state religion of Ahura Mazda: but their wars were waged without barbarity, justice was obtainable, the good of the subject peoples was, as never before, a constant objective of government. Local ways were largely unchallenged, and wide provincial freedom was allowed even under the sternest of the satraps: a freedom which, on the fringes of the Empire— the desert tribes, the marshmen, and (as Xenophon's great march in 401 B.C. was to prove) the Kurds of northern Iraq—became ungoverned independence. But Persian culture was receptive of foreign, including notably Babylonian and Assyrian, influences, and her administrators themselves took over much of the civilised legacy of Babel. A measure of empire-wide uniformity, and the due collection of the annual lump-sum provincial taxation assessments, were assured by the famous system of roads and fast couriers. Persian military supremacy was guaranteed, for most of the Empire's lifetime, by the virile quality of its troops and its novel use of light archers and mobile tactics; but essentially the Persian Empire was a grouping of dependent nations, whose existence as such, as long as they behaved, it was no part of the policy of the King of Kings to question.

If the satrapy of Assyria and its cities enjoyed the average treatment due to a conquered warrior-nation, Babylonia was, like Egypt, initially given the special favour proper to an ancient and honoured civilisation. Cyrus declared himself King of Babel, the internal government of its territory was little changed, its own gods held sway, and the transplanted foreign peoples, including the Jews, were allowed or bidden to return home. The eastern-Semitic Babylonian language continued, with the cognate Assyrian dialect in the north, to be the speech of Iraq, though Aramaic (the language of the Aramaean wave of Semitic invaders from desert Arabia) was destined first to modify, then to supplant these as the prevailing tongue of towns and peasantry alike. But the Babylonians sought persistently for opportunities to reassert their independence, and futile rebellions by these Iraqi plainsmen, in 520 and 484 B.C. and again in 479, cost them their privileged status. The statue of the god Marduk was removed from Babylon, the 'Kingship of Babylon' renounced, and a firmer régime imposed. The city was, however, still used by the Great King as his normal winter residence.

While the relations of the Persian Empire on its western fringes with the Greek city-states, now approaching the apex of their vitality and culture, was for the first time to familiarise east and west, Asia and Europe, and to lead to the extraordinary expansion of Hellenism in the 4th to 2nd centuries B.C., the Achaemenid empire was itself, after its first triumphant century, declining in power and cohesion. Its greatest achievement, the system of communications and provincial government, continued in being well into the 4th century, but the revolts of subject peoples grew more formidable, the Persian ruling class were deeply corrupted by power and wealth, the influences of the harem increased, intestine struggles multiplied, and the later kings fell far short of the great founders of the dynasty. By the time that the east had become, by its vast extent and revealed riches, a possible expansion-area for the Greeks, and a man of genius had arisen to make the attempt, the Persian satrapies were profoundly weakened and ready, at the approach of an Alexander, to fall feebly to his arms.

Darius III, an amiable but weak ruler, ascended the Persian throne in 336 B.C. He was to lose it three years later to the invading forces of the youthful, brilliant, ill-balanced, drunken Greek-Macedonian, whose conquest of the known world marked for all time a stage in human affairs. His almost effortless occupation of Asia Minor, of the Levant and of Egypt (334–331) was quickly followed by his advance to the Euphrates and Tigris, where he engaged the Persian main army some miles north of Arbil. The King of Kings was defeated and driven from the field, his forces scattered. Northern and southern Iraq lay without resistance at the mercy of the Greek conqueror, and took their place in his dominions while he, after a rapid visit to Babylon, led his army into and across Persia and Afghanistan, and deeply into India. From these remote conquests he returned to Iraq by way of southern and central Persia, where a series of rebellions, and the gross misconduct of his governors, recalled him to tasks of organisation. He sailed up the Tigris, crossed to its twin river, feasted in Babylon and, with a hundred plans still forming for sea power in the Persian Gulf and the conquest of Arabia, died a week later (June, 323).

Alexander the Great, for all his dreams of empire on the fullest oriental scale with himself as King of Kings, his urge to unite east and west in a common society, his foundation of Greek cities in the heart of Asia, the marriage of thousands of his followers with eastern women, had in his short life no time to develop even the foundations of a stable régime. He had broken the power of Achaemenid Persia, had opened the doors of Greek civilisation to the east, had suggested possibilities of a world-state; but, meanwhile, he bequeathed a mere fragmented anarchy. The peoples whom he had overthrown or liberated, among them those of Assyria (or Mesopotamia) and Babylonia, must look thenceforward where they could for a permanent rule and way of life.

In the absence of an heir to Alexander's unique position and world-empire, twenty years of bargained partitions, broken agreements and assassinations among the Greek candidates for power elapsed before the eastern part of the empire fell securely to the able commander and statesman Seleucus. Never free from interruption by his rivals, he was able forcibly to reoccupy the provinces of Iraq, Persia and the Levant, and to move his capital to Antioch while shifting the provincial capital of Babylonia, or lower Iraq, to his new Greek city of Seleucia on the Tigris. His murder in 281 B.C. was followed by a half-century more of rivalry among 'the successors', of indecisive campaigns, murders, revolts, and the setting up of new dynasties—Greek, Anatolian or Iranian—in many of the ever-seceding provinces. A succession of feeble 'Seleucid' monarchs failed to establish order until the long reign of Antiochus the Great (223–187) witnessed a successful reassertion of the royal power: royal, since the Seleucid rulers were now kings in the oriental manner. He imposed himself by vigorous campaigns and settlements in most of the eastern provinces, including Media and Persia; those of Anatolia he was forced finally to abandon. But Iraq, which formed now the two provinces of Mesopotamia and Babylonia, was, with western Persia, firmly under Seleucid rule at the time of his death (187 B.C.). He was killed in a punitive campaign in Luristan.

The later Seleucid monarchy, never well-based or integrated, produced no ruler adequate to the government of a distracted, turbulent and disloyal empire. The best-remembered, Antiochus IV Epiphanes, maintained himself in the Levant and prevented the secession of Iraq and Persia; but under his obscure successors even the semblance of an empire was ever harder to maintain. Rivals appeared at every point, all cohesion was lacking; and among the pretenders, upstart dynasties and ungoverned regions one power more formidable than the rest had already, since the end of the third century B.C., been busily advancing its pretensions in the east.

The Parthians, from the north-east of Persia (the modern Khurasan)—or, ultimately, from the nomadic Caspian steppe-people—were an half-Iranianised group of tribes, welded together by a dominant family and enriched by the cultivated lands and cities they had acquired. Since the decline and fall of the Mace-donian satraps of the area, the Parthian people, now united under a monarchy, had spread across northern Persia, absorbed a more authentic Iranian population, and made their capital at Ecbatana (Hamadan). Their further advance into Iraq and across both its rivers, with the defeat of the last Seleucid forces and the expulsion of their decrepit garrisons, was the work of a few years. Seleucid rule vanished for ever from Iraq; the place of Greeks as rulers was taken by an upstart, half-Iranian power new not only to the area but to civilisation itself.

From the first appearance of the Macedonian to the expulsion of the last Seleucid, what had the Greek, or Hellenistic, presence in Iraq contributed to its life or culture? To the rural, or even the urban, masses, very little: their way of life and speech, their skills and resources were unmodified by the relatively few Greeks, or half-Greeks, who haunted the towns and garrisons but were rarely seen in the toiling villages. Among the more educated Iraqis, in daily touch with Greek resident merchants and officials, a widening of mental horizons could not but result from this presence and authority of foreigners with their different speech, manners, experience, and abilities. The Greek language became, to a few, familiar in speech and writing, and in the Greek city of Seleucia, and perhaps elsewhere, much could be seen of Greek art, drama, housing and living-standards, even though, as elsewhere in the east, the purity of the Greek tradition was, like their blood, soon heavily contaminated by oriental admixtures. Received grudgingly by the intelligentsia of Babylonia and its still powerful priests, and never seen in Iraq at its freshest, Greek culture excited, it is probable, as much of disapproval or doubt as of admiration. Even the Macedonian techniques of war, the victorious phalanx, were soon lost in these surroundings, and warfare itself came to mean the disastrous raids and reprisals of bastard Seleucid armies, with levies of unwilling Iraqis to swell their ranks.

PARTHIAN AND SASSANIAN

THE EMPIRE of the Parthians, under its Arsacid dynasty, was never accepted by true Persians as other than that of usurpers and half-barbarians, yet was to endure in Iraq and Persia for more than three centuries. The rulers, as alien in the Tigris-Euphrates valley as the Greeks themselves, acquired as time went on a mixed civilisation formed from nomadic (or Scythian), Iranian and Hellenistic elements; and while they did little actively to extirpate the Greek survivals—such as the great city of Seleucia itself—and indeed their earlier kings were glad to adopt Greek titles and tastes, governmental procedures and coinage, the latter half of the period witnessed the gradual fading of such influences, and the stiffening of an eastern self-consciousness against the west. They accepted, if half-heartedly, the Zoroastrian religion of Iran, spoke and wrote (in Aramaic script) their own Pahlevi dialect of early Persian, were in ceaseless political conflict with the west, and were forced to reckon with a strong oriental patriotism in their own ruling class. The Parthian empire was, from the first, weak and ill-knit: it lacked the virtues alike of rugged Achaemenid Persia, to whom it aspired to succeed, and of the subtler Greeks. It was distracted by internal feuds and dynastic disputes, lacked a firm provincial administration, permitted (because powerless to prevent) excessive local authority leading to secession or revolt, and failed, in spite of its famous light mounted archers with their 'Parthian shots', to produce an adequate military machine. Many of the kings were mere puppets of the powerful nobles, and ever-repeated inroads by central-Asian nomads weakened the dynasty. Much of northern and north-eastern Iraq and neighbouring territory—the district of Osroene (the northern Jazira), Gordyne (central Kurdistan), Adiabene (between the two Zabs), and Chalonitis (astride the middle and lower Diyala) continually changed its allegiance between Parthia, Rome and aspiring Armenia; tribal 'kingdoms', with considerable capital cities, arose on the western desert-fringe, and in the far south, astride the Shatt al-'Arab, a seemingly independent state could survive for three centuries, with its own ruling house, currency and trade.

The kingdom of the Arsacids, who built a new capital, Ctesi-phon, on the Tigris, immediately below the obscure village of Baghdad, suffered both from unending disorders at its heart and on its eastern borders, and from the perpetual menace of Roman advance. The latter power, already thrusting into Asia, aspired to succeed to the empire of Alexander. It did more than prevent a westward expansion of Parthia, who in spite of some successful campaigns in the Levant could be sure only of its Persian and Iraqi provinces; it expanded its power steadily among the statelets into which Asia Minor was now fragmented, sought bases in northern Iraq itself, and released itself at will from treaties made (as in 92 and 69 B.C.) with the Arsacid Phraates, Mithridates, Orodes or Tiridates of the time. War between the two empires, of which even a Rome distraught by civil war was by far the stronger, broke out in 53 B.C. Its first phase ended with the defeat and death of Crassus. Julius Caesar planned a campaign of revenge in the east, but his murder prevented it. Pompey the Great tried again in 36 B.C., but lost a campaign in Kurdistan, and was glad to retreat. In 20 B.C. the Arsacid handed back to the Emperor

Augustus the standards captured a generation earlier, and peace
between the powers was signed a few years later, but with all their
rivalries still unresolved; it lasted for sixty years, during which
constant diplomatic activity was maintained, the Parthian
attitude varying from subservience to defiance.

The first century of the Christian era witnessed an increasingly
anti-western attitude in Parthia: the privileged position of Greek
Seleucia was threatened, and the city itself was at times in open
revolt. War with Rome began again in A.D. 113–7, through the
ambitions of the Emperor Trajan who, dreaming of a revival of
Alexander's empire, forced his way into Iraq. He occupied the
Arbil plain, descended the Tharthar depression and captured
Hatra, sailed down the Euphrates to Babylon, then seized
Ctesiphon itself. But the great expedition ended in fiasco, thanks
to a Parthian reaction and an uprising in the conquered territory;
Trajan was forced to withdraw discomfited, and his successor,
Hadrian, preferred a policy of restoration and peace. This lasted
for half a century until, under Marcus Aurelius in 162, another
Roman army entered Iraq, and this time destroyed Seleucia, a
blow which proved fatal to such of Greek culture as survived in
the territory. A Partho-Roman peace was made in 165, whereby
north-western Iraq, but no more, remained under Roman sway.
Further wars between Ctesiphon and Rome were waged in 195–
202 (Septimius Severus) and in 216–7 (Caracalla); the latter was
one of extraordinary brutality.

But successors to the feeble, mongrel Arsacids were at hand.
The great southern province of Persis had, under weak central
rule, long since split into small local principalities. One of these
was that of Bebek, descendent of Sassan and father of Ardashir.
This prince, in the first decade of the third century, killed off his
immediate rivals, absorbed his neighbours and created a united
kingdom. He could then challenge his suzerain, the Parthian
Artabanus IV, and defeat him in a succession of battles. Within
a few years the other great satrapies of the Empire fell under
'Sassanian' power, and the palace of Ctesiphon, with all Iraq,
was to be theirs without question until the Islamic conquest.

The new dynasty, firmly Persian and national, revived the
Zoroastrian religion with its intolerance and its powerful priest-
hood, took steps to suppress Christianity (including the famous
Manichaean heresy) which had already spread fast into the
Empire, insisted on the reign of law and justice among its subjects,

curbed (where it could) the power of the great nobles. It imitated orthodox Achaemenid methods and procedures, claimed (as they had done) world-empire, and dazzled Persia and Iraq by its ceremonial splendour. It gave Persia probably the most glorious four centuries of its history; but its essential military weakness forbade any permanence to the westward—or eastward—expansion at which it aimed, and limited its power to Persia itself and Iraq. The far greater, and often aggressive, power of Rome barred the way equally to Asia Minor and the Levant.

Hellenism and the Greek language almost disappeared during these centuries (A.D. 225–635) from Iraq and Iran, although western scholars were on occasion made welcome at Ctesiphon, and Christian divines and missionaries (mainly Syrians) kept alive many contacts with western thought; the leaning of the considerable, probably predominant, Christian population of Iraq towards Rome (officially Christian after A.D. 324) was, indeed, a constant thorn in the Sassanian side. The culture of the latter, considerable by any standards, was itself composite. It showed itself in an extensive Pahlevi literature, excellent carving and metal-work, silken fabrics and seal-engraving, and town-planning and palatial buildings which included the still-standing Arch of Ctesiphon, Taq-i-Kesra, south of Baghdad. Their architecture shows mixed influences, not excluding Greek, their buildings were to serve as models for the Islamic period.

Just as the Iraq of 1500–1900 never became Turkish in culture or sentiment, still less in blood or language, so the Iraq of the third to seventh centuries A.D., accepting almost without question its Sassanian Persian masters, and forming a major part of that empire, derived therefrom its protection from Roman or Byzantine aggressors, its governmental and fiscal machine, its official procedures and terminologies; it submitted to Sassanian justice, was (at least in the cities) subject to Persian-nationalist and Zoroastrian exigencies, and could share if it liked in Persian cultural and perhaps social life; but there still remained, between and even within the great centres of Persian power, an Iraqi public which, while lacking even the elements of nationhood, yet had its own very different and characteristic environment, racial blend, means of livelihood, past history, religions and political traditions. It could be as improbably 'an integral part of Persia' (as Sassanid patriots may have claimed) as could Algeria of France, or Herzegovina of Austria. The period was one, moreover, of significant

changes in Iraqi society; upward movements of Arab tribes from
their deserts swept into and dominated all country west of
Euphrates, the essentially Arab city (and miniature empire) of
Hira endured for generations as a vassal of Ctesiphon, Arab tribes
still nomadic occupied wide lands between the Rivers, and
their blood and speech contributed even to the Aramaic-speaking
(and largely Christian) town populations. One more of the age-
long Semitic invasions was in progress.

The political history of contemporary Iraq was that of the
Empire to which it belonged, except that its position as the western-
most province made it, more frequently than any other Sassanian
region, the battlefield in wars with the west; and these, though
separated indeed by long periods of peace, formed the outstanding
feature—the repeated, wearisome, and wholly futile and destructive feature—of external national life for all this four-century
period. These wars between the Roman and the Persian power
were occasioned by no essential clash of interest; geographically
separate and each self-sufficient, the two powers could well have
peacefully co-existed. But human affairs are otherwise, and in
deep east-west uncomprehension or antipathy, religious difference
and intolerance, inflated nationalism, personal and commercial
jealousies, the vain-glory of princes, the disputed allegiances of
Anatolian states, the flight of fugitive younger-sons or statesmen
to this or that capital craving support, the inevitable frontier
clashes, there were occasions enough to keep two empires
habitually in a state of war, precarious armistice, or sullen peace.
The effect of these conditions on society, notably in an Iraq
constantly exposed, drained for military levies, and frequently
invaded, can be imagined.

During the first century of Sassanid rule, under Ardashir, the
first Shapur, Bahram, Narses and lesser monarchs, the Persian
objectives were, as ever, the line of Roman forts sited defensively
from the Mediterranean to the Jazira, and the unstable principalities of Asia Minor. Many of the campaigns were indecisive,
conquests short-lived, battles more bloody than conclusive;
and the Persian empire, in spite of victories over Alexander
Severus and the capture of Valerian, in spite even of the sacking
of Antioch and other Levantine cities, did not otherwise than
momentarily extend its frontiers beyond the Euphrates. The
Romans, on the other hand, with occasional help from Arab or
half-Arab potentates of the Shamiya desert—the rich, settled

chieftains of Hira or Palmyra—could invade Iraq, threaten or occupy Ctesiphon itself, grant peace (as did Diocletian) on payment of indemnity, receive Sassanian pretenders at Rome or Byzantium, gain ground in the Anatolian states and even annex for some years parts of northern Jazira and the Kurdish hills, but could not otherwise dislodge or subdue the Persian power. No more definitive result was gained, in the second century of struggle, by wars between Shapur II and the Emperor Constantine, by the determined but ultimately futile invasion of Iraq by Julian the Apostate (who was killed in battle there in 363), by agreed and later repudiated partitions of disputed Armenia, or by unreal peace-treaties between Yazdegerd I and Theodosius. Nor was the Sassanid power able to devote itself exclusively to wars with the west; the eastern provinces of its empire lay under the threat of Turkish or Hunnish pressure or invasion, revolts of outlying areas were habitual, and ceaseless schism or pretension distracted the royal dynasty itself.

From the second quarter of the 5th to the corresponding quarter of the 6th century A.D.—the period during and after which the Nestorian doctrine prevailed in Perso-Iraqi Christianity, under the patriarch of Seleucia—wars with Rome were relatively infrequent, and as ever indecisive; the Sassanian state was in decline, and at intervals separated by long peaceful periods could do no more than attack frontier fortresses, which the great Belisarius was well able to defend. But the last century of the Sassanid period, 530–633, was marked by a resumption of the exhausting struggle. Chosroes the First, in a reign outstanding for its improved administration, religious zeal and cultural activity, waged successful wars on the Emperor Justinian, sacked Antioch, transplanted thousands of Syrians to Iraq, helped the far-off Yaman against Ethiopian invaders, and exercised a precarious sway from Central Asia to the Caucasus, Aegean and Red Sea. But a period of distracting civil strife in Persia caused the loss of these advantages, and the monarch finally enthroned at Ctesiphon, after long confusion, owed much to the aid of the Roman Emperor himself. After a period of peace with Rome, war was renewed in 608, 615 and again in 626 under Chosroes II, who founded a new capital, Dastagerd, near Shahruban. The war turned for a time greatly to the Persian advantage, with victorious expeditions to the Levant, Egypt, and almost to Byzantium; but the Emperor Heraclius restored the position by able diplomatic

approaches to Turkish hordes and disaffected Persians, invaded
Iraq, defeated the Persian army near Nineveh, sacked Dastagerd,
and secured the abdication of Chosroes. The years following
(628–32) were a time of confusion and near-anarchy in Persia
and Iraq: but terms of peace were arranged with Rome, a King
of Kings emerged from dynastic anarchy and bloodshed in the
youthful person of Yazdegerd III (633), and there seemed no
reason why the general lines of the history of the last four centuries
in Western Asia should not be repeated for four more. But fate
planned otherwise; the greatest turning point in all Iraqi history
was instantly at hand.

Chapter 3

Muslim Iraq

THE FIRST CENTURY OF ISLAM

THE IRAQ of the last years of its pre-Islamic period, the third decade of the 7th century A.D., was, as we have seen, a land of mixed race which had received repeated additions to its aboriginal stock or stocks from Anatolian, Syrian, Persian, Greek and Arabian sources; and such additions themselves represented not single but various races immigrant from those countries. Culturally, its languages were, at this period, Aramaic among the urban masses, Pahlevi Persian as the speech of government and the ruling class, Greek perhaps that of a small learned circle and the foreign-commercial houses, and Arabic, in its then fully evolved form—the tongue of the Prophet himself—among the considerable Arab population of the fringes, the Jazira and riverain lower Iraq. The accepted religions were those of Nestorian or Greek Christianity or Manichaeism, of Zoroaster, of Judaism, and of varied pagan cults of many origins, with Babylonian survivals among a tenacious priesthood. The arts and crafts of the country showed a distinctive blend of the autochthonous with the foreign (Persian, Greek and Roman); the manner of life—housing, clothes, food, social manners—was one evolved under those same influences in a strongly characteristic Iraqi setting; and in the material field, the practices of irrigation and agriculture, the crafts of boat-building and brick-making, the use of bitumen and of reeds, were elaborately developed on long-traditional Iraqi lines, of which many survive into our own age.

Previous invasions or infiltrations into Iraq, including those of Arabs or proto-Arabs—Sea-landers, Amorites, Aramaeans—had been absorbed, with their contributions of blood, prowess and culture, invisibly and integrally into the body of the Iraq people. It was left now to the Arabs of the earliest Islamic period to alter profoundly, in ten years, not indeed the country's racial amalgam but its national consciousness and character, religion, language, manners, and international orientation. Iraq became in a single decade an Arab and a Muslim country, and would never again be otherwise.

The appearance of the Prophet Muhammad in the Hijaz, his revealed monotheistic religion—itself no mere dogmatic system but a comprehensive and satisfying way of life—his extraordinary success and personal dominance, his virtual unification of the squabbling, feckless tribes of peninsular Arabia, cannot be narrated here, desirable as is some understanding of these circumstances for an appreciation of the new forces which, less than two years after the Prophet's death (632), were to appear on the southwestern fringes of Iraq.

These forces, no more at first than scanty tribal levies, represented the striking force of an Arabia always hungry, prone (because forced) for millennia to persistent emigration, but now for the first time unified (if but temporarily), inspired, convinced, and resolute in its conviction of the superiority of its new-found religion and way of life. Its sons, led by dashing commanders and confronted by undreamed of opportunities for loot, wealth and captive women, proved irresistible in their assault on a country in which the Arab (and therefore potentially friendly) population was already considerable, in which no religion and no loyalty was firmly held, and which the decadence of its foreign rulers and the centuries of futile and weakening war with Byzantium had long enfeebled.

Every episode, every personality of the Arab invasion and occupation of Iraq has become legendary. The great commanders were Muthanna, Khalid ibn al-Walid, and Sa'd, names which rank among the greatest in early Islam. The well-remembered battles were those of The Chains and of Walaja, of the Bridge and of Buwaib (the 'Field of Tens'), and the long-drawn, finally decisive struggle at Qadisiya (635). Punctuated by some Persian counter-successes, by the rallying of Muslim reinforcements, and by famous sieges of Hira, 'Anbar, and 'the Cities'—that is, Seleucia and Ctesiphon—the campaigns from 633 to 637 could have but one ending; by 638 the whole of Iraq was under the power of the Caliph at Mecca, represented by his vigorous generals in Iraq. Incalculable riches had been ransacked from the fallen Persian armies and cities, Sassanid military power had been finally destroyed, the ruling dynasty itself had fled. Iraqi converts in scores of thousands joined the body of Islam by conviction or interest. The important military garrison-cities of Kufa and Basra were founded, and a rough beginning was made, on inherited Sassanian lines, at a fiscal and provincial system, and at the administration of Muslim justice. The last Persian attempt at re-occupation was foiled at Nihavend in western Persia (642), and the whole empire of Iran lay open thenceforward to the Caliph's commanders.

But the Muslim occupation of Iraq, unthreatened thereafter by Sassanids, Greeks or Babylonians, was yet uneasy. The score of years between Nihavend and the transfer of the Caliphate from Mecca to Damascus (661) saw not only the progressive Islamisation and Arabisation of all areas of Iraq (save those parts of the Christian and Jewish communities which refused conversion), but also dissentions within victorious Islam itself. These broke out first under the feeble rule of the third Caliph, 'Uthman, and then, in bitter civil war, continued between his successor 'Ali (the Prophet's cousin and son-in-law) and the powerful governor of Syria, Mu'awiya, who belonged to the Umayyad branch of the Quraish clan as distinct from the Hashimite, which could claim the Prophet himself. This struggle ended with the assassination of 'Ali in Iraq, near Najaf, in 661. The same period witnessed the beginning of deep disunity between the Quraish and the rest of the Islamic community, as well as fierce rivalries within the privileged clan itself; tribal groupings, centering on ancient (and largely mythical) patriarchal kinship, began to appear in Islamic politics as motives of inter-Arab enmity: the great influence—and the dangerous politics and turbulence—of Kufa and Basra made themselves felt, and added to the high importance of Islamic Iraq as a vital province in the still growing Muslim world-empire; and the foundation of the fanatical Khariji sect in Iraq, uncompromising religious extremists, was thenceforward continually to create disorder and ruin.

The death of 'Ali, the abdication of his son Hasan, and the tragic failure and murder of his second son Husain at Karbala in 680, left the field free for the consolidation of the Umayyad Caliphate at Damascus, under Mu'awiya, his son Yazid, and the line of their successors; but the claims of the followers of 'Ali and Husain persisted. It gave rise, on the theological side, to the great dissident sect of the Shi'a (itself later deeply subdivided) and, on the political, to bitter feeling in Iraq and Persia against the Umayyads. Meanwhile, the uneasy, reluctant position of Iraq as a group of garrisoned, seditious provinces under the viceroys of a hated Caliph, was a constant embarrassment to his empire; rebellious generals, pretenders to the Caliphate, religious sectarians were all sure of a following, and called repeatedly for military operations of suppression.

These were constant phenomena in the Iraq of the first century following the rise of the Umayyads, while the great empire in east and west, acquired with astounding speed by Muslim armies, was barely held together by the Caliph's prestige and his imperial officers against secession, revolt and local proclamations of independence. In spite of the endless intrigues of Kufa and Basra, and the growing feeling in the Iraqi countryside against rule from Syria, and in Arab circles everywhere against the growing power of Persian converts, and the covert or open designs of the ambitious or the desperate, and the ceaseless uprisings and atrocities of Khariji mob-armies, some sort of order was maintained in Iraq under viceroys (notably the famous Hajjaj) sent to secure obedience to the Caliph, whose own position and luxurious court at Damascus, those of an oriental despot, were now in striking contrast to the simplicity of earliest Islam. A strong military centre was established at Wasit in central Iraq; all official correspondence was conducted, not in Persian as at first, but in Arabic; an Arabic coinage appeared; and leading families from the Hijaz sought new homes in the fast growing Islamic cities of lower Iraq.

THE HOUSE OF 'ABBAS

THE SECOND phase of Iraq's history under Islam began with an event which no observer could have foretold: the transfer of the seat of the Caliphate from Damascus to Iraq, and its continuance there for the next five centuries. That the already degenerate line of the Umayyads, disturbed by constant weakening civil wars, would be replaced by an uprising of the strong elements of Shi'i devotion and other malcontents was clearly probable; but in fact, on the contrary, the successful rival was to appear from the line of the Quraish which descended from 'Abbas, the Prophet's uncle. After patient years of intrigue in eastern Persia, conducted from a secret base first in Palestine and later in Iraq during the second quarter of the eighth century, statesmen of the House of 'Abbas, of unusual ability and few scruples, by deceiving the 'Alid faction with false hopes, denigrating the Syrian Caliphate, and inspiring a strong following of their own (almost entirely Persian, but by now Arabised in faith and language), succeeded by 749 in establishing themselves at Kufa, and making good their claim to the Caliphate itself. Abandoning at last all concealment of his long-hidden ambitions, rallying supporters in Iraq, defeating the forces of the last Umayyad, Marwan, at the Battle of the Zab, and then occupying Damascus itself, Abu'l-'Abbas, great-great-grandson of the Prophet's uncle, was to reign for five years from his capital, Kufa. By his fierce methods of suppression of rebellion wherever it broke out, his contempt for human life, and in particular his slaughter of all survivors of the Umayyad house, he well earned him his chosen nickname of al-Saffah, the Shedder of Blood. But he powerfully established his throne and authority, and the long line of 'Abbasid Caliphs were, to a man, the descendants of his brother Abu Ja'far (better known as al-Mansur), to whom he left his immense inheritance.

The period of the 'Abbasid Caliphate is the best remembered and most appreciated of all Iraqi history. It has left an immense volume of tradition, many famous names, the record of great achievements; and although its glories in the political field were almost confined to the first century of its life, and were followed by four centuries of weakness, corruption and domination by Turkish or Persian secular rulers, yet the cultural and economic achievements of the period, the consolidation of Islam by the 'Abbasid dynasty, the high civilisation evolved, the central position of Iraq and its Caliph amid the shifting politics of the time, render the period one of singular interest.

No attempt can here be made to follow the full sequence of events in these five crowded centuries. During the first eighty years from the accession of al-Mansur the Caliphate, in spite of grave defects of administration, much insecurity and many uprisings, possessed unquestioned political as well as religious authority, was great in prestige as in wealth and glory, and was adorned by exceptional rulers in the persons of Mansur himself, the grim, efficient and imaginative builder of Baghdad (762): Harun al-Rashid, the brilliant, wayward, glamorous hero of legend: and al-Ma'mun, the cultivated, theologically-minded patron of science and the arts. In these three reigns, rivals' uprisings and 'Alid pretensions were suppressed, Islam exalted, civil government highly developed, wars waged against Byzantium,

an embassy received from Charlemagne himself; but the seeds of
future trouble were already sown. In the ensuing century, from
833 to 945, the prestige, powers and merits of the 'Abbasid
Caliphate declined with extraordinary rapidity. Under fifteen
Caliphs, all direct descendents of Mansur but none of high
personal consequence, the violence and abuses of the Caliphate's
Turkish mercenary troops horrified their capital, and led to the
removal of the seat of Government for sixty years (836–895) to
Samarra. Arab influence and personalities took less and less place
as compared with Persian, and Arab forces compared with
Turkish. Theological argument rent the political world, and
produced the bitterest intolerance. In the recurring wars against
the Greeks the Caliphate fared badly. Rioting and insecurity
were widespread and endemic, including a serious slave-rising
in southern Iraq (900), and gross and bloody campaigns by
Carmathians—fanatical Isma'ili sectarians—as well as Kharijis.
Administration was capricious and exercised often with brutal
cruelty, while the Caliph was at times no more than a prisoner
puppet of warring factions. In northern Iraq an Arab dynasty of
tribal origin, the Hamdanids (930–1000), secured well-nigh
sovereign power at Mosul and in the Jazira, and could threaten—
indeed, once occupied—Baghdad itself.

Meanwhile the eastern provinces of the Empire, by a natural
process which the rulers of Baghdad were powerless to prevent,
had split into a dozen independent states under dynasties which
soon rendered no trace of temporal homage to the 'Abbasid.
One of these, the Shi'i state of the Buwaihids, succeeded in
mastering southern Persia by 935, spread into Iraq and occupied
Baghdad in 945, and had its ruler saluted by the Caliph as
'Amir of Amirs' and commander of his armed forces. For a century
thereafter, till 1055, the Buwaihid Sultans effectively ruled Iraq
or most of it, with an authority questioned by none and least of all
by the puppet Caliphs who, whether or not treated still with
signs of outward respect, existed on sufferance under these Shi'i
overlords, as they had existed before under Turkish troop-leaders
or intriguing ministers. On the Euphrates, an Arab state of the
Bani Mazyad tribe-group maintained itself in effective independence for a hundred years from the mid-eleventh century; in the
north the Kurdish Marwanid Amirs of Diyarbakr (990 to 1100)
pushed their authority southwards deep into the Iraqi Jazira;
and in Mosul authority, during most of the eleventh century,

passed from the Hamdanids to the equally Arab house of the 'Uqailids, who ruled a wide group of cities of northern Iraq. This phase of division and weakness in the Iraqi provinces ended with the decay and fragmentation of Buwaihid power, and the scarcely opposed entry on the scene, in 1055, of the ruler and forces of the now formidable Turkish, or Turkoman, Seljuq power. This virile and uncorrupted race, recent converts to Sunni Islam, had emerged from Turkestan, conquered the greatest part of Persia, and with ease occupied all of Iraq as a stage towards the political reunification of all western Asia, which they achieved. Under their outstanding Sultans—Toghril, Alp Arslan, Malik Shah—and the earlier successors of these, resident normally in Isfahan but often in Baghdad, an order and security revisited the territory which it had not known for two centuries; and the Caliph was permitted to regain not only wide spiritual recognition but, in the temporal field, the overt respect of powerful rulers, and even some show of territorial and military authority. He could suppress local dynasties, lead an army, form marriage-connections with the Seljuq Royal House, and consider (though with little result) the despatch of aid to the Muslims of Syria, now at grips with the Crusaders.

Nor, even in the final century of 'Abbasid history, was the Commander of the Faithful ever to relapse completely to his abject decadence of the Buwaihid period. By no means all his efforts to re-assert his temporal sovereignty were successful; powerful Amirs arisen from commands in the Seljuq armies set up States of their own in and around Iraq—those of the great Zangi (leader of anti-Crusader armies) and its offshoots at Mosul (from 1130), at Sinjar (from 1170) and in the Jazira (from 1180), and those of the house of Begtigin at Arbil (from 1144), and of Ortuk at Diyarbakr (from 1100). The Caliph too was repeatedly involved in struggles with the remnants of the original Seljuk state, and with half-independent Turkish or Kurdish (but rarely Arab) captains and would-be dynasty-founders. But in the decline of the Seljuq power, the absence of any imperial successor, and the preoccupation of other potential overlords with the Crusaders, more than one of the last 'Abbasids could claim at least to enjoy a precarious independence, to be sole master of Baghdad and all central and southern Iraq. If the north and the Jazira fell after 1175 to the originally Kurdish, but now Syrian and Egyptian, dynasty of the Ayyubids, under the famous Saladin (Salah al-Din),

the Caliph could still command important forces, and negotiate
as an equal with powerful neighbours. The reigns of the Caliphs
Mustarshid (1118), Muqtafi (1136), Nasir (1180) and Mustansir
(1226) covered a period of striking revival, even though a world
removed from the imperial glories of the Golden Age.

But the end was at hand. The last of the 'Abbasids, Musta'sim
(1242), a mean and feeble ruler, mishandled the approaches
made to him by the inexorably oncoming Mongol hordes, now
looming up across Persia from central Asia. Jenghis Khan had
already, a generation earlier, cast a menacing shadow towards
the Two Rivers, and had even been invited by al-Nasir, with
credulous folly, to protect him from the Turkish Shah of Khiva;
his grandson, Hulagu, advanced in 1256 in earnest upon Iraq,
was rather provoked than pacified by Musta'sim's inept
diplomacy, and in the space of a few days (February, 1258)
stormed, occupied, and, with savage barbarity, substantially
destroyed the peerless City of Peace. Its citizens, with their ruler,
were put to the sword in tens of thousands, incalculable treasures,
of 500 years accumulation, were looted and dissipated, seats
of learning were rifled or destroyed, industries and commerce
trampled to nothing. From this calamity, which ended in a day
a half-millennium of Iraqi history, the capital and its fellow-cities,
and indeed the wide country-side itself were destined never to
recover; the great canals and their head-works were left in ruins,
the age-long irrigation system destroyed, flooding and desolation
took its place.

The territory and its citizens had witnessed, despite so many
vicissitudes, upheavals and changes of master, a substantially
continuous and elaborated system of fiscal and provincial administration, evolved upon the basis of the Sassanids but modified
by Islamic conceptions and requirements and social-religious
stratification. They had known, for better or worse, the justice
of the Qadhis and the Caliph, based as it was on the Qur'an,
tradition, equity, and simplicity of procedure; no other law could
exist. They had seen the military power of mercenaries and
foreigners at its worst, with scarcely a relic of a virile self-defending
Iraqi peasantry or tribe. They had seen periods of safety and ease
alternating with those of near-anarchy and rapine. The wealth of
the territory, which in spite of later legends could doubtless have
been far greater under stable and enlightened government, was
nevertheless secured by its fertility, its developed irrigation, its

teeming man-power, its far-flung trade with Islamic neighbours on every hand. A rich market existed for its crafts and products, while artisans from every land improved and varied its output. The intellectual and scientific, religious and legal achievements of the age are indeed proverbial: a score of great names in learning and speculation, poetry and theology adorn the annals of Iraq from the ninth to the thirteenth centuries. Public buildings and amenities in the cities, and above all in Baghdad—even the Baghdad which, on the left bank of the Tigris, succeeded to the short-lived Round City of al-Mansur—were reckoned as superb. The Iraqi people, even in the frequent and prolonged periods of disorder and foreign government, were continuously in the presence of great events, great spectacles and the, however fallen, Commander of the Faithful himself. The country was always a main centre, and for long the unique centre, of the civilisation of the age. Complete habituation to Islamic speech and thought, pride and superiority was established; the older faiths lingered only in the small unconverted Jewish and Christian minorities, while those of earlier Persia and ancient Iraq vanished for ever from the scene, together with almost every trace of the great cities and shrines of the first millennia of history.

Was this an Arab civilisation—and were the Iraqis Arabs? The prevailing culture of the Muslim lands was never, obviously, that of the primitive Arabia which saw the birth of Islam; and with the disappearance or enervation of the earliest Arabian fire and fervour, it soon shed also almost all of such Arab elements as their military victory had introduced. In Iraq, particularly, the manners, character, arts and culture of Persia, modified more outwardly than essentially by Arab speech and learning, soon and permanently prevailed. Little or nothing was to remain of Arab asceticism or strictness, and the subtle speculations of the Persian mind penetrated the religion of Islam itself, as well as dominating the fields of learning and science in which Arabism could have nothing to offer. The officials of the 'Abbasid state, and the rulers who later controlled it, were by majority Persians, Turks, Christians, or Jews. Almost from the outset the military reliance of the Caliph, during the periods of his temporal independence, was on Turkish, Persian and barbarian bodyguards and mercenaries; his Court was of a luxury and splendour utterly remote from Arab tradition. Nevertheless, the dominance of the Arab language, the pride in tracing family origins to

C

ancient Arabian sources, a persisting sentimental loyalty to
tribalism, the acquired and asserted self-consciousness as 'Arabs'
of the racially almost unchanged rural masses and even of the
cosmopolitan cities, the unique position of Arabism and its speech
—that of the Prophet and the Traditions—in the whole Islamic
world, made of Iraq beyond denial an 'Arab country', state-
member or province of the Arab world, in a sense as valid ten
centuries ago as it is to-day.

THE DARKEST AGE

Two AND three-quarter centuries were to elapse between the
catastrophic fall and disappearance of the 'Abbasids, and the
entry of the imperial power of Ottoman Turkey on the Iraqi
scene. No period in its history was darker, more obscure, less
happy. The status of Baghdad was, save briefly under the Jala'irs,
no longer that of a capital. Five separate governments, Mongol,
Turkoman and Persian, were to exercise authority in its lifeless,
impoverished provinces: governments which (except the last and
shortest-lived) stood for nothing considerable in the field of culture
or even of material achievement, and cared little enough for
Iraqi welfare—or for human rights. A second visitation of Mongol
barbarity, under Timur the Lame, worthy successor of Hulagu,
crushed whatever was left of Iraqi prosperity.

Little was done in these centuries, from lack of leadership,
wealth or security, towards restoring the ruined, all-important
canal-system, replanting gardens, or rebuilding villages; desolation remained, the population, halved by Hulagu's massacres
and by starvation, further decreased, living standards in town
and country sank lower, learning barely survived, trade was
meagre and restricted. Emboldened tribes from the western
desert occupied ever wider areas and turned ploughed-land into
camel-pasture. The infusion into Iraq of Arab blood, tradition
and habits was stronger than ever before.

The successors of Hulagu, the Il Khans, as nominal vassals
of the supreme Mongol emperor, held the government of the
Iraqi provinces for three full generations. They imposed from their
capital in Isfahan an administration which, though not without
pretensions and conducted by high-ranking governors who had
accepted conversion to Islam, could not but be ill-regulated, capricious, and effectively limited to urban and suburban areas.

Some good, nevertheless, is remembered of Ghazan Khan (1295) and of Abu Sa'id (1316), and it seems that at least the constant internal factions and urban violence of Caliphate days were, perhaps from very lack of vitality, no more.

The second quarter of the fourteenth century witnessed the appearance in Persia, and the extension into Iraq, of the invariable phenomena of an eastern monarchy in decline—the intrigues and jealousies of kinsmen, ministers and generals. From these struggles for power the house of the Jala'ir Amirs, Persianised Mongols, emerged triumphant, and could by 1340 establish its sway firmly over the greatest part of the Il Khan empire, including most of Iraq. The son of the first Jala'iri Sultan extended his power over northern Persia to the Caspian, and added Mosul and Diyarbakr. The dynasty, no longer one of Mongol barbarians, more than held its own with the rival offshoots of the Mongol power, gave Iraq half a century of peace, and even vouchsafed some support to the arts and to works of charity. But the ninth decade of the century saw the outbreak of civil war between the royal heirs, and the habitual evils of a divided empire; and the tenth was to usher in another visitation of Mongol armies at their most bloodily destructive. Timur and his horde overran Persia and Armenia in 1384–7, paused at Baghdad to instal a governor to replace the Jala'iri who had incontinently fled, but revisited it in anger when, in 1401, the Jala'iri had returned and the city called accordingly for punishment. The second sack of Baghdad, scarcely less appalling than that of Hulagu, with its wholesale destruction of life and property and ravishing of the surrounding towns and country-side, was a blow to which Iraq owed largely, for ensuing centuries, its place as a backward and forgotten country.

For the moment, the withdrawal and death of Timur (1405) allowed the re-establishment, for another half-dozen years, of the former ruler. But he and his were too fatally weakened to survive. Among covetous neighbours was the growing power of the Turkoman Qara-Qoyunli—'Black Sheep'—principality, which had risen from clan to empire in eastern Anatolia and, after a period of subservience to the Jala'irs, had survived the visitation of Timur and could emerge as rivals of the Perso-Iraqi Jala'ir kingdom. Some years of bad relations between them were followed by armed clashes; fortune favoured the Turkoman Sultan, Qara Yusif; and after a major trial of arms he entered Baghdad in 1410

to establish for sixty years a rule which, inferior in enlightenment
to the Jala'ir, was delegated, from the capital at Tabriz, to
viceroys and governors of miscellaneous origin and little skill in
administration. Later quarrels between the Black Sheep ruler
and his western neighbours turned to his advantage, and the rule
of Jihan Shah (1444), the greatest of his line, seems to have
covered all northern and western Persia, and all Iraq.

But the usual factors of dissolution were at work. A royal prince,
governor of Baghdad, rebelled, assumed sovereign powers, was
besieged and expelled (1465). There and elsewhere the story was
the familiar one of local secession and uprising; nor did the
imperial line of Timur, surviving in eastern Persia, ever accept
the Black Sheep claim to independence. A rival Turkoman
dynasty, the Aq-Qoyunli (White Sheep) had meanwhile established itself at Diyarbakr, and threatened the land of the Two
Rivers from the north. The fourth ruler of this hitherto obscure
principality, Hasan the Long, ventured at last in 1467 to try con-
clusions with the Black Sheep forces. He won the first and
subsequent battles, placed garrisons, governors and tax-collectors
in the Iraqi towns, and, at the last, captured Baghdad itself after
a siege, and installed what passed for government.

The White Sheep, overlords of the impoverished and distracted
territory for 35 years, had little to contribute but the wars of rival
candidates for its throne vacated by the conqueror in 1478. Ten
rulers or nominal rulers of the White Sheep kingdom and its un-
fortunate provinces claimed authority in the ensuing two decades,
each calling vainly for aid to such neighbours in Turkey or Persia
as would heed them, and caring for Iraq solely as a source of funds
or levies; and only when, in 1499, a semblance of order was
restored among the warring candidates could less disastrous
conditions be hoped for.

But it could not be long before Iraq, now largely depopulated,
militarily defenceless and economically ruined, must become the
appanage, or the battleground, of one or other of the two States,
to north and east, whom power and ambition were even now
calling to important destinies in western Asia. In north Persia a
genuinely national revival, strongly Shi'i and well rooted in
Iranian soil, was by 1500 in full evidence. Its inspirer and leader,
Isma'il, of the pious Safawi family, could confidently challenge
the unsure authority of the White Sheep sultan, defeat him in
the important battle of Nakhchawan, drive him from Persia, and

occupy that country and much of Asia Minor with a settled and confident administration. His capital was at Tabriz. In 1508 he turned to Iraq, occupied Baghdad and all parts of the country, and had time before his death in 1524 to come in person on pilgrimage to the Shi'i shrines on the Euphrates, ostentatiously to destroy Sunni mosques and their attendant divines, and to ensure some years of formidable peace to town and tribe through his vice-regal Khans. Iraq was a Persian province for a quarter-century, and its indefinite continuance as such must to contemporary eyes have appeared certain.

But the Ottoman ('Uthmanli, or Osmanli) Turks had by now been, for two centuries, a virile and growing power which their arms and outstanding leadership and discipline had raised from a tiny clan to wide imperial rule in the Balkans and all western, northern and central Asia Minor, and their destined moment for eastward expansion corresponded with the Safawi rise and aggressions. The Kurdish princes and valley-lords of eastern Anatolia were already playing one power against the other, and providing an abundant field for clashing ambitions; and the religious bitterness of Sunni against Shi'i, and a total difference, or indeed antipathy, between Turk and Persian in tradition, manners, gifts and character completed the certainty of imminent strife. The first campaign, of exceptional scale and violence, led to the victory of the relentless Turk, Salim the Grim, at the battle of Chaldiran, and to the at least nominal submission of the north-Iraqi Kurds, and Mosul and the Upper Jazira, to the Sultan. The next operations, delayed for some years, were led in person by one of the greatest of Ottoman rulers, Sultan Sulaiman the Lawgiver, and, delivering Baghdad without bloodshed into his hands, opened the way to a peaceful occupation of the whole country. Basra and all outlying towns, country-side and tribes sent delegations of submission; the Sultan visited in person the Holy Places and offered large benefactions, military fiefs were bestowed on his captains, and a system of what passed for civil government, on the Turkish model of the period, was installed and operated.

THE TURKISH EMPIRE

IRAQ WAS to form part of the Ottoman Empire, whose despotic ruler was also (by his own arbitrary assumption) the Caliph of Islam, for nearly four centuries. During this period sometimes effective, sometimes nominal Turkish authority was exercised, through the governors sent from the capital, over most, or infrequently all, parts of Iraq. Under these Pashas, who varied almost infinitely in type and character, methods and merits, the territory was normally organised in three, or at times four, vilayets or provinces, though the status of Basra and Mosul as such was discontinuous, and the province of Shahrizur, and its capital Kirkuk, early lost their vilayet rank. The regions of Mardin, and even Diyarbakr, formed at times part of the Iraq command. Baghdad retained throughout the period its primacy of status and pretention. The minor subdivision of the country for administrative purposes tended, with succeeding years, to approach nearer and nearer to its modern form.

The long and inglorious period of Turkish government falls into a number of easily recognisable stages. The first, from 1534 to 1621, was that of the early phase of Ottoman dominion, with imperfect control, wide areas of virtual non-government, administration (where it existed) of medieval and decentralised type with the grossest local abuses, and an almost continuous state of war with the Safawi rulers of Persia. This period was ended by the recapture of Baghdad and occupation of all northern Iraq by the forces of Shah 'Abbas the Great, accompanied by great damage to Iraqi property and life and by savage repression of Sunni interests. The restored Persian rule lasted for 17 years (1621–1638); it gave place in turn to a restoration of Turkish authority after a victorious expedition to the territory by Sultan Murad IV. This was followed by two full generations during which the Turkish empire, already corrupt and weakened, enjoyed peace from Persian pressure, but failed to impose a civil government of reasonable adequacy; unless by the building of an occasional mosque, caravanserai or flood-dyke, the tyrannical Pashas conferred, in their brief tenures of office, little of benefit to Iraqi security, enrichment or progress. Administration was corrupt, maladroit and rapacious, high office normally for sale, self-enrichment the prevailing motive. Some meagre contribution of revenue from the Iraqi vilayets was, in most years, remitted to Istanbul. Basra and its neighbourhood fell, for eighty years (1620–1700), to the authority of a local ruler.

The first half of the 18th century, less obscure and inglorious than the foregoing period, was marked by two outstanding events. The first was yet another Persian invasion, under the great

conqueror Nadir Shah; it led to a prolonged siege of Baghdad
(1730) and later of Mosul, and to campaigns led vigorously, on
the Turkish side, by Hasan Pasha, Ahmad Pasha his son, and the
chivalrous veteran general 'Uthman Pasha 'the Lame' (1733).
The country was, in the end, delivered from the Persian threat
by the murder of Nadir Shah in 1747. The second feature of this
period was the proved inability of the Sultan-Caliph to nominate,
now or for the next full century, officers of his own choice to the
government of these vilayets; he was compelled, instead, to
accept and confirm, often after abortive counter-efforts, the
candidates preferred by Baghdad or Mosul themselves. Indeed,
in the ensuing period, 1747–1831, the Pashas of these provinces,
while formally correct in their treatment of their Sovereign,
and willing at times even to remit some token revenue, enjoyed,
in all but name, effective independence. The Walis of Mosul were
drawn from an eminent local family, the Jalilis, those of Baghdad
and Basra from the ranks of the Circassian slaves or freedmen
whose presence, and whose paramount power in the highest
governmental circles, was a remarkable feature of Iraqi, and
Turkish, public life prior to the nineteenth-century reforms.

The period from 1747 to 1831 was pre-eminently that of the
Slave-Pashas. Chief among these are remembered the astute and
vigorous Sulaiman abu Laila (1747–62): 'Umar Pasha (1764–80),
in whose reign the Persians under Karim Khan occupied Basra
for three years (1776–79): Sulaiman the Great (1780-1802),
who gave Iraq two decades of relatively firm and enlightened
government: and the last ruler of the old régime, Da'ud Pasha
(1817–31), whose catastrophic fall and surrender came after a
devastating visitation of plague and flood. The Iraq of these eighty
years remained, despite the rich courts and almost royal
pretentions of its rulers, a remote, oppressed and impoverished
province, in which medieval conceptions of life and government
still prevailed, and those of Europe had yet to appear.

The final Turkish period, from 1831 to 1914 is, to the student
and analyst of twentieth-century Iraq, the most directly interesting in its long history, since it set the scene, and introduced the
conceptions and institutions, which lasted till 1914; even though
the modern state of Iraq is the child of Arab nationalism, yet its
immediately preceding Turkish background was deeply formative.
The nineteenth century saw the attempted introduction, with
some goodwill but much feeble inefficiency, of the 'reformed'

system of government towards which the Turkish Empire, itself
by now incurably the Sick Man, had striven fitfully from the early
years of the century. The great names in Turkish Iraq of this
period were those of 'Ali Ridha Pasha (successor to Da'ud), Najib
Pasha, Muhammad Rashid 'the Spectacled', Namiq Pasha, the
great reformer and statesman Midhat Pasha (1869–72) whose
enlightenment and relative efficiency were far above habitual
Turkish levels, and the dynamic but short-lived Nadhim Pasha
(1911–12). The Revolution of 1908–9 gave fresh impulse to the
forces of reform and modernisation, and did something, but dis-
appointingly little, to produce better government—or at least
the conditions to make it possible.

The long-drawn Turkish régime in Iraq suffered at all times
from the weakness, distraction and poverty of that Power: from
its lack of a tolerable system—or even, in its first three centuries,
a reasonably humane conception—of government: from its geographical and moral remoteness, its lack of adequate communications, its ill-disciplined and outmoded Janissary or feudal forces,
and the absence of any tradition of law-abiding among its unwilling subjects. At least until the middle of the 19th century, the
bestowal of office was capricious, venal and entirely blind to the
public interest, while local candidates for power, and flagrant
abuses of authority, were rarely absent. The civil service was
archaic, or scarcely existed. Among the Arab tribes, which
dominated the larger part of the Iraqi country-side, there was as
little willingness to obey foreign and hated masters as there was,
in the latter, little sympathy for the disorderly, marauding,
resentful tribesmen; from this antipathy it resulted that the
abiding problem of tribal indiscipline and transgression—those of
the 'Aniza, Shammar, Dhafir, Muntafiq, Cha'ab, Bani Lam,
Zubaid, and many more—was never solved, the consequent
country-wide insecurity was never brought to an end, even though
conditions improved considerably towards the end of the century.
In Kurdistan, the principalities founded at Jazira ibn 'Umar,
'Amadiya, Keui Sanjaq, Sulaimaniya and elsewhere by Kurdish
rulers, and the lesser 'valley lords' who were their vassals or rivals,
continued until 1850 to defy (or insincerely to placate) the Turkish
Pashas, to preserve a practical independence, and to play off
Turk against Persian in the wide and restless border-country.
Only with the fall of the famous Baban dynasty in the eighteen-
fifties, after more than a century of independent (if unhappy and

divided) rule, could direct Turkish authority make itself felt, precariously enough, in most of Iraqi Kurdistan. The rule of Basra presented its own problems of powerful riverain tribesmen, the proximity of uncontrolled Arabia, and the rivalries of Europeans—Portuguese, Dutch, British, French—for position in the Persian Gulf. At Mosul, whose government was for a century the perquisite of the Jalili family, the enemies of tranquillity were the foothill Kurds, the fierce Yazidis, the unsafety of every road, and the starvation which recurrent drought and locust visitations could produce. The Euphrates region and cities, always vulnerable to descents by the desert tribesmen, had witnessed, during the earlier centuries, the independent power of desert potentates; and, when these ceased to be, were constantly threatened, after 1775, by the rising power of the Wahhabi Amirate of Najd, whose forces in 1802 attacked and ransacked the holy shrine of Karbala itself. Town life in all areas, though its tempo and character were found by many not disagreeable, was commonly distracted by the indiscipline of the Turkish forces, by criminals to whom (as in Najaf and Karbala) gang-organisation appealed, and by disorderly tribal visitors; the life of the citizens was conditioned by the callous attitudes of a government frankly archaic till 1830 and its many follies and inhumanities in matters of taxation and demands for service, by the deep suspicion within Islam itself between Sunni and Shi'i, and by the exclusion of the Shi'is from all public careers.

The last eighty years of the régime witnessed, admittedly, considerable efforts at improvement and at a modernisation which was rendered the more necessary by the strong Turkish desire to stand well with the powers of Europe, the presence in Iraq of foreign consular representatives and men of commerce, the increasing interest of Europe in the territory, the importance of the land-route and the steamer-lines to India, the opening up of river-steamer and telegraphic communications. These were all circumstances which must render anachronistic the régime of the Slave Pashas or anything like it: and Iraq had, indeed, by the mid-century, and still more after the epoch-marking governorship of Midhat Pasha, left behind most of the antiquated (but often picturesque) phenomena of the public life of preceeding centuries. It stood committed beyond recall to the ways of Reform. If roads and useful public works were few, railways (till 1914) non-existent, agricultural improvement neglected, modern industry unknown,

C*

the social services scanty and starved, the cities filthy, officialdom
shabby and ill-educated, the tribes still sullen or unruly, the Kurds
disloyal and turbulent, yet much had been accomplished in instal-
ling at least a system (the 'vilayet system') of civil administration,
developing a specialised civil service, half-modernising both the
codes and courts of justice, regularising the armed forces and the
police, attempting (though with woefully inadequate resources
and techniques) a form of land settlement (the Tapu system),
settling tribes and encouraging municipalities. In the disappearance in 1909 of the long and stagnant dictatorship of
Sultan 'Abd al-Hamid, the genuine enthusiasm for progress of
the Young Turks (who had their substantial following in Iraq),
and the good intentions of the best officials, both Turkish or Iraqi,
there was, in 1914, fair hope for the future. Meanwhile the problems of irrigation had at least, for the first time, been studied (by
British consultants) and the Hindiya Barrage built in 1912; a first
sector of the German railway (Baghdad-Samarra) had been
completed; the possibility of oil-deposits had attracted interest,
local tests had been made, and in remote Istanbul, an Anglo-
German group (the Turkish Petroleum Company) had obtained
a vizirial promise for an oil-concession over the Mosul and
Baghdad vilayets. Security had markedly improved. The minority
communities, which since the formation of the Chaldean Uniate
community (by Catholicising Nestorians) had assumed their
modern forms, had no great cause for complaint. European
consuls and interests were, if little favoured, not quite ignored.
The fruitless adventures in Arabia initiated by Midhat Pasha,
and pursued again in 1906-7, had been fortunately abandoned,
though Kuwait and Najd itself were recorded, solely on paper,
as Turkish dependencies. The Persian frontier was finally delimited
in 1913-14, under international auspices; and the three vilayets
which, together forming the eastern half of the Fertile Crescent,
were to constitute the future State of Iraq, were by that date
bounded almost exactly as are the fourteen Iraqi *liwas* of to-day.
Since the foundation in the later 19th century of new towns as
military bases or river-steamer fuelling points—Nasiriya, Diwaniya, Ramadi, 'Amara, Kut al-Amara—the urban centres of the
territory were, like nine-tenths of its villages, those of our own
age. The old walls of Baghdad, built by the Jala'ir Sultans, were
demolished by Midhat Pasha; the city, half Jewish in population,
was, after a thousand years of life, still commercially active and

not unprosperous. Basra was still the worst equipped of sea-ports, Mosul, through changes of trade-routes, had heavily declined since its great days.

Still the most forlorn and stagnant of Turkish provinces, Iraq had nevertheless by 1914 a greater international interest than at any time since the middle ages. It lay notoriously on the land routes to India; it was believed capable of rich development; it was important in Islam, in the worlds of history and archaeology, perhaps of commerce, certainly of missionary effort and cultural expansion. It had been visited, since the first British travellers in 1583, by scores of foreign visitors. British interest, moving northward from the Gulf, was established at Basra in the eighteenth, and at Baghdad in the early nineteenth centuries, with unquestioned primacy over other European powers; the river-steamers, a permitted system of British post offices, the bulk of foreign trade, and the Gulf steamship services (and a well-earned special position in those waters) were British. Goods and pilgrims came in quantity from British India, and the installation of the British Resident at Baghdad was upon a scale of considerable formality and some privilege. The Russian power was active, though largely invisible, in penetrating northern Iraq, and had known designs on neighbouring Persia. The French by their missionaries and teachers had proved successful pioneers of western, or specifically French and Catholic, culture. The Americans carried out some educational and missionary work. The Germans, cherishing wide schemes of eastern penetration and expansion since 1900—the famous *Drang nach Osten*—had planned and partly completed the Iraqi sections of the Bagdadbahn.

The extent of Turkish permeation of Iraqi society is debatable. Though in terms of culture (other than a superficial Europeanisation) the Turks had had little to contribute, and their racial contribution to the three million Iraqis of the time had been minimal, yet in the administration, civil and military, their position was paramount, all procedures and standards were theirs alone, and the whole legacy awaiting post-1918 Iraq in those fields was that of Turkey; the governmental conceptions and methods, the laws, offices and procedures inherited by Great Britain during and after the War of 1914–18 were Turkish. In the middle strata of town society Turkish was widely spoken, the vocabulary of Iraqi Arabic was perceptibly influenced by that of Turkish, urban manners and social life were much affected from the same source, marriage with Turkish ladies was common. The few and ill-found government schools taught in that language, and higher education was to be had only in Istanbul. The veneration of the Caliph, and the exclusively Sunni flavour of all public life, conferred great advantages within Iraq on that section (about one-half) of local society. Pro-Turkish, and especially pro-Hamidian, sentiment was strong though far from unanimous in upper-class urban circles, while the opposite was generally true among the lower orders, throughout the country-side and the tribes, and everywhere in the Shi'i community.

Arab nationalism was already alive by 1914 and could be judged as a movement certain to gather force in the near future. It was based upon the active but hitherto non-political Arabism of scholars and divines, upon the racial-cultural self-consciousness of an awkening people, and, lately, upon the specific efforts being made by publicists (though less in Iraq than other Arab countries) to move towards a form of administrative decentralisation, or Home Rule within the Ottoman Empire or even, in the last resort, detachment from it. Such ideas had as yet little or no popular following, no inter-regional organisation, no agreed programme; yet they existed, and, as in Syria and Egypt, were yearly becoming more widely known and a greater menace to the existing régime. Arab, or Iraqi, nationalism was in the early years of the 20th century already a discernible movement within that class, the educated urban upper or middle-class, to whom its full development was to be due; and it had already attracted to its service some of the potential political leaders of the future kingdom.

If the handling of local nationalism could be felt in 1914 as an emerging problem for the rulers of Iraq, it was far from being their only problem. An adequate system of representative government was still to be evolved—or, more broadly, a tolerable relationship was still to be established between government and public. In the field of public enlightenment, everything remained to be done among the backward, ignorant population by education at every level and by every means. National physique was poor, disease endemic and neglected. An almost universal and long-familiar poverty, accepted with hopeless fatalism, afflicted and retarded the public, and precluded all but the lowest standards in nourishment, clothing and manner of life; only immense economic advance on a wide front could improve this, by the comprehensive betterment of agriculture, quantitative and qualitative, the re-establishment of control over the Rivers and their scientific exploitation, the intelligent fostering of industry and commerce, the discovery and development of natural resources, the creation and equipment of modern communications. The problem of tribal disorder must be transferred into one of tribal welfare. The difficulties of Kurdish government must be overcome by intelligent tact, and firmness. The minority communities must be re-assured and protected. Security of life and property and land-tenure demanded the firm establishment it had never had. The legal and judicial systems cried out for reform, or for complete refashioning. Officialdom, and official procedures and standards, stood in need of purging, re-basing, elevating; this must cover in particular revenue-assessment and collection, local administration, the army and the gendarmerie. Adequate public services must be created, and the benefits of benevolent government made manifest to town and country.

Such were, in outline, the tasks and problems which, whether so recognised or not, confronted the Turkish government of Iraq as the storm-clouds of 1914 gathered. It was, however, after all to no Turks that their solution, or their burden, was to fall.

Chapter 4

The British Mandate

FIRST WORLD WAR, AND AFTER

THE decision of Great Britain, in the autumn of 1914, to invade 'Turkish Arabia' from her bases in India was due to the already threatening signs of Turkish adhesion to the German enemy, to fears for her 'special position' and her friends in the Persian Gulf—and ultimately, perhaps, for the security of India itself; and to these was added the immediate need to safeguard British oil production in southern Persia, a new and important asset, dating only from 1912. The landing of a small force in the Shatt al-'Arab, the bloodless occupation of Basra, and the restoration of the position in the Persian oil-fields, were the work of a few weeks in and after early November 1914. A Turkish counter-attack was unsuccessful, and the spread of British forces in lower Iraq, to Qurna, Nasiriya and 'Amara, arduous and costly as it proved, was complete by mid-summer 1915. The autumn of that year saw the ill-fated, because ill-timed, attempt on Baghdad by General Townshend, followed by the 140-day siege of his forces in Kut. His garrison, in spite of determined efforts to relieve it, was forced to surrender unconditionally in April 1916; but meanwhile the British hold on southern Iraq had been strengthened, many contacts with the local public were established, and an embryo Administration, staffed by military officers, was created.

The surrender of Kut, an outstanding reverse to British arms, was nevertheless followed by a comprehensive regrouping and reinforcement of the invading forces which, originally known as 'Indian Expeditionary Force D.', were now renamed the Mesopotamian Expeditionary Force. These steps, to which not without reluctance the British Government were led by military and in part political exigencies, made possible not only the firm establishment of all port, base, road and railway communication, and supply facilities between Kut and the Gulf, but the recapture also of that city and a powerful forward movement from it by General

Maude in December 1916. The Turks were dislodged from their riverain positions and pursued up-river, and Baghdad fell to British arms on 11 March 1917. Mobile forces occupied the districts northward of the city, touch was for a time established with a Russian column in western Persia, and preparations were made for Turkish counter-moves in force, with which rumour was active.

The expected counter-stroke did not materialise; and in the spring of 1918, after the lamented death of Maude, the Anglo-Indian armies advanced their front far up the Euphrates to 'Ana, and along the Mosul road to Kifri and Tuz. Kirkuk was taken in May, but for supply reasons could not be held. In early autumn the advance was resumed against light opposition, Kirkuk and Sharqat were entered and passed, and the advance pressed on to Mosul itself, which was entered a few days after the Armistice of Mudros (30 October). The city was held in spite of Turkish protest, and in the weeks following Turkish troops withdrew from all parts of the Mosul vilayet. The whole of Iraq, from Zakho to Fao, from the Persian frontier to Dair-al-Zur, was thus effectively in British occupation before the close of the year 1918.

That it would present exceptional difficulties in government during the coming months, that post-war nervousness, reactions and uncertainties would certainly render the immediately ensuing period one of peculiar delicacy, was already clear, from growing experience of its problems and daily incidents, to the Chief Political Officer, Sir Percy Cox, and his deputy Colonel Arnold Wilson, and to the officers of the Political Department—in effect, the civil government of the territory—which they had formed. The tribes of southern Iraq, almost strangers to orderly government, and resentful of it in whatever form, presented baffling problems of shaikh-peasant relationship; the middle-Euphrates Holy Cities, with their satellite tribes and towns, relapsed into a congenial near-anarchy; the attitude of the powerful Shi'i *mujtahids* was doubtful or antagonistic, and at Najaf the murder of a British officer was unavoidably followed by coercive measures. In the Jazira and western desert, 'Aniza and Shammar and Jubur problems multiplied within these tribes and between them. In Kurdistan favourable contacts had been made, but administration of the wilder mountain areas had not yet been attempted. From the Hakkari mountains beyond the Iraqi northern frontier, and from the plains of Urmiya in Persia, had arrived thousands of

'Assyrian' (that is, Nestorian Christian, see p. 27) refugees from Turkish and Kurdish barbarity, in the last stages of want and weakness; these were rescued, fed, rehabilitated, and housed in a vast camp near Ba'quba.

But the greatest of immediate problems was that of the disposal of the occupied territory itself. The country, or at least the vilayets of Baghdad and Basra, had been specifically excepted from the ill-formulated promises of Arab government made by Sir Henry MacMahon to King Husain of the Hijaz, late in 1915; but in the ill-fated Franco-British 'Sykes-Picot' agreement of May 1916— condemned by its critics as a sad example of secret, and amateur, diplomacy at its worst—the Mosul area had been allotted to France as a sphere of influence and privilege, part of northern and most of western Iraq was assigned similarly to Great Britain, while the centre and south of the territory was to be available for direct British government. The Sykes-Picot agreement was by the end of 1918 already a dead letter—or at least so treated in Whitehall; Mosul was transferred, by agreement between Lloyd George and Clemenceau in December of that year, from the French to the British sphere, and distinctions between the various areas of Iraq were, because unreal and inapplicable, no longer envisaged. But a Franco-British declaration made on 7 November 1918 spoke of their joint intention to install, in Syria and in Iraq, 'national governments . . . which shall derive their authority from the free exercise of the initiative and choice of the indigenous population'; and much the same could already have been deduced (at least by Arab optimists) from the terms of Maude's proclamation on the occupation of Baghdad.

The earliest post-war period, indeed, revealed Iraqi aspirations strictly on such lines. Colonel Wilson, unsympathetic to local nationalism and to administrative inefficiency, favoured little or no British surrender of control; but under instructions he was willing to conduct a rough-and-ready referendum, and himself inclined to the formation of a (largely nominal) Arab State, with Cox as ruler. In Great Britain, cabinet and popular opinion was divided, with at least some support for the cautious grant of a self-determined régime. International statesmanship, in the persons, notably, of President Woodrow Wilson and General Smuts, was already devising the 'Mandate System' for the ex-Turkish Arab regions, and provision for this was specifically included in the Charter of the League of Nations (Article 22), and in the Treaty of Versailles. The long delay in reaching a decision was due to the multiplicity of interests involved and opinions held (Great Britain herself speaking with far from a single voice), to the delay in peace-making with a Turkey still nominally sovereign over Iraq, and to the actually disturbed conditions in that country, which could be variously interpreted. Meanwhile an attempt to set up a Kurdish principality, under Shaikh Mahmud Barzinji, had sadly failed through his own excessive ambition; trouble-makers from northern Syria were entering the upper-Euphrates area of Iraq; anti-British propaganda was pouring from the Shi'i *mujtahids*; the Sunni politicians of Baghdad in growing numbers were uniting on a warmly nationalistic programme; and British forces were melting, with post-war demobilisation, to a level far below that of safety.

The news that the Principal Allied Powers, meeting at San Remo in April 1920, had conferred a Mandate for Iraq upon Great Britain reached Baghdad at a moment when committees both there and in London were considering, in a spirit of caution, what forms Iraqi constitutional development could take. The temporary administration of the territory (now, in some areas, already five years old) retained a character which, while it assured a security, honesty, and progressiveness far in advance of anything the three vilayets had seen before, was nevertheless inevitably authoritarian, foreign, Christian, and, largely for these reasons, uncongenial and increasingly unpopular.

This wide-spread though far from universal attitude to the British administration, with the announcement of the Mandate and the increased activation of subversive movements from Syria and Turkey and in Iraq itself—and the presence, as ever, of strong tribal antipathy to restraint or government in any form—led in the summer of 1920 to a tribal and country-side uprising upon a considerable scale, later acclaimed by nationalists as a National Rebellion. Lacking adequate leadership, co-ordination or timing, or the visible support of the town populations, it nevertheless gained ground in many parts of southern and central Iraq and in lesser areas of the north where it led to general disorder, the cutting of communications (including the new-made Basra-Baghdad Railway), and allowed the formation of local 'governments' by shaikhs or urban notables in outlying districts. The British, unprepared for opposition on this scale and having (in part through defective civil-military understanding) sustained

distressing early reverses, were forced, at a moment when peace
and economy were their paramount desiderata, to expend very
considerable treasure, resources, troops and time in restoring
order. This was done by a wide series of small operations, the
recovery of key points and reopening of communications, the
collection of rifles, and the rewarding of the loyal. The revolt, in
which many leading figures in the country had refused to partici-
pate, was over in the late autumn of 1920, though restorative or
punitive columns were still in movement throughout the
winter.

Sir Percy Cox, relieving his deputy, Wilson, returned to
Baghdad in October 1920. His instructions from London were on
the basis of British acceptance of the Mandate, the operation of
which would be on liberal lines and not without regard to the
principles of self-determination; it would include the establishment of an Iraq Government, with the due forms of statehood
even though possessing at first an independence limited by the
advice and control of its Mandatory. For such a programme he
expected, and in fact obtained, much support; the events of mid-
summer 1920 had alarmed all but the extreme nationalists, and
more moderate councils now prevailed. The High Commissioner
(as was Cox's new designation) secured the support of the ven-
erated Naqib of Baghdad, Sayyid 'Abd al-Rahman al-Gailani,
and invited ministers, including competent and representative
figures, to join the cabinet of a provisional government over which
the Naqib would preside. The Council of Ministers thus formed
met on 2 November, assumed their charges as responsible ministers
—each, however, aided by a British adviser—undertook the
drafting of an Electoral Law, recalled to their own country many
expatriated Iraqi officers now in Syria (where the Amir Faisal
had been dethroned by the French in July), installed Iraqi
governors (also British-advised) in all administrative units, and
began the formation of an Iraqi Army.

A Government of Iraq, neither easily nor quickly achieved,
existed and was operating.

THE MANDATE

THE IMPOSITION of the British Mandate was, when and where
understood, received with apathy or with satisfaction by a large
part of the non-political public, as being a guarantee at least of

safety from Turkish reappearance, a defence against their own politicians, and an assurance that security and progress could be expected: but almost the entirety of the intelligentsia and the political world, which the war and post-war periods had much augmented, and to which now full 'liberation' and national independence alone appealed, the Mandate was from the first unpopular and resented, and its unconditional abrogation became the chief of objectives. The British attitude, which their policy and actions were substantially to make good, was one of accepting the duties and obligations of the Mandate, of conducting it with economy and for as short a time as possible, and of expecting from it little or no material (but, doubtless, some general strategic) advantage, while preserving—an essential mandatory conception —the Open Door to all League members. They hoped to protect the territory, if need be, with their imperial forces, in addition to others raised locally, to secure its international position, and to safeguard internal order. They intended to establish an effectively workable administrative régime, and to entrust this to a maximum of selected and trained Iraqi personnel with a minimum of British interference or control, with a view to their own earliest withdrawal. How far these unexceptionable objectives were realised in the event, will appear hereinafter; at least they contrasted favourably, in practical operation and certainly in popular acceptability, with the policies and methods of the French mandatory in contemporary Syria.

The period of twelve years covered by the Mandate was, for all its brevity, extraordinarily formative for the Iraqi people, and significant for their future. Although, from lack of funds, material development was restricted to humble levels (a fact with which the British were at times, and later, frequently reproached) the public was nevertheless in a few years habituated to new conceptions and standards in public life, a new atmosphere and new opportunities; and this in spite of the substantial continuity not only of local society but also, until progressively modified, of law and governmental procedure and the administrative machine. The territory was delimited, assured of its integrity. Its relations with other nations, and above all with Great Britain, were established: indeed, Anglo-Iraqi relations from 1920 to 1932 formed the main, the absorbing, interest of nationalist politics in these years. A Kingdom was erected, a constitution and elective parliament were installed, governmental institutions and techniques were

created (or those in existence were reviewed and modified) at
every level, and were made to operate at the hands of keen and
self-respecting officials. Iraqi political life gained vitality and the
beginnings of organisation, the dominant personalities emerged.
Determined efforts were made to solve, or palliate, certain of the
abiding problems of the territory—of its lands and waters, its
tribes and minorities, its security and its livelihood. The present
and next section will deal summarily with these matters.

Four months after the installation of the Provisional Government at Baghdad with the Naqib as Prime Minister, the convening
of a Conference by Great Britain at Cairo was announced, with
the object of settling, under the chairmanship of Mr. Winston
Churchill (then Secretary of State for the Colonies) Britain's
immediate and tangled middle-eastern problems. Attended by
Cox and higher Iraqi and British officials, the Conference took
important decisions. One was to 'encourage' the candidature to
the Iraqi throne of ex-King Faisal, now in Europe and without
employment: another, dictated by the hope of greater efficiency
and economy, was to substitute the Royal Air Force for the Army
as the controlling force for the maintenance of order. The arrival of
Faisal in Iraq revealed him from the outset as by far the most
acceptable of possible candidates: and, not without a negative
attitude in certain Shi'i and some Kurdish circles, his selection
was confirmed first by the cabinet and later by a hastily im-
provised nation-wide referendum. His enthronement took place
in Baghdad on 23 August 1921. The King quickly established
good relations with his ministers and his subjects, and with the
British element still inevitably dominant, though no longer
executive, in the administration; and the twelve years of his reign
gave opportunity for his charm, political flair and good sense to
make an outstanding contribution to his adopted country.

The first year of the monarchy witnessed, with much consolidation and some innovation, some growing-pains in the current
administration of the country, and the hardening of Shi'i theocratic sentiment as well as of urban Sunni nationalism against
the British connection. This was specifically directed against the
Anglo-Iraq Treaty now designed as the least offensive means of
interpreting the Mandate. The Najaf and Karbala *mujtahids*, and
eager politicians in Baghdad (and even in the King's own
entourage) opposed on varying grounds the suggested twenty-year
commitment to a foreign alliance which must necessarily involve

(as did the Mandate itself) some incompleteness of independence. The Treaty with its subsidiary Agreements (financial, military and judicial) were, nevertheless, signed by the High Commissioner and the Naqib on 10 October 1922. It was to be followed by country-wide elections for a Constituent Assembly, of which the function would be to ratify it and produce a Constitution and an Electoral Law. The aged Naqib at this point gave way as Prime Minister to 'Abd al-Muhsin Bey, of the famous Sa'dun family, as did Sir Percy Cox, in May 1923, as High Commissioner, to Sir Henry Dobbs.

The twenty-year Treaty period was, to the general satisfaction, shortened to four years by a Protocol signed in April 1923: but continued Shi'i opposition to, or indeed categorical veto of, the elections for the Constituent Assembly was modified only by the retirement to Persia of the leading Shi'i *mujtahids* (all Persian by nationality) following an alleged insult to their order, and their chastened return to Iraq some months later: an episode not displeasing to the King and the orthodox nationalists, and one from which *mujtahid* influence never fully recovered. The elections were held; Ja'far Pasha al-'Askari (a veteran of the Hijaz campaign of 1916–18, and a staunch supporter of Faisal in Syria) succeeded 'Abd al-Muhsin as head of the government; and the Constituent Assembly met in March 1924. In the face of considerable, at times physically violent, opposition the Treaty was ratified by a narrow majority, and the Assembly proceeded with greater calm to complete drafts of the Electoral Law and of a Constitution which provided for a modern-type, two chamber parliament. Ja'far Pasha was in turn succeeded as Premier by an outstanding nationalist and ex-Turkish Corps Commander, Yasin Pasha al-Hashimi.

Meanwhile, widespread disorders in Kurdistan during 1921–24 reflected the feebleness of the governmental hold in that region, the centrifugal tendencies of the ever recalcitrant Aghas, and, in particular, the strong infiltration of the Turks into frontier areas both before and after the Armistice of Mudania (November 1922) had ended the Greco-Turkish war: by which date determined Turkish claims to the retrocession of the Mosul vilayet had already begun to be advanced. Thereafter, three years of anarchy, largely Turkish-inspired but also traditional, in all but the the inlying Kurdish areas ended in 1924–25 with the eviction of disturbing elements (notably Shaikh Mahmud) and the re-establishment, by military columns and air action, of substantial government control.

The Turkish claim to Mosul, highly alarming to the Iraq authorities, was formally advanced at the first Lausanne Conference (February 1923), and, opposed by Great Britain on Iraq's behalf, was referred to the League of Nations for settlement. The League Council laid down a 'Brussels Line' as a provisional frontier intended to reflect the *status quo*, and sent a three-man Commission of Enquiry to the territory. It arrived in January 1925. Its excellent report, discrediting the Turkish claims (which were in fact based on misleading or fabricated population-figures), assigned the vilayet definitely to Iraq, but suggested that, for the better reassurance of the Kurdish minority, antagonistic to or suspicious of the Baghdad Government, the four years of the current Anglo-Iraq Treaty should be lengthened to twenty-five; and, moreover, that in administering the Kurdish areas due regard should be paid to their language, racial distinctness, and susceptibilities. The treaty prolongation, though disliked by all nationalist groups, was adopted by parliament in January 1926, with the significant proviso that the question of Iraq's admission to the League of Nations should be reconsidered by its Ally every four years. Turkey, after a strong and indeed menacing initial reaction, accepted the position, and a tripartite Anglo-Turco-Iraqi Treaty (July 1926) stabilised the arrangement, and, as a partial *douceur*, assigned to Turkey in compensation one-tenth of eventual oil-royalties which one day might accrue in the Mosul vilayet. (No discovery of commercially-producible oil had as yet been made in the vilayet). Machinery was provided in the Treaty for the delimitation of the frontier and the adjustment of disputes.

This extremely important settlement, a striking British achievement on Iraq's behalf, made final the scale and area of the Iraq kingdom and endowed it (as the near future would show) with vast wealth from petroleum, even though it involved Iraq also in all the problems of administering the mainly Arabophobe, well-armed, and chronically restless Kurds. Elsewhere on the frontiers, a temporary (to become in 1933 a permanent) boundary was established with Syria; relations with Persia, always strained by current incidents and by a measure of mutual antipathy, were at least prevented from further deterioration. With Sa'udi Arabia (as the Sultanate of Najd became in 1932) an agreement on boundaries, involving the construction of a Neutral Zone, was concluded in 1922; but thereafter a phase of violent frontier raiding across Iraq's south-west border, due to tribal animosities and to Sa'udi-Hashimite dynastic bitterness, was ended with difficulty, through British intervention, by a series of conferences and a royal meeting in January 1930 on a warship in the Persian Gulf. An Iraqi-Sa'udi treaty was concluded in April 1931. In northern Iraq the settlement of the hapless Assyrian remnant (p. 80) in hill-villages was attempted, but was rendered the more difficult by their own divisions, the shortages of suitable un-occupied land, and the long-drawn political uncertainties of the region. Thousands took service in the Assyrian units of the Iraq Levies, a British-paid and British-officered force distinct from the Iraq Army; some drifted to the towns; parties that foolhardily sought to regain their ancient homes in Turkey were rudely disappointed; and the majority, still discontented, were settled and subsidised, village by village, in areas near the Turkish and Persian frontiers. All these and Mar Sham'un their Patriarch, anti-Arab in sentiment and heavily committed to the British, could not but view with great apprehension the nearer approach of full Iraqi independence.

In the administration of the country, the part played by British officers—always, of course, entirely distinct from the functions and establishment of the High Commissioner—grew progressively less, with fewer officials and executive duties confined to the technical departments. The innumerable cases of, and disputes arising from, tribal misdoing, land-tenancy, water-rights, revenue assessments and all other sources occupied them (and particularly the provincial Administrative Inspectors) and their Iraqi col-leagues, under a collaborative régime predominantly happy and successful, but by its nature temporary. In politics, while the power of the *mujtahids* diminished, the aspirations of the long-excluded Shi'i urban rank-and-file to their due place in public life persistently increased; these were correspondingly resented by Sunni elements, which were accustomed for centuries to a monopoly of influence and appointments in the government. Political organisation in these years, in spite of much activity and an increasing (and almost solely political) Press, did not transcend the few 'parties' formed by leading personalities; these could claim few members, announced stereotyped and always imprecisely Utopian nationalist programmes, had little appeal other than personal, and enjoyed scanty or no support outside the main cities—or indeed, usually, outside Baghdad itself. Such parties came into ephemeral existence in 1921—the 'Nationalist' party, the 'Free' party, the 'Awakening'—and were increased by others—the People's, the Popular, and that of National Independence—in subsequent years. They showed the immaturity of local political organisation and the limitation of aspiration, at present, to the sole objective of shedding the Mandate; and they showed also the ominous possibility that the politicians would be ready to use both religious (especially Shi'i) emotion and armed tribal strength as weapons, however dangerous, in their campaigns. Towards pan-Arabism, the creation of the unitary or federal Arab State alleged to have been promised by the British in 1915, no specific steps were taken, or were possible, at this period, though the ideal remained in many Arab minds for ultimate realisation. Social reform, as an objective of the political parties, had no visible place before 1932. Communism was not unknown, though it could claim but few and obscure followers.

The leading statesmen of the time, besides the Prime Ministers already mentioned, were glad, meanwhile, to accept ministerial office in the brittle and ever-changing cabinets. Such notably were General Nuri Pasha al-Sa'id, Rashid 'Ali al-Gailani, Ra'uf al-Chadirchi, Hikmat Sulaiman, the Suwaidi brothers—Naji and Tawfiq—Naji Shaukat, Rustum Haidar, 'Ali Jaudat, Jamil al-Midfa 'i, Arshad al-'Umari, and a score of other Sunni ministers or *ministrables*; and among the Shi'is, 'Abd al-Husain al-Chalabi, Muhammad al-Sadr, Muhammad Ridha al-Shabibi, and the young Salih Jabr. Christian ministers were not unknown, and a Jew, Sasun Haskail, had been the first Minister of Finance. Many leading personalities among the more articulate tribal shaikhs gained a place in politics, predominantly nationalist on the middle Euphrates, 'moderate' elsewhere. The work of parliament, in which the British took no part, was, from the first, conducted creditably and with dignity. The Press, rhetorical and unrealistic, was of value as a provocative but little as an educative factor. But at least the Iraq State was offering liberty and careers in politics, and abundant national self-expression, in a sense undreamed of before.

A revised and more favourable Anglo-Iraqi treaty was initialled in December 1927, with the promise of amended financial and military agreements and of a British recommendation, 'provided the present rate of progress in Iraq is maintained', for the country's entry to the League in 1932: an entry involving, of course, the end of the Mandate and of the *wadh' al-shadh* (the 'preposterous situation' of Anglo-Iraqi dyarchy) ridiculed by Iraqi humorists. The treaty was, however, viewed as disappointing or ungenerous by Iraqi nationalist opinion, and remained unratified. In 1929 the promise to recommend Iraq as a League candidate was made unconditional by the incoming High Commissioner, Sir Gilbert Clayton, and the Council of the League was informed accordingly. Even so, the path to independence was not yet clear. The Prime Minister, 'Abd al-Muhsin al-Sa'dun, committed suicide in November 1929, to the general consternation; and Clayton died suddenly, to be succeeded by Sir Francis Humphrys, lately Minister in Afghanistan. The text of a new Treaty was gradually established. Nuri al-Sa'id became Premier in succession to a short tenure of that office by Naji al-Suwaidi, and on 30 June, 1930 the new Treaty was signed.

The Treaty provided for full Iraqi independence, close alliance with Great Britain, a variety of not unfavourable financial provisions, and arrangements, in the field of Defence, whereby two R.A.F. bases would be maintained on the fringes of Iraq, at Shu'aiba and Habbaniya. New judicial arrangements, with a higher complement of British judges, were accepted by all ex-capitulatory powers; nothing more would be, or was, heard of the ancient Turkish-granted Capitulations. In Iraq some organisation of die-hard anti-Treaty elements was carried out, and a Party of National Brotherhood was formed to oppose it as being too favourable to Great Britain; strikes were arranged on a considerable scale, and something was even done by irresponsible politicians to foment Kurdish opposition. The British Government meanwhile used all its efforts to convince the League of Nations that Iraq was fit for its new status, and in particular could be trusted to deal correctly with its minorities, of whom the Assyrian (which had attracted considerable European interest) was the most vulnerable—and the most provocative. Guarantees to this end were given by the cabinet in Baghdad, and after further months of negotiation and reassurance Iraq was, under firm British pressure, formally admitted to full League membership, in an atmosphere of great cordiality, on 3 October 1932. The Mandate was over, independence achieved; a new 'Nation of the Modern World' had taken its place.

THE BRITISH CONTRIBUTION, 1920-32

THE BRITISH had begun in 1914 the occupation of an Iraq
where they had long been known and had already exercised a
progressive influence; they remained in military possession, and
as civil governors in all but in name, for the years from 1915 to
1920; and in relinquishing their Mandate in 1932—with relief,
and with the general approbation of the world—they were far,
as the future was to show, from forfeiting the possibility of render-
ing further service to the country. It is, however, of their specific
contribution as Mandatories, between the years 1920 and 1932,
that the present Section will chiefly deal.

There were, indeed, obvious limits to the possible services
which a Mandatory could hope to render. There was lack of time,
since the internationally-imposed régime was fated to last twelve
years only. There was lack of freedom; the views and interests
of other nations, who had ratified the Mandate and continuously
scrutinised its application, must always be considered. There were
the abiding geographical and hydrological difficulties of the
territory itself, as an earlier page has made clear (pp. 31-2), and
these could not be rapidly soluble. There were the abiding evils
of the Turkish inheritance, the age-long general habituation to
low standards, insecurity and antipathy to government as such.
There were the deep divisions within Iraqi society (urban-tribal,
Kurd-Arab, Sunni-Shi'i) and the widely various stages of evolution reached by different elements in the population, from
cultured intelligentsia to the mass illiteracy of tribesmen. There
was the exclusive concern of the best-qualified Iraqi minds with
politics—and a narrow, egocentric range of politics—with little
to spare for social or economic matters. There was an uncompromising national character, uncorrected by previous experience
in public life, and by its extreme individualism ill-adapted for
the working of any real democracy, yet intolerant of other forms
of government. And there was, throughout the period, thanks to
the extreme meagreness of Iraq's revenues, and Britain's unwillingness to expend more from her own resources, a continuing financial
stringency which must inevitably limit practical results and retard
progress, and of which the end was not, at this period, in sight.

Nevertheless, the achievement of the years 1920-32, in which
the British can claim not, obviously, an exclusive part but one

of predominant initiative and control, was very considerable; it caused the Mandate for Iraq to be generally acclaimed, by Arab critics among others, as the most successfully operated of all those assigned after the war of 1914–18. Without it, modern Iraq would be beyond doubt a very different, a less advanced, less equipped, less stable and less hopeful nation.

Something has been said already of the rescue of the threatened Mosul vilayet, the stabilisation of frontiers, the creation of an acceptable monarchy, constitution and smoothly-operating elected parliament, and the establishment of an adequate modern-type administration in all its range and operation throughout the territory, with far higher standards of honesty and efficiency than anything seen for centuries past—an administration in which service was sought eagerly by all grades of educated Iraqis. In particular can be claimed the installation of a well-adapted system of law-courts at every level, administering new or suitably revised codes of civil and criminal law. The important Auqaf (Religious Endowments) of the Muslim community were pre-served, improved, and utilised for their proper objects. In town and country alike, a modern police force, with all its specialised activities, attained a higher standard and commanded general confidence. The small and youthful Iraq Army attained in these years a respectable status and discipline, aided by a British Military Mission and modern training and arms. Security through-out the country, never perfect, stood higher than at any period since, at least, the Caliphate. The inherited and highly defective Turkish land-revenue system was indeed, largely retained, but was overhauled and amended, its ultimate supersession planned, and an Income Tax added. The Customs were rationalised, honestly administered, and productive. The financial structure and mach-inery of the State ensured the control of expenditure, and national solvency; the Iraqi share of the inherited Ottoman Public Debt was extinguished, from current revenues, so that the country entered the League of Nations free from debt. A new sterling-based Iraqi currency was introduced, in supersession of the Indian currency used since 1915; it commanded complete con-fidence. To such examples can be added an enlightened trade-policy (the more necessary in the years of severe depression, 1930 and onwards), and the important assistance to commerce offered by the European banks which soon opened branches, as well as by the improved communications. Such infant industries (brick-making, cotton-ginning, cigarette-making, wool-mills, soap-making, tanning) as local resources and conditions seemed to permit were fostered by fiscal privileges and exemptions, and, on no impressive scale, took root. The oil-concession covering northern and central Iraq, assigned in March 1925 by the Iraq Government to the international Turkish Petroleum Company (p. 74), led to immediate large-scale exploration and drilling, and in 1927 oil in highly important quantities was located by the Company in a structure of great magnitude close to Kirkuk. Exploitation was put in hand, and construction of a pipe-line to the Mediterranean, with shipping terminals at Haifa in Palestine and Tripoli in the Lebanon, was begun; the way was open towards realisation of an immense national asset, upon which the Iraq of the future would, above all, depend. Oil on a smaller scale had been discovered by the Anglo-Persian Oil Company at Naftkhana, near Khanaqin, in 1923, and was already under small-scale exploitation. No other minerals of importance were discovered.

The social services, scarce almost to non-existence under the Ottoman régime, were in this period established and developed within the too-narrow limits set by lack of funds and of trained personnel. Elementary, primary, secondary and technical schools were set up, if on a scale and diffusion admittedly inadequate, with higher colleges for law, theology, medicine and engineering, even though all of these, whose quality and equipment great efforts were made to improve, could make but a small impression on the prevailing illiteracy and could supply too few of the trained and professional personnel demanded. An Antiquities Service cared for the uniquely valuable ancient remains in the territory, dealt with visiting archaeological expeditions, and founded a Museum. Hospitals, specialist institutions, clinics, dispensaries were established in all major and some smaller towns, and efforts made to combat the endemic and epidemic diseases. If little could be done for the amenities, or almost the essentials, of still primitive village life, much was achieved in town improvement, by cleaning and restoring, planning, building and street-opening, the installation of water-systems and electricity, and guidance offered to the pride and progressiveness of the urban communities. The immense advances of the period 1932–57 should not lead to forgetfulness of less striking but more arduous achievement of 1918–32. This applies justly to the whole field of social services.

In the highly important sphere of agriculture, scientific studies and experiments were made, a Research Institute and model farm were maintained, expert instruction was given, new plant-types introduced, cotton-growing initiated; but it cannot be claimed that, otherwise than locally, any major impact was, or could have been, made upon traditional local cultures, methods or productivity. One important and a large number of minor land-development schemes were carried out. Nothing appreciable could be done towards forest rehabilitation or planting. A small veterinary department dealt with the control of animal disease, and the improvement of stock and animal-products. Irrigation by water mechanically pumped from the rivers greatly, indeed strikingly, increased and extended many-fold the area of summer cultivation. A number of controlled flow-irrigation works of medium magnitude were completed in central Iraq, and studies were made for future and greater works calculated in part to restore (as the Hindiya Barrage of 1912 had done) the long-deteriorated régime of the rivers and of the soil. Such works could be carried out only when funds, further study, and time permitted; they would include provision for large-scale drainage and desalination. All that was possible was done meanwhile to strengthen the 'bunds', or flood-dykes, along the rivers, but serious inundation (not sparing the outskirts of Baghdad itself) was still frequent and costly. Land settlement, an essential condition for agricultural and, in a measure, for social advance, was for some years attempted on various lines; in 1930 a comprehensive expert study laid the foundation for major progress in this field.

In no section was visible advance more apparent than in that of communications, one of the few (with Surveys) in which the war-time effort of 1914-18 could be fruitful for later civilian purposes. The railway (Basra-Baghdad-Kirkuk, and Baghdad-Sharqat, with lesser branch-lines) was quickly repaired after the troubles of 1920, locally improved and extended, and, treated rightly as a now indispensable traffic-link and produce-carrier, maintained a fair service. It remained for some years under British ownership, but with Iraq Government operation through British experts; traffic fluctuated, interruption by flooding was not infrequent. To the construction and upkeep of the rapidly increased (or indeed new-born) road system, necessitated as it was by the great increase of wheeled and motor vehicles, a serious obstacle was the total lack of road-making materials in lower

Iraq, and this, save in rare stretches, normally rendered the highways—and even the town-streets—no better than passable. A new motor-route, due to British enterprise based in Syria, linked Baghdad with Damascus and Beirut; another, as a temporary expedient, coupled the Iraqi and Turkish railway systems, while others ran into Persia and to Transjordan. Important river bridges were completed, others planned. Post and telegraph services, internal and external—Iraq joined the Postal Union in 1929—reached a respectable standard; they were helped by the appearance, from 1927 onwards, of civilian international air services, for which an airport was created at Baghdad and fair landing-grounds at Basra, Rutba (in mid-desert), and elsewhere. The British, and some Iraqi-owned, river-steamers held their own on the Tigris, with traffic greater than before 1914, if far below that of the war years. The Port of Basra, created by the Army in 1916–18, was maintained as an Iraq Government directorate, with well-qualified British officers and fully adequate modern facilities. Dredging operations at the Fao bar permitted deep-draught vessels, for the first time, to use the port.

PART TWO

The Independent Kingdom

Chapter 5

The Course of Events

WHEN Iraq gained her independence in October 1932 King Faisal wished to set about her consolidation and development within the framework of the new treaty with Great Britain. Such a programme required, however, the co-operation of the powerful Party of National Brotherhood, led by Yasin al-Hashimi, Rashid 'Ali al-Gailani and Hikmat Sulaiman, whose policy was one of treaty revision (p. 89). After four months of neutral government under Naji Shaukat, the King persuaded the dissidents to accept the treaty and to form a cabinet under Rashid 'Ali in coalition with several treaty supporters.

Six months later, in September 1933, King Faisal died in Switzerland; the burden of his achievement was aggravated by anxiety at the Assyrian incident which had occurred in the summer of that year. Settled, as we have seen (p. 87), in northern villages and widely employed in a British imperial force, the Assyrians were obstinately opposed to Arab rule, and their young spiritual leader, the Mar Sham'un, sought the autonomous temporal authority of an Ottoman ethnarch. Failing to win either the Iraqi Government or the League of Nations to his views he refused to co-operate in the government's plan for settlement, while in north Iraq some of his followers flaunted armed strength with little regard for the administration. In July, for a reason never adequately explained, an armed band of eight hundred of them suddenly sought refuge in Syria, were turned back by the French authorities and became involved in an engagement with the Iraqi army. Without the knowledge of the civil administration, the army thereupon killed some hundreds of Assyrian villagers and was acclaimed as a saviour by the public, misled by the Press into suspecting an Anglo-French-Assyrian plot against the State. The Mar Sham'un, as an Iraqi pensioner in exile, continued his pretensions; his people were either absorbed

in the State as individual families and villages, or emigrated to
Syria. Those who remained still preserved some unity in the
Levies which the British Government maintained in Iraq until
1955 to guard its air bases.

King Faisal was succeeded by his son Ghazi, at the age of twenty-
one. With Faisal's guiding hand removed political leaders pursued
their rivalries unchecked, invoked powerful and dangerous forces
for political ends and were finally, in 1941, to involve the country
in the conflict of the European Powers.

The first faction to use unconstitutional weapons successfully
was the National Brotherhood. A month after Ghazi acceded he
declined to dissolve an unco-operative Chamber at the request
of Rashid 'Ali, who thereupon resigned (October 1933), to be
followed by three cabinets under Jamil al-Midfa'i, with one of
'Ali Jaudat al-Ayyubi between. To regain office the Brotherhood
had recourse to tribal disaffection and Shi'i sectarianism on the
Middle Euphrates, and thereby succeeded in unseating successively
'Ali Jaudat and Jamil al-Midfa'i and engineering their own return
to power under the premiership of Yasin al-Hashimi (March 1935).

The Hashimi Government, resolute and enterprising, was in
some ways the most successful of the period; with its tenure of
eighteen months it was also the longest lived. When the tribal
disturbances which had frustrated its predecessors refused to abate
they were suppressed with ruthless rapidity by General Bakr
Sidqi. Irrigation works were encouraged, industries planned, an
Agricultural and Industrial Bank established, a labour code
introduced, municipal development promoted and conscription
enforced. The Hashimi Government's nationalism was immacu-
late: it maintained close relations with other Arab countries,
proclaimed pan-Arabism, took a firm stand over Palestine and
taught the same doctrine in the schools. But its clear intention to
retain its position, its dictatorial attitude towards Parliament and
its intolerance of criticism aroused resentment, particularly in
the queue for office. Hikmat Sulaiman was especially incensed;
he had sponsored the tribal intervention which brought the
government to power and then been disappointed in its composition. He formed an alliance with two new political forces,
left-wing reformists and the army. The reformists ranged from
communism through orthodox to unorthodox socialism and were
not primarily inspired by Arab nationalism; the more moderate
of them were associated in the *Ahali* group, named after its news-

paper. The younger army officers looked with distaste at the disputes of professional politicians, and with some envy at the part the army had played in Turkey and Persia. Their leader was the victorious general Bakr Sidqi. In October 1936, by prearrangement with Hikmat Sulaiman and the *Ahali* group, he moved military units against Baghdad and demanded the resignation of the Cabinet. The Prime Minister yielded and Hikmat Sulaiman formed a largely *Ahali* cabinet, with one of Bakr Sidqi's army associates as Minister of Defence and Bakr himself as Chief of Staff. Yasin al-Hashimi and Rashid 'Ali were banished, the former to die the following year in Damascus; Nuri al-Sa'id escaped to Egypt. He had a personal feud with the new government, for in their advance on Baghdad the officers had murdered his brother-in-law Ja'far al-'Askari, Minister of Defence in the Hashimi as in many previous cabinets and creator of the Iraqi army.

The alliance of Hikmat Sulaiman, *Ahali* and army did not last. The *Ahali*, concerned rather with agrarian reform than pan-Arabism, alienated tribal landlords and nationalists alike; and the officers, more disposed to Kemalist dictatorship than to democracy, were also hostile. Hikmat was forced to submit to majority opinion; he withdrew support from the *Ahali*, suppressed their organisation, and expelled some of the leaders and their communist associates from the country. By devout professions of pan-Arabism he propitiated the nationalists. He could not, despite appeasement, check tribal disorder, which the army continued to crush with severity; and for the first time there was serious labour unrest. The army itself became an embarrassment to him: it came increasingly to dominate the State machine and lost public sympathy through the excesses of General Bakr Sidqi's entourage. In August 1937 the General was assassinated by a disaffected military group, which thereupon attracted sufficient army units to its side to force the resignation of the government. Although the government had adduced the despotism of its predecessor as justification for its own *coup d'état*, it had itself respected civil liberties no more, had intervened no less in elections and administrative appointments, and had quelled tribal unrest with equal severity. Of its programme of reform and development, the reform was renounced and the development impeded by financial difficulties; it nevertheless undertook certain works of irrigation and communications. It was the first independent government

to conclude agreements with other States: these were a treaty of
alliance with Sa'udi Arabia in 1936, a treaty with Persia in 1937,
which settled a long-standing dispute over the Shatt al-'Arab
waterway, and in the same year the Sa'dabad Pact of mutual
defence with Persia, Turkey and Afghanistan (p. 226).

When Bakr Sidqi introduced the army into politics in 1936
he undertook to withdraw it once a new civilian government
was established—a promise in which he was probably sincere.
Withdrawal was, however, unwelcome not only to his personal
followers but to other officers with dictatorial sympathies. The
army, although internally divided, had become a powerful force;
it had developed a mystique and considered itself the arbiter of
national destiny. In the following four years (1937–41) it intervened time and again in politics, usually, however, from personal
rather than political motives, and in conjunction with civilian
politicians. The government of Jamil al-Midfa'i, which succeeded
the régime of Hikmat Sulaiman and Bakr Sidqi, incurred the
hostility of the latter's bitterest opponents, Nuri al-Sa'id and
Rashid 'Ali. A third military *coup d'état*, in December 1938,
resolved an internal army dispute and set Nuri al-Sa'id in the
premiership, with Rashid 'Ali as head of the Royal Diwan. A
fourth, in February 1940, returned Nuri to office in difficult
circumstances and gave dominant influence in the army to four
generals—the 'Golden Square'—who held key commands.

In April 1939 King Ghazi died in consequence of a motor
accident and was succeeded by his infant son Faisal, for whom
Prince 'Abdul-Ilah, Ghazi's first cousin, assumed the regency.

Hitherto the rivalry of the political leaders had been personal;
after the autumn of 1939 it was drawn into the struggle of the
European Powers. Extreme nationalist opinion had for some years
past been courted by the Axis States, and would have liked their
support in breaking the British connexion. Under pressure from
the extremists, and himself no Anglophile, Rashid 'Ali, who
succeeded Nuri al-Sa'id as premier in March 1940, hesitated to
break with the potentially victorious Axis Powers. Iraq had indeed
severed diplomatic relations with Germany in 1939; but the
Rashidist cabinet had imposed conditions on the passage of
British troops across the country, refused to break off relations
with Italy, whose legation was a centre of anti-British activity,
and permitted one of its members to make informal contact
with von Papen in Turkey, with the prospect of formal relations

to follow. This policy involved the premier in disagreement with advocates of close co-operation with Great Britain, notably the Regent and Nuri al-Sa'id, and he became increasingly identified with extreme nationalists and Axis-sympathisers. The Regent eventually pressed him to resign and refused to dissolve a Chamber that was unfavourable to his cabinet. Rashid thereupon, in January 1941, invoked the dominant generals in a fifth military intervention; he was forced to resign, however, later in the month, when the Regent made government impossible for him by withdrawing from Baghdad. The generals now intervened once more, to impose a cabinet under General Taha al-Hashimi, in whom alone they had confidence, and again in April to unseat him, when they believed their confidence betrayed. On this occasion Rashid 'Ali renewed his alliance with them, in an attempt to coerce the Regent. The latter, however, escaped to Transjordan, where he was joined by Nuri al-Sa'id and other statesmen loyal to him. Rashid 'Ali, now the nominal head of a self-constituted military government, had Parliament unconstitutionally convoked and intimidated it into deposing the Regent and appointing an obscure member of the royal family in his place. He then formed a strongly nationalist civilian cabinet, which the British Government refused to recognise.

Just as he had drifted into leadership of extremist opinion Rashid now drifted into hostilities with Great Britain. In April 1941 the British Government made two requests for permission to land troops; this was on the first occasion granted conditionally, and on the second withheld until the first contingent should have left the country. When the troops were nevertheless landed, Iraqi forces were moved to a position commanding the British base at Habbaniya. On 2 May R.A.F. aircraft attempted to dislodge them by bombing, and hostilities, thus commenced, lasted until the end of the month. During this period the Iraqi Government sought military aid from the Axis, and in fact received a number of aircraft before British reinforcements, advancing from Transjordan, made its position untenable. Had their campaign in Crete and preparations for invading Russia allowed the Germans to send more assistance, the British position in the Middle East might have been imperilled, for, although there is no evidence of pre-arrangement in detail between Rashid 'Ali and the Axis, his movement offered a conveniently open door. As it was, he and his government escaped before the British advance, an armistice was signed on 30 May and two days later the Regent returned from exile. The leading Rashidists were tried in absence, Rashid 'Ali himself and the four generals being sentenced to death. The generals were subsequently captured and executed; Rashid 'Ali has continued to live in exile in Sa'udi Arabia and Egypt.

For the remainder of the war, under the premiership of Jamil al-Midfa'i (1941), Nuri al-Sa'id (1941–44) and the veteran nationalist Hamdi al-Pachachi (1944–46), Iraq co-operated fully with her British ally. She became a base for the military occupation of the Levant and Persia, a channel of supply to Russia and, until the Axis pincers were withdrawn, a defensive position against possible attack through the Western Desert or the Caucasus. In 1943 she declared war on the Axis Powers and subsequently took her place among the United Nations, where she has played an active part; and in 1944, for the first time, she established diplomatic relations with the Soviet Union. In 1943 there was a rising of Barzani Kurds under Mulla Mustafa, whose brother, Shaikh Ahmad, had been in intermittent revolt until 1935. In 1945 the Mulla withdrew to Persia, in 1947 to Russia; and Kurdish nationalism has since tended to maintain communist or Soviet connexions. From the end of 1941 Iraq was active in the movement towards Arab unity which was to lead, four years later, to the formation of the Arab League. In the 1930's, as the only self-consciously nationalist Arab State to have achieved independence, she had been acknowledged as the centre and refuge of pan-Arabism. She had interested herself particularly in the cause of the Palestinian Arabs, in whose interest she had made repeated attempts to mediate with Great Britain.

The post-war history of Iraq displayed four main aspects. The first was the vastly increased wealth which accrued from her oil resources, and the possibility it afforded of extending her economy, consolidating her national strength and raising her standard of living. The second was the conflict between different conceptions of Arab unity in which she was involved, and her rivalry with Egypt for Arab leadership. The third was her alignment with the West in the cold war. The fourth was a new political division within Iraq herself, no longer so significantly within the ministerial group as between that group and upholders of a new form of nationalism opposed to many of that group's policies. The newer school combined a desire for neutrality between the world blocs (often, in effect, hostility to the West and benevolence to the East), a passionate desire for Arab unity and latterly an inclination towards Egypt and Syria, and—far more forcefully than pre-war nationalism—a desire for rapid and radical social reform. Finally, the attitude of Government and Opposition alike was marked indelibly by the war in Palestine and the establishment of Israel, which influenced every sphere of political life.

By the end of the war Iraqi nationalists were demanding the restoration of free political activity, which had been suspended in the interest of war-time security, and early revision of the Anglo-Iraqi treaty of 1930. The first was effected under the premiership of Taufiq al-Suwaidi (February-May 1946). Six parties were formed, representing equally the old and the new nationalism—or a standpoint rather left of the new nationalism. They set about the task of opposition so enthusiastically, with Press attacks and strike action, that the government of the ex-Mayor of Baghdad, Arshad al-'Umari, (June-November 1946) thought it expedient to curtail their activities. Succeeding premiers, Nuri al-Sa'id (1946–47) and Salih Jabr (1947–8)—the first Shi'i to hold this office—took stern measures against communist groups established illegally during and after the war, and closed the more extreme of the left-wing registered parties.

The programme of Salih Jabr's cabinet included treaty revision, and in January 1948 he signed a new treaty with Great Britain at Portsmouth (p. 224). It was greeted with an outburst of political feeling. The opposition were incensed at governmental action against their parties and newspapers and complained of the conduct of elections. They were exercised by the signs of friction between Arab governments (p. 214), by the situation in Palestine, by the newly signed treaty with Turkey (p. 227) and by the permission given for a precautionary landing of British troops at Basra in view of disorders across the Shatt al-'Arab at 'Abadan. They disapproved of the Portsmouth Treaty, the conclusion of which, moreover, coincided with popular anxiety at an acute grain shortage and indignation at the continued export of grain. In the capital opposition to the treaty began with student demonstrations and labour strikes; these were reinforced by political parties and communist groups and soon turned to rioting, in which there were numerous casualties. The administration lost control, the government resigned and the treaty was repudiated. Disturbances continued in Baghdad and other towns during

the premierships of the Shi'i divine Muhammad al-Sadr
(January-June 1948) and Muzahim al-Pachachi (June 1948–
January 1949), but were mastered under the martial law which
accompanied the Palestine War. Muzahim and his successor,
Nuri al-Sa'id (January-December 1949) renewed the government's attack on communism: in 1949 four communist leaders
were hanged.

Iraq took her place with the other Arab States in the Palestine
War of 1948, and alone of them concluded no armistice with
Israel. She had objected bitterly to the United Nations decision to
partition Palestine in November 1947, and provided some
hundreds of recruits for the irregular 'Arab Liberation Army'
which began to enter Palestine by January 1948. On 15 May 1948,
the day after the mandate for Palestine expired, units of the regular
Iraqi army entered that country, and were later reinforced to a
total strength of between eight and ten thousand, consisting of
a mechanised brigade, seven or eight battalions of infantry and
three squadrons of supporting aircraft. They relieved the Arab
Legion of Jordan and the Arab Liberation Army in the triangle
Nablus-Tulkarm-Jenin, which they continued to hold until
recalled in 1949; public opinion would not permit an earlier
withdrawal. Iraq has thereafter continued formally in a state of
war with Israel. Her southern oil pipeline to the Mediterranean,
disconnected at the Jordan-Palestine frontier on the outbreak of
war, has remained out of use; this, combined with bad harvests
and the expenses of the war, was for some years an added
embarrassment to her finances. To Iraqi Arabs Israel continues
to be the primary enemy, and a source of bitterness against the
West.

The events and consequences of the Palestine War also
affected Iraq's relations with other Arab States. The aspirations
of Jordan, Iraq's sister Hashimite monarchy, towards Syria and
Arab Palestine had before 1948 led to a certain tension with Egypt,
which reacted on Iraqi relations with the latter; Egypt regarded
the treaties which Iraq and Jordan ratified with Turkey in 1947
as a further provocation. Friction continued during and after the
Palestine War, particularly when Jordan annexed Eastern
Palestine. In 1949 Iraq and Egypt were rivals for the partnership
of Syria, where a military régime had been established in the
wake of the Palestine War. On two occasions the possibility of
Iraqi-Syrian union, always the hope of certain Iraqi and Syrian

statesmen, was frustrated, partly by Egyptian opposition. Although Iraq continued to support Egypt and Syria against Israel, and Egypt in her exchanges with Great Britain, her relations with the two countries remained uneasy. The cabinet of 'Ali Jaudat al-Ayyubi (December 1949–February 1950), indeed, attempted to gain Egyptian goodwill by renouncing schemes of unity with Syria, but the commitment was unacceptable even to some of its members and led to its fall (pp. 215–216).

Party activity, trammelled with the security measures imposed during the Palestine War, was resumed under the premiership of Taufiq al-Suwaidi (February–September 1950) and intensified under his successor Nuri al-Sa'id (September 1950–July 1952). The latter had already united his followers in the Constitutional Union Party; in 1951 Salih Jabr founded a rival party of moderates, the Socialist Party of the Nation, which depended largely on Shi'i support, and the surviving opposition groups—the Independence and National Democratic Parties—were augmented by a small coalition of elder politicians which called itself the United Popular Front. For the next three years the political scene was doubly divided, between the two moderate parties and, more fundamentally, between the moderate and the three opposition groups, which represented aspects of the new nationalism. The latter united with Salih Jabr to oppose, unsuccessfully, the passage of a new oil agreement in February 1952, and the following November were concerned in a riot which led to the fall of Mustafa al-'Umari's cabinet, (July–November 1952). The riot began as a display of student grievances but was transformed by opposition parties and communists into a demonstration for single-stage parliamentary elections. The police lost control, communists carried out organised destruction, the army was finally summoned to restore order, and its Chief of Staff, General Nur al-Din Mahmud, was called to the premiership. He vacated it in January 1953 when stability had been re-established and single-stage elections introduced, and was succeeded by Jamil al-Midfa'i (January–September 1953).

King Faisal II came of age in 1953 and assumed sovereign powers on 2 May. In September he entrusted the premiership to the young Shi'i statesman Dr. Fadhil al-Jamali, an eloquent exponent of the Arab case in the United Nations. His cabinet was liberal in spirit, and contained two members of the United Popular Front and Iraq's most distinguished advocate of agrarian

D*

reform, 'Abdul-Karim al-Uzri. It attempted to reintroduce a land tax and to organise a comprehensive information service; it was the first post-war government officially to acknowledge the importance of public opinion. It received little support from the hard core of the opposition, which distrusted its western connexions and censured its attitude towards communist-exploited strikes. The phenomenal and well-nigh calamitous Tigris floods in the spring of 1954 provoked criticism of its measures for flood control, and, in consequence of this and lack of parliamentary support, it resigned in April with its projects unfulfilled.

Meanwhile a vast programme of national development had been undertaken which included defence against destructive flooding. Before the Second War Iraq's will to develop had been frustrated by lack of funds. The export of oil from 1934 onwards had, however, laid the foundation of prosperity. After the war oil revenues greatly increased in consequence of growing production and the new profit-sharing agreement of 1952, and 70 per cent of them was allocated to a Development Board created in 1950 to develop the country's economy and raise its standard of living. Plans have been drawn up and are in process of execution for systematic progress in most fields of national life; they provide for agronomy, flood control, industry, power, communications, town and country development, health, social security and education (pp. 143–145). It was the Vice-President of this Board, Arshad al-'Umari, who succeeded Dr Fadhil al-Jamali as premier, himself to give way in August 1954 to Nuri al-Sa'id.

This was General Nuri's twelfth premiership and, lasting nearly three years, was the longest in Iraqi history; it was also one of the most important. Nuri intended to effect the revision of the Anglo-Iraqi Treaty and—matters on which he believed the safety and well-being of the country to depend—to ensure defence against possible Soviet aggression and uninterrupted execution of the development programme.

The negotiations which were to lead to Iraq's membership of the Baghdad Pact had begun during the Jamali ministry. The Iraqi Government had been interested in the conception of a 'Northern Tier' which had appeared in the spring of 1953; and when it was announced, in February 1954, that Turkey and Pakistan were to consider closer collaboration and that Pakistan was to receive American military aid, the Jamali cabinet similarly applied to the United States for arms. In March King Faisal and Nuri al-Sa'id visited Pakistan and in October discussions were held in Turkey. A Turco-Pakistani treaty of friendly co-operation in April 1954 was followed in February 1955 by a Turco-Iraqi defence treaty, which was the nucleus of what came to be known as the Baghdad Pact; in the previous month Iraq had severed diplomatic relations with the Soviet Union. Pakistan acceded to the Pact in July and Persia in October 1955. In the new alignments both the British and Iraqi Governments had seen a solution to the problem of their joint treaty, unrevised in consequence of the riots of January 1948 and due to expire in 1957. In April 1955 Great Britain ratified her adherence to the Baghdad Pact and on that basis the two countries simultaneously concluded a new treaty of alliance by which the British bases were to pass under Iraqi command and British forces to be withdrawn (p. 225).

General Nuri believed that the aims of external and domestic consolidation which he had set himself were endangered by party turbulence and communist conspiracy and would justify a considerable measure of control. Before entering on office he had dissolved his Constitutional Union Party, an example followed by Salih Jabr. In September 1954 he abolished all parties—of which those in opposition continued, however, to operate unofficially—and tightened the Press Law. Vigorous action was taken against communism and the allied Partisans of Peace, and a law was passed depriving convicted communists of Iraqi nationality. The agreements which constituted the Baghdad Pact were ratified without disturbance and the work of development proceeded briskly; but outward stability was purchased at the price of much bitterness on the part of frustrated intellectuals and adherents of the new nationalism, many of whom condemned the Pact and sympathised with the policies of Egypt and Syria.

From these two countries, indeed, the Pact seemed to have severed Iraq irrevocably, at a time when relations had slightly improved. The Egyptian Government set about organising a network of Arab military alliances that was specifically directed against it, and attacked it with all the resources of their propaganda. The Iraqi Government was increasingly disturbed by the association of Egypt and, even more, of her ally Syria, with the Soviet bloc; the climax of tension was reached during the Suez crisis, when Iraq's export of oil was stopped by sabotage of the pipeline pump-stations in Syria. With Sa'udi Arabia, on the other hand, long a supporter of Egyptian policy, the crisis revealed common interests and led to closer relations (pp. 216–220).

In Iraq herself the Anglo-French intervention in Egypt served to detonate a mass of nationalist opinion already under pressure and, since the nationalisation of the Suez Canal, in a highly explosive state. The resulting outburst would have overthrown a less resolute government. As it was, there were disturbances in Baghdad, in which 60 police and 9 civilians were officially reported injured, and in Najaf, Mosul and other centres. Faced with widespread public bitterness against the two western Powers, the government broke off diplomatic relations with France, maintained them with Great Britain, but refused to sit with British representatives at any Pact meeting, a position which it maintained until March, 1957. Martial law was maintained from December 1956 to June 1957; in that month, with order restored and the economic consequences of the crisis partly overcome, Nuri al-Sai'd withdrew from office. The approaches of his successor, 'Ali Jaudat al-Ayyubi, to Syria and Egypt, combined with a certain increase in prosperity among white-collar workers, allowed the passions of Suez somewhat to abate. In December 1957 'Abdul-Wahhab Mirjan, a Shi'i supporter of Nuri al-Sa'id, became premier.

On 14th February 1958 King Faisal and King Husain of Jordan signed an agreement uniting their countries in an Arab Federation (pp. 219–220). The two Hashimite monarchies had on several previous occasions seemed on the point of union and had until 1956 tended to maintain a common front in their Arab and international policies. With the appearance of a short-lived pro-Egyptian government in Jordan in that year a certain coolness had supervened, to be dispelled in April 1956 by King Husain's royal *coup d'état*. The combination of Egypt and Syria in the United Arab Republic, announced on February 1958, was followed, thirteen days later, by the federation of Iraq and Jordan, and on 3 March Nuri al-Sa'id resumed office to watch over its formation. General elections were held on 5 May, in accordance with the provisions of the Iraqi constitution that constitutional amendments, such as those demanded by the new Federation, must be ratified both by the existing and by a newly elected chamber. The new deputies were all supporters of the government, and the revised constitution was passed unanimously by that chamber and, after some bitter exchanges, by the senate. On 19 May the first federal cabinet was formed, with Nuri al-Sa'id at its head; his place as premier of Iraq was taken by Ahmad Mukhtar Baban. There was initially some hope that Sa'udi Arabia might join the Federation; this was not realised (p. 220) and, largely in view of Iraq's financial commitments towards her federal partner, attention was turned to Kuwait, also without result (p. 220).

In June and July the Iraqi Government was preoccupied increasingly with the political strife in the Lebanon and expressed its readiness, under certain conditions, for both western and Iraqi intervention in favour of President Chamoun. It was believed that joint action by the Muslim members of the Baghdad Pact was to be discussed at their meeting in Istanbul arranged for 14 July. On that morning, immediately before the King and Nuri al-Sa'id were to leave Baghdad by air for the meeting, the régime was overwhelmed by the military revolution.

Chapter 6

The Economy

I N THE last days of the Ottoman Empire the poverty of Iraq was in startling contrast with her natural resources and with her past prosperity. Oil has provided her with the means of economic rebirth. The rapid increase in oil revenues since 1952 has made her indeed a laboratory of national development, in which to gauge the power of abundant foreign exchange and unlimited technical skill to transform an economy and a society of undoubted potentiality but not yet fully attuned to the modern world.

The natural economy of Iraq has been indicated in an earlier chapter. The demands of oil and its derivative industries on manpower will remain relatively small and other raw materials have still to be found in significant quantities. The greater part of the population will continue to earn a living from agriculture and animal husbandry and from the industries they supply. Development of the natural economy is likely to consist in increasing agronomic production and fitting it for competitive marketing abroad, and in establishing competitive industries which may reasonably reduce foreign imports and provide products for at least regional export.

Three-fifths of Iraq's 6,500,000 inhabitants live in the rural areas. Of her working population, it is known or estimated that some 1,400,000 are employed in sedentary and 160,000 in nomadic agronomy, 90,000 in manufacturing industries, 14,000 in the oil fields and refineries, 20,000 in the railways and port, 29,000 in road and 5,000 in river transport, 200,000 in trade and other forms of business, 20,000 in hotels and catering, 5,000 in the professions, 13,000 in education, 37,000 in the civil service (of whom 14,000 are permanent officials) and 21,000 in the police. In agriculture, where they work within the family unit, women provide over a quarter of the labour force, and in industry about a seventh, employed mainly in a few specialised branches;

otherwise relatively few of them are engaged in paid occupations.

AGRONOMY

IRAQI AGRONOMY was at the beginning of the First World War in a primitive condition. Natural disadvantages had been aggravated by insecurity, ignorance, apathy and neglect. Fertile soil, inadequately watered by the rain, owed most of its production to the Two Rivers; their flooding could nevertheless be disastrous to crop and habitation and was unhelpful in its timing. Irrigation could be undertaken only by relatively complicated methods, and even so there was too little water for summer crops. Great works of water control had been planned but only one completed. In the absence of proper drainage land was ruined by salination. Cultivation was threatened by soil erosion, in which deforestation played a part, by dust storms and by plant diseases, noxious weeds and pests; of the last, locusts were the most feared but not necessarily, over a period, the most destructive. The population was too small to permit large production and was seriously weakened by malnutrition and endemic disease. Its life and its tenure of land were insecure. Its instruments and methods of cultivation were primitive; its ploughs barely scratched the surface, and draft animals were poor and few. The fertility of the soil was not adequately maintained; fertilisers were unknown and animal manure required for fuel. Crops were limited in variety and determined by custom as well as suitability: dates around Basra, rice in the marshes, fruit and tobacco among the Kurds, the winter crops, wheat and barley, almost universally, and a limited cultivation of grains and vegetables in summer. There was little crop rotation; for half the year most of the land, like its cultivators, was idle. Irrigation was carried out wastefully and for lack of direction or communal effort the vital works were menaced by silting and by disrepair. Crops cultivated inefficiently yielded a meagre harvest; it was the date, tended with long-learnt skill, which gave the most generous return.

Animal husbandry was equally neglected, except the rearing of camels and the Arab horse, which creates its own canons of criticism. Sheep and goats mainly among the pastoral Arab and Kurdish semi-nomads, cattle among settled cultivators everywhere, buffaloes among those of the southern riverain and marsh areas, mules and donkeys—none of them were bred, fed or tended systematically or with care. Outside the cities they were left to forage for themselves, in competition with the ubiquitous goat. Among the nomads no organisation existed to control grazing or reseed natural pasturage, which was consequently threatened with denudation. Among the settled cultivators there was no mixed farming; animal husbandry was a mere adjunct of agriculture. Without proper winter fodder, feeding was adequate for only half the year and at starvation level for half the rest. Animals died when water-holes dried up in the south, and of exposure in the severe winters of the north. Diseases, particularly of the parasitic type, were rife. In the face of this manifold affliction livestock developed a certain hardiness of strain; but their quality was poor and their productivity low.

To improve and extend so retarded an agronomy was a formidable task for the young Iraqi State. It demanded a vast outlay of capital, a strong, efficient and technically competent administration and a radical change of tradition and outlook in the agricultural and nomadic communities. It is only with the vast increase in national revenue after the Second World War that comprehensive development has been attempted on a large scale, facilitated by the new organs of international co-operation. The inter-war years were less spectacular in their undertakings, but played nevertheless an essential part of preparation. None of the problems were solved; but a specialist minority recognised them and was studying their solution or even attempting its implementation. The administrative and psychological basis of improvement was slowly being created. Security was established, effective government extended over the provinces and a more adequate administrative machine constructed. Cultivation could proceed unmolested and measures of development and control could more successfully be applied. Iraqis had been trained to plan and some to execute. If not the peasant, at least some of the landowners had come to appreciate the benefits of innovation. It was a situation ready for fertilisation by that urge towards material progress and reform which followed the Second War, encouraged by the young men trained in increasing numbers abroad and by the stimulus of an increasing national income.

The material progress that was made between the Wars was by the tentative, painstaking work of small departments, using such resources as the country itself provided and still struggling against social and administrative impediments and lack of funds. The one modern heritage from the Ottoman Government in this field was the programme of irrigation drawn up by Sir William Willcocks, of which the Hindiya Barrage had been completed in 1912 and the scheme for Euphrates flood control had been started. The Iraqi Government did not complete the latter, but did accomplish, before the Second War, one major project of the Ottoman programme, the barrage across the Tigris at Kut. Apart from this the department of irrigation worked systematically on a valuable programme of survey, experiment and secondary works, some of them nevertheless of considerable dimensions. New canals were constructed, old canals improved, revived or realigned, regulators installed, the simple existing measures of flood control extended and improved and the area of cultivation thereby enlarged. A parallel development, though encouraged by the government, was due essentially to private initiative: the rapid extension of pump irrigation to supplement irrigation by direct flow. By the end of the Second War some third of Euphrates and two-thirds of Tigris cultivation was by this method, with a considerable expansion of cultivation in consequence. Otherwise mechanisation was insignificant and confined to large land-owners. The government established an Agricultural Bank just before the Second War, designed to encourage private enterprise by advancing money and selling and servicing agricultural machinery; but its influence was limited by inadequate resources. Nor were agricultural experiments uniformly successful. The cultivation of tobacco progressed in the northern hills, though with ample scope for improvement; but sericulture proved less successful than expected and cotton, after a promising beginning, suffered from pests, inexperience and low world prices, from which, however, it was beginning to recover before the Second War. Several private attempts at scientific farming foundered on the conservatism of the cultivator. A locust campaign, co-ordinated with neighbouring states, made valuable headway but was financially hampered. The veterinary department continued to take active measures against rinderpest, glanders and rabies, within the bounds, however, of its own inadequate size and the still limited influence of the state administration.

The course of development created its own problems, of which the most serious was salination. Inevitable in the absence of proper drainage, it was accelerated by the wasteful use of water in irrigation and attempted remedy; lavish washing of the roots of crops eventually defeated its own purpose by raising the water table still higher. A large proportion of the irrigated land was affected, with a consequent decrease in yield.

Since the Second War Iraq has at last been in a position to set about the systematic increase and improvement of her crop and animal production and to attack her agronomic problems as a whole. The great projects of water control and storage in particular have an element of majesty. To them and to smaller irrigation projects were devoted £50 million out of the total £155 million allocated for the first six-year plan of development and £150 million out of the £500 million for the current six-year plan. The control and utilisation of water lie at the heart of the country's natural economy and its improvement and development offer the quickest means to larger and better production.

The first priority has been to control the annual spring flood, whose periodic excesses caused loss and ruin; the need was emphasised by the Tigris flood of 1954, which threatened to overwhelm the capital and its population and inundated a large area of central and southern Iraq, washing away crops, animals and houses and destroying roads and railways. Two major schemes of control have been completed and are saving the country at least twenty million pounds' worth of damage a year: they are the Wadi Tharthar scheme for the Tigris and the Habbaniya for the Euphrates. Barrages across the rivers raise their level so that the water flows in each case into a natural depression. The Habbaniya Lake, thus formed from the Euphrates, has an outlet channel through which the stored waters can be fed back into the river in the summer, when the need is great and the natural supply of the river is small. In the case of the second depression, the Wadi Tharthar, surveys are in hand to establish finally whether or not it can also be used as a reservoir. It it can, outlet channels will no doubt be dug so that the stored waters can be fed into either the Tigris or the Euphrates, between which the Wadi Tharthar lies; the Wadi could also be made to receive Euphrates water.

In addition to these two schemes, dams are under construction at Dokan and Darband-i-Khan in the head-waters of the Lesser Zab and the Diyala, both tributaries of the Tigris. They will serve both for storage and for flood control. Other dams are under study, but their future is uncertain until it is finally determined whether or not the Wadi Tharthar can be used as a reservoir.

Barrages for diversion of waters (as opposed to dams for storage) will be built at various points on the river system, at Batma, for example, on the Lesser Zab, near 'Amara, and on the Shatt al-Gharraf. A comprehensive hydrological survey is nearing completion; it will provide the factual basis of a decision for or against other major projects of water control and storage, and will provide operating rules for the complex system of water-routing which is being created.

Together with these monumental schemes of control a programme of dependent irrigation projects is in course of planning and execution. In the Musaiyib area, some forty miles south of Baghdad and the site of a large project of peasant resettlement, irrigation works have been completed, linking with the Euphrates; and control structures on the Euphrates tail reaches at Nasiriya are nearing completion. Work is in progress on a scheme to irrigate the 'Udhaim lands, between the Tigris and the Jabal Hamrin, by water diverted from the Lesser Zab; on canals using the water of the Diyala, which will be increased by the Darband-i-Khan dam; on regulators and barrages in the 'Amara area; on cross-regulators on the Shatt al-Gharraf; and on the enlargement of the Hilla canal. Other projects are being studied or awaiting decision for bringing new land under irrigation: for example, in the areas of Mosul, Arbil and Kirkuk, in the Ishaqi area south of Samarra, in the Nahrawan area south-east of Baghdad and in the area of the Shatt al-Gharraf. By means of these and other projects it is hoped to increase the cultivated area by three thousand square miles—a seventh of its present extent.

Drainage, the absence of which has permitted ruinous salination, has a high priority in the programme of development. A comprehensive programme is in hand to save or sweeten land already under cultivation, and drains are being provided for all new irrigation schemes.

It is proposed to support the better supply of water with improvements in plant varieties and in agricultural method. Research and experiment are being conducted in soil science, fertilisers, comparative varieties of crops and fruit trees, and plant pests and diseases. Proved varieties are grown in government experimental farms for sale to the cultivator; at the same time the best methods of cultivation and types of fertiliser are sought for each. Experiments are in particular being carried out with wheat, barley, cotton, flax, jute, alfalfa, sesame, peanut, fodder crops, potatoes, dates and citrus. A fertiliser plant is planned in Basra, which will use as raw material the natural gas of the local oilfields. The State is itself conducting a campaign against the *sunn* pest, which destroys cereals in the mountain districts, the cotton bollworm and red spider mite, the *dubas* hopper of date palms, and wheat and barley smut; and means have been devised to enable the cultivator himself to control the destructive grasshopper and the insect enemies of the date, the apple and summer vegetables. The common citrus wilt and inflorescence rot of date palms are also under study. Precautions against the desert locust are methodically organised; reports are exchanged with neighbouring countries and watching posts have been established along their frontiers. An extension service of agricultural guidance has been created to bring the results of research and experiment to the cultivator; it now employs some 150 trained officials. Using the radio and audio-visual aids in addition to personal demonstration, it has given instruction on the use of improved varieties, tools and methods, the use of fertilisers, and the cultivation of fodder crops for soil improvement. A five-year extension campaign is planned; newly settled areas are in particular to be centres of instruction, where horticulture and crop rotation will be encouraged.

An increasing number of agricultural specialists is being trained abroad, mainly in the United States, and higher training in agricultural subjects is also given in the country itself; the College of Agriculture, established in 1950 near Baghdad, has now some 400 students and is being equipped with new buildings and laboratories.

Forestry has, for the first time in Iraq, received serious attention. At the end of the Second War some 2,800 of her 172,000 square miles were classified as forest land; it was highly desirable to extend this area as a measure against erosion, the silting of irrigation canals and waterways and the shortage of timber. Forests were, moreover, confined to the mountain areas of the north; in the southern plains windbreaks were needed to protect the crops from desiccating winds. The State has in the past had competent forestry officials, but they lacked the staff and resources even to combat the periodical forest fires, and had no adequate legal sanction against the inroads of woodcutters, charcoal burners, cultivators and livestock.

In 1955 a Forest Law was passed. Regulations have followed for establishing State forests, charcoal manufacture for commercial purposes has been forbidden for a trial period pending a system of controlled cutting, and a forest police has been created. Lookout stations and forest roads are being built against fires. A fifty-year programme for afforesting an area of 2,000 square miles is under consideration. Meanwhile a twenty-year plan of afforestation has been drawn up to cover 100 square miles, most of the area to be furnished by the major irrigation projects; it will both provide for the protection of crops and serve the commercial needs of the country, including those of industrial hardwood, firewood, domestic and industrial charcoal, and wood pulp. Over the same period it is proposed to plant 750 miles of avenue between the main towns. An organisation has, moreover, been created for research and experiment on the varieties of tree most suited to the country's conditions and requirements and on the control of insects and pests which attack them. It is experimenting on poplar and eucalyptus, and the plane, tamarisk and exotic conifers are also under trial. The poplar is already widely grown and used for building in the north; a suitable supply of heavier timber has still to be found. Of the vastly increased staff which the programme requires a number of senior officials have already been trained and others, with subordinate staff, are under training abroad. Senior officials will continue to receive foreign training; but the Iraq Agricultural College may be extended to train forest officers at university level and new forest schools be established for training subordinate staff.

A major obstacle to the development of the country's forests is the lack of public feeling for trees and their preservation. This the government is trying to remedy by all available means of publicity; in particular a Tree Day has been instituted all over the country, on which the public, and particularly the school children, are asked to join in symbolic tree planting.

In the field of animal husbandry there are experiments to improve feeding, breeding and the quality of animal products and to control animal diseases and parasites. The effect of controlled grazing and reseeding of pasturage is being studied, and the use of dates and protein concentrates in providing a richer feed. The attempt to introduce fodder crops has already been noted. There is a large well-drilling programme for the north and there too the provision of shelters is being considered. Livestock and poultry centres are to be established in different climatic

regions of the country; in experimental farms breeding is already
in process, consisting of selection within native stock and crossing
native stock with foreign breeds. Improved rams, bulls, poultry
and eggs are being distributed to farmers. Special allocations from
development funds have been made for projects of breeding and
parasite control, for the establishment of hygienic slaughter-
houses and the improvement of hides, and for the establishment
of a Veterinary College to train further staff.

There are few problems to which thought has not been given,
which have not, on paper, been accounted for in some project.
When these projects have been executed successfully Iraq's rural
economy will be able to support itself on a commendably high
level. But execution has its own problems, not to be measured by
the relative ease and speed with which the great projects of water
control are being completed. There is in fact a division of development projects into those whose fulfilment can be bought from
foreigners, given only the money and a supply of labour, and those,
often costing far less, which can be achieved only by domestic
skill, experience, administrative capacity, patient and unselfish
service, enthusiasm and co-operation. The great water projects,
like the oil production which finances them, have made relatively few demands on Iraq. It is what must accompany and
follow from them that is demanding: the efficient and equitable
use of the new water, the maintenance of irrigation works, the
improvement of plant and livestock production and of the standard
of living of the rural population. The technical skill required for
research exists already and is being multiplied yearly; its use to
transform the system of agriculture and to benefit the cultivator
is more difficult. To the changes which are necessary in the
social and administrative tradition and outlook of Iraq we shall
return in a wider context. There are in addition two connected
problems which lie at the heart of the agrarian community and
its operations: those of land tenure and the organisation of agricultural production.

The economic problem presented by Iraqi land tenure is
that on much of the cultivated land the right to its produce is
held by persons—often absentees—other than the actual cultivator,
and the latter, particularly in the south, must pay them a crippling
rent for its use. In a country as primitive in its agriculture as Iraq
has been, the total produce may amount to very little and the
proportion retained by the cultivator barely support life. The

system works viciously: malnutrition, itself debilitating, encourages disease, and as the capacity for work declines so does production. The tenant, lucky if his share feeds him till the next harvest, is in no position to store grain for seed and must borrow it from the landlord. If he has a bad harvest or falls sick he will have to borrow his food as well, and while the debt remains unpaid he cannot by law leave the land; he then sinks to virtual serfdom. His landlord may in some cases determine the plot he cultivates, the crop he grows, the water he uses and the agricultural methods he follows; there is neither the incentive nor the scope for improving the holding. Hearing of an easier living in the towns, more and more peasants go to seek it.

The need for reform is widely accepted. The remedies proposed have as much a political as an economic basis, for some reformers would change the system of land tenure on principle. It concentrates a large part of the cultivated land in a few hands. By ensuring a parliamentary majority of large landholders or their representatives, it has provided a constitutional obstacle to reform. It may equally be criticised for its social effect, for in the south it has introduced a relationship of landlord and tenant into a system that was tribal and patriarchal. The unit of cultivation was originally the tribe, which occupied land and allotted and reallotted it among its members, without, for the most part, establishing individual or legal tribal rights. By degrees legal right to the cultivation and disposal of land, subject to the State's ultimate ownership, was granted, first by the Ottoman Government and then more systematically by the Iraqi Government from the early thirties onwards (p. 93); for in the prevailing confusion cultivation had suffered from insecurity of tenure and the public peace from land disputes. But the legal assignment of rights often removed confusion at the price of social distortion, for wide areas of common tribal cultivation were registered in the name of the shaikh.

To dispossess the holders of land titles or to limit individual holdings has so far been considered outside the sphere of practical politics. Nor has it proved possible effectively to limit the landlord's share of the crop. Recent laws have, however, empowered the government to reoccupy a proportion of the land so held, so far only in the vicinity of the towns, and to recover half the valuable 'Amara lands, which the shaikhs held only on short lease but treated as their own. The object of the latter law was specifically to create small holdings for peasants; its outcome is still to be seen. In both cases the landlords were conciliated with firmer tenure of the land they retained. A simpler means of releasing areas from the landlords might be to impose a heavy enough land tax, for much of their holding is inefficiently cultivated and would then become a liability. Until 1939 the State levied a tax on some categories of assigned land and on water; in that year the tax was compounded by a limited payment. Since 1953 governments have been discussing its renewal in various forms.

Another remedy under trial would by-pass the agrarian system and resettle the peasant on such unassigned State land as can be brought under cultivation; the new projects for water control could irrigate large areas of such land. It is possible, moreover, that under threat of losing their labour in this way landlords might be forced to offer better terms, though hitherto they have not been so moved by spontaneous migration from the land; backward landlords have been unwilling to make concessions of status even for financial gain, and the more businesslike are prepared to substitute machines for human labour. Resettlement has been under way for some time. A law of 1951 indeed provided that all State land thereafter reclaimed should be divided into small holdings, and a special section has been created in the Development Board to supervise its application. There remains a danger that, although the land is legally registered in the name of the small holder, his tribal shaikh will for some time have sufficient influence to claim a share of his crop. A contrary danger, until the State decides to impose rent or taxation on the new small holders, is of creating another privileged class, even—unless strict supervision is maintained—of absentee landlords, especially as some of the holdings are perhaps unnecessarily large. The first attempt at peasant resettlement was made as early as 1945 at Dujaila, near Kut, but organisational difficulties limited its success.

Resettlement of this kind in fact makes severe administrative demands. It must not only provide for health and security, but also replace the paternalism of the shaikh, which, too often grim and grasping indeed, has offered nevertheless a form of agricultural credit, technical guidance, marketing organisation and social security—a structure of society, agriculture and finance which, with all its shortcomings, springs naturally from a traditional setting and is in actual existence; whereas when the government

takes share croppers out of this system and settles them as independent small holders, it has to act in a social vacuum, among
uprooted peasants and on land where the most suitable crops
and methods of cultivation have still to be determined. At
Musaiyib, the most important area at present under settlement,
the situation is being treated particularly by encouragement of
co-operative institutions; these seem to offer a solution to many
problems, including the supply of agricultural credit to a peasantry
not yet habituated to thrift. But it is doubtful whether enough
competent and experienced officials exist on an executive level to
apply similar methods to many areas simultaneously. Yet speed is
important. Since resettlement began less than two thousand
families a year have been settled and even this has been a formidable task for the organisation which exists; and the number of
families which need assistance might perhaps be estimated at half
a million.

These difficulties are avoided in another, very different
proposal. The water made available by the new projects of control
would be used for the most part on already irrigated land, some of
it already assigned to small holders, but much of it held by large
landlords and worked by sharecroppers; a proper system of
drainage would at the same time be provided. This is calculated
not only to make the most efficient use of water and labour but
also to bring the peasant immediate benefit within the old paternal
framework. He is thus not dependent on a still maturing administration for capital and guidance and if the landlord, taking the
same share of the produce, gains more in quantity than does the
tenant, the latter's gain is one of kind, for it means the difference
between enough and too little. It might be hoped that the tenant
would in time be in a position to supply his own seed and implements and that the cultivation of a summer cash crop would
modify the whole agrarian relationship. As for the larger bene-
ficiaries, if draft legislation to that effect can be ratified and
implemented, they will be charged for additional water and for
drainage.

Meanwhile, with a change in national outlook, the position of
the landlords is changing. They are on the defensive against public
opinion and measures of reform. Their tenants are less docile,
more conscious of present disabilities and claimed rights; and
repression is psychologically more difficult. The landlord class
is itself changing from within. Its sons are more liberal and

progressive in their outlook, they go to school, share the political aspirations of the other students, and sometimes graduate to specialised agricultural training. In the past the tribal landlords, complacent and unimaginative, have been a drag on agricultural development. Part of the new generation, as businesslike as any large western farmer, is, insofar as it can obtain capital, modernising and mechanising its production.

The supply of capital for major agricultural development has never been systematically organised, as it has, for example, for commercial enterprise.   Landholders who wanted to extend their holdings provided the funds from their own capital or took urban capitalists into partnership, while a number of the latter have turned to agriculture on their own account. The State Agricultural Bank, limited in its capital and liquid resources and impeded also by social pressures, by its inability to recover loans and by too short a period of repayment, has been more suited to routine activity than to development. Assistance of another kind is offered by the government's Department of Agricultural Machinery, which advises on its selection and use and gives training in its operation. On the larger estates tractor drivers are likely to form a new skilled class of agricultural labour, whose growth will assist the change from subsistence to cash economy and may to some extent counteract the drift of peasants to the town. At the same time estate managers are being trained in the agricultural colleges, and will be employed on the large estates to supervise modern farming. Within a quarter-century the condition of agriculture and of the rural population should improve enormously, and not only by a multiplication of independent small holdings.

INDUSTRY

WHILE IRAQ has continued to supply her own agricultural requirements, in the field of industry she has inevitably declined from the comparative self-sufficiency of Ottoman times, when the manufactured goods required by the majority of her population were simple and could be supplied by local crafts.

Between the two wars the demand for imported manufactures grew steadily. The official and professional classes multiplied and adopted increasingly the material manifestations of western life. Motor vehicles were required for passengers and freight. Development in irrigation, urban construction and communications demanded the importation of irrigation pumps and engines, iron, steel, cement and other constructional material, machinery and electrical equipment. Cheap foreign goods, moreover, competed with some of the traditional handicrafts and caused them to wither, though many of them continued to supply the rural population and expanded with it. Domestic industry also developed in other ways. On the one hand, it turned to new products: matches, mineral waters and, with the cultivation of tobacco and cotton, cigarettes, ginned cotton and cotton textiles, On the other, it introduced a measure of mechanisation, both in these new processes and in some of the old, such as milling, distilling, tanning, and the manufacture of bricks, woollen textiles, vegetable oils and soap. Repair shops were set up for vehicles and machinery. The new industry was nevertheless limited in variety and scale. It could claim a few factories, of only moderate size, but was mostly housed in small workshops or conducted in a single room by a master and one or two assistants. It was only in the oil companies, the railways and the Basra port organisation that modern industrial processes were carried out on a considerable scale.

The limitation had several causes. There was little variety of raw materials; industry did, indeed, employ the few available and as new ones, such as cotton and tobacco, appeared, brought them into use. Capital was in short supply, the government commanding no surplus money, private individuals having other uses for theirs and the banks concerning themselves rather with commercial transactions. There was no tradition of industrial investment and there was traditionally a social division between the landowning and mercantile capitalists on the one hand and, on the other, the artisans turned workshop owners who formed the industrial class. Much capital, particularly that accumulated from agriculture, was simply hoarded, and the balance was usually invested in urban or rural property, which secured adequate profits at little risk, or in commerce, where the return was even larger and more rapid. Industry, by contrast, offered few temptations and many problems. The bulk of the population was too poor to provide an attractive market. There was no cheap source of power in sufficient quantity. There were few skilled workmen to operate or maintain the machinery. Wastage in material and machinery was proportionately great and the quality of the product poor.

On the part of governments and of the political public, however, there was, after 1921, considerable enthusiasm for industrialisation. It was an issue of national prestige, a symbol of liberation from 'colonialism' and of progress to modern statehood. It was expected to increase the national income, raise the standard of living, support a larger educated electorate and promote political consciousness and solidarity. In 1929 an attempt was made to encourage it by granting fiscal privileges to industrial concerns; but there was no provision for the supply of capital and no very spectacular response. More significant assistance was offered by a law of 1950, which was reinforced with import duties and the prohibition of a number of foreign products. Shortages during the Second War and changes in social outlook had meanwhile stimulated a new interest in industry and a State Industrial Bank had been established to advance capital to private enterprises or purchase shares in them. Private capital is now being invested in industry much more readily than before. There is not yet any wide public investment, nor is there a stock market, though the establishment of a Stock Exchange is being considered; hitherto capital has usually been subscribed privately by the initiators and their associates. The post-war development programme of the government is of great importance to industry: it provides for an adequate supply of power, for communications and for technical training, and has equipped a section of the public with increased spending power; at the same time it has allocated funds for the establishment of State industries.

Modern industries established privately since the Second War include cotton and wool spinning and weaving, jute spinning, rayon weaving, mechanised baking, brewing and the manufacture of date syrup, footwear, cement, reed 'thatchboard' for building, aluminium ware and light steel products; and pre-war mechanised industries have been considerably extended. The Industrial Bank holds shares in fourteen of the largest companies, representing an investment of some two million pounds; it has indeed been criticised for ignoring the economic and social advantage of assisting smaller enterprises. Its policy is gradually to dispose of its shares, thus releasing its capital for other enterprises and accustoming the public to investment in industry. Large factories, although increasing in number, are still the exception. Of the thousands of industrial and artisan establishments in the country in 1954, some ninety employed over a hundred workers, twelve over five hundred and four over a thousand, while half the total were one-man concerns; they represented altogether a capital investment of some thirty million pounds.

Industry has hitherto tended to provide its own power, using petroleum products to work its plant directly, or to generate electricity. The electricity produced for public consumption has been inadequate and in some places too expensive for industrial purposes, and has served primarily for lighting. In Baghdad it was generated by a commercial company, which was nationalised in 1955, and elsewhere by small municipal power stations. These are to be supplanted by three central power stations, scheduled for completion in 1958, which will be situated in Baghdad, in Basra and at Dibis on the Lesser Zab. They will supply all important centres with light and power. The development of hydro-electric power will not be undertaken without careful study, for the use of water for this purpose would complicate the processes of flood control and especially summer irrigation; and the production of thermal electricity, for which the oilfields provide cheap and abundant fuel, can meet the country's immediate requirements. Nevertheless major works of water control are providently being designed for hydro-electric generation.

In its development programme the State has itself undertaken to establish industries. The respective role of State and private enterprise has still to be defined and is under consideration by the government. Official opinion tends to the view that public utilities (such as electric power) and industries which require special skill or specialised marketing (such as oil refining and the manufacture of sulphur) might reasonably be undertaken by the State, but that as much initiative as possible, especially in consumer industry, should be left to private enterprise, with the Industrial Bank where necessary supplementing private capital. In some cases the government may set up an industry and dispose of it as a going concern to a private company; the public may, however, have to be convinced that State-founded industries are a profitable investment for private capital.

The government intends its encouragement of industry to be appreciable—the current development programme allocates £67 million to it—but accepts limits to industrial expansion. It considers the basis of the Iraqi economy to be agronomic, and will concentrate on industries for which Iraq offers a natural market and natural advantages and which may hope to become competitive. Undertakings within this category which are in hand or already completed include a cotton textile factory, two cement plants and a steel-rolling mill using both domestic and imported scrap. It has been decided to build two sugar plants using Iraqi beet and imported cane, a paper plant using reeds from the southern marshes, a fertiliser and a sulphur plant using natural gas from respectively the Basra and the Kirkuk oilfields, and a rayon fibre plant using imported and later perhaps domestic pulp; this and other industries might be expected to develop with afforestation. There must surely be expansion in the manufacture of building materials, of light metal products, mechanical and otherwise, and of clothing, and in the processing and transformation of agricultural products, such as the use of dates to provide animal feed and syrup. Further development might follow the detailed mineral survey which is in progress. Oil refining is described elsewhere (p. 151).

Although domestic demand will clearly increase with evolving habits and growing wealth, to support any considerable industrialisation Iraq must seek foreign markets. She is already exporting small quantities of date juice to Syria and cement, bricks, reed 'thatchboard', straw products, clothing and cigarettes to Kuwait or Sa'udi Arabia; but except in the case of these southern areas, whose population is in any case small, most of her existing industries duplicate rather than supplement those of neighbouring countries. For the manufacture of petrochemicals from natural gas she is, however, if not uniquely equipped, at least likely to be the first in the Middle-Eastern field and may supply much more than a regional market with them; they may include not only fertiliser but plastics, and it is further proposed, as we have seen, to derive sulphur from the natural gas of the Kirkuk oilfield.

With the availability of State and private capital, provision made for an adequate supply of power, and the services of foreign engineering companies at hand, there is no difficulty in establishing the mechanical framework of an industry of any size or complexity. The greater problem is to find the men to run it; there has hitherto been neither the apparatus for training them nor the tradition of industrial management and organisation, of mechanical knowledge and maintenance, and of research and marketing on which effective training must rest. The educational system has been ill-suited to provide either managers or foremen and technicians, nor has the prevailing social outlook favoured the existence of the latter class; the acquisition of any degree of education has been thought if anything to raise the student above practical work. Technical schools, founded intermittently since the First War, have in the past been hampered by this prejudice. There has consequently been a gap between the qualified engineer and the illiterate artisan, bridged only in specialised State departments and the oil companies. There it has been found that prejudice can be overcome if a suitable example is set; the technical training centre of the Iraq Petroleum Company in Kirkuk, which trains its apprentices to accepted British technical standards, has been particularly happy in its experience. Faced with its industrial programme, the government, with the assistance of foreign specialists, is giving the problem its serious attention. Reformed technical training as a branch of regular State education is dealt with elsewhere (p. 179); there is little indication that difficulties will diminish in the immediate future, though a changing outlook encouraged by attractive pay may effect an eventual transformation. A proposal to give further training to existing artisans may produce competent and willing technicians more quickly, and men are being trained on the constructional projects themselves. The Development Board is optimistic about the outcome.

TRADE

A DEVELOPING ECONOMY and changing tastes have, as we have seen, led Iraq to import more and more manufactured and mechanical articles. She has also imported basic foodstuffs, such as tea, coffee and on occasion grain, and raw materials for construction and for her domestic industries, particularly for tanning and wood and metal crafts. She has not so far supplied her own metals, nor has her heavier timber been commercially adequate.

Exports, apart from oil, have been almost entirely agronomic. These are hardly more varied now than at the beginning of the century: dates; grains and pulses; oil seeds; gall nuts for tannin, used in preparing ink, leather and medicine; gum tragacanth used in pharmacy and calico printing; liquorice root for pharmacy and the manufacture of cigarettes; livestock, comprising camels, sheep, cattle, buffaloes and Arab horses; and such animal products as hides and skins, fat, intestines for sausage making, pressed wool and mohair. To these items the only appreciable addition between the two World Wars was cotton; but, after a promising start, export declined to practically nothing in the early nineteen-thirties, rising again to exceed previous quantities by 1938. Since the Second War its export has fluctuated greatly between 300 tons (in 1949) and 4,300 (in 1951); in some years it is a major item of trade. There has also been a certain export of cotton seed and tobacco. Among these agricultural and animal products dates and grains take first place, often amounting to three-quarters of the total value of exports; they are followed in order by wool, hides and skins. Until the late nineteen-thirties dates were a more important item of export than grain. The grains have subsequently overtaken them, the most important being barley, followed in most years by millet, wheat and rice in that order. (Most of the very considerable rice crop is consumed in Iraq.) Since 1932 the annual export of grains has increased from some 170,000 to some 500,000 tons, of wool from some 3,000 to some 5,000–7,000 and of dates from some 100,000 to rather more than 200,000. Industry, as we have seen, is beginning to export its products, but not yet in appreciable quantities; exports of date juice, cement, bricks, reed and straw manufactures, clothing and cigarettes account for less than a thirtieth of the total, excluding oil.

Iraq's markets and sources of supply have varied. Except for a period during and after the Second War Great Britain has been her largest supplier and customer. Before the Second War she provided nearly a third of Iraq's imports, and after the war a proportion varying from a third to a half. She is the main supplier of woollens, machinery and electrical apparatus, chemicals and pharmaceuticals and many other products, and a leading supplier of motor vehicles. At the end of the Mandate she bought nearly a third of Iraq's exports, immediately before the Second War a quarter, and since the war a proportion which had risen from a tenth to nearly a third in the early nineteen-fifties but has since fallen to about a fifth. As a supplier she was followed in the nineteen-twenties by India (with cotton goods) and Belgium (with woollen textiles, iron and steel) and in the later thirties by Japan (with cotton and artificial silk goods), the United States, Germany, India, and by Holland and the Dutch East Indies, which together supplied half of Iraq's increasing requirements of sugar. Since the Second War the United States have continued to hold second place with a wide variety of goods, particularly motor vehicles and agricultural machinery, iron and steel manufactures, paper products, artificial silk and clothing. Other prominent post-war suppliers have been India, with cotton goods, timber, rope, jute sacks, leather, coffee, and tea (of which Ceylon has, however, been the main source), and Japan and Italy with cotton, artificial silk and woollen goods. Belgium has continued to supply much of Iraq's iron and steel and from Sweden and Canada she imports much of her timber. Until the establishment of her own refining facilities in 1955 her southern districts drew their supply of petroleum products from Persia.

Apart from Great Britain her main customers before the Second War were the United States and India. Great Britain bought dates, grain, wool and hides; the United States dates, intestines and liquorice; India dates, grain, animal fat and horses. Syria, Palestine and Transjordan also imported large numbers of Iraqi livestock. After the Second War India was for several years the largest importer, especially of grain and dates, but in 1950 Great Britain resumed her pre-eminence. Otherwise no firm order has been established among buyers. Considerable purchases have been made by Holland (chiefly of grain), Syria (of dates, livestock, hides and intestines) and Japan (of grain, cotton and seeds). The United States have remained a leading importer of dates, intestines and liquorice, but Iraq's dollar exports are less than before the war.

A major change in Iraq's pattern of trade has followed her relations with Persia. Before the First War she commanded most of Persia's western trade routes; in particular she had in Basra the adequate port which Persia lacked. The Persian transit trade, which was assisted by the close relations between Persia and the Shi'i Holy Cities, was consequently a major element in the economic life of Iraq. From the late nineteen-twenties onwards it diminished in consequence of renewed and increased Russian commercial connexions with Persia and the nationalist policies of Riza Shah, who diverted Persia's sea-borne trade first through Muhammara on the Shatt al-'Arab and later through a new deep-water port at Bandar Shahpur. His currency restrictions, moreover, reduced the total volume of Persian trade. Since the Second War the Iraqi transit trade with Persia has survived on a

E

greatly reduced scale; it deals mainly with Persian exports to the United States.

Until the great increase in her oil production after the Second War Iraq's requirements from abroad always exceeded what she could export in exchange. Oil revenue, received outside the country, is omitted from statements of the visible trade balance; and there are other invisible receipts—from the pilgrim traffic, for example—which may combine with it to create a more favourable balance of payments. Nevertheless, with the demands of economic development in the late 1930's, an increasing annual trade deficit of several million pounds was accompanied by a deficit in payments, which was met by loans. The outburst of public and private spending when the restrictions of the Second War were removed enlarged both trade and payment deficit enormously, until in 1948, after two bad harvests and the closing of the Haifa pipeline, they both stood at about £25 million. They were rectified largely by releases from the sterling balance of nearly £60 million which the government had accumulated during the war. Since then the new programme of development has increased imports to an unprecedented figure, while the value, though not necessarily the quantity, of exports (other than oil), after a brief boom at the time of the Korean war, has declined. The visible trade deficit had by 1955 reached some £74 million; but by 1951 greater oil production had already created a surplus in the balance of payments. This was much increased after the oil agreement of 1952 and had by 1955 exceeded £10 million.

One desirable result of the expansion and diversification of agriculture and industry would be to make Iraq less vulnerable to the fluctuation of world prices. Her commercial position would also benefit if the quality of her exports were raised. To improve the crops and animals themselves is a major task, which is being undertaken indeed but will require time. Improvement in processing and packing is an immediate possibility and is being pursued with some success, the former in the case of skins and wool, the latter in the case of dates. A Date and a Grain Board exercise surveillance and control and also study and develop markets, and the existing Hides and Skins Association is to be converted into a Board with similar functions. Equal attention might well increase the importance of tobacco as an export. With the establishment of a modern industry the quality of industrial products is also improving. Iraq is furthermore beginning to display her goods in foreign countries and to negotiate foreign trade agreements. She is feeling her way towards an active commercial policy.

Short-term credit for mercantile transactions is adequately provided by the commercial banks, whose main function it has been. In its indigenous form commercial banking is represented by *sarrafs* (small bankers), who, by reason of the Islamic prohibition of usury, have mostly been Jews. Since the Jewish exodus in the early 1950's this form of banking has been of secondary importance; there are at present only six licensed *sarrafs* in Baghdad and eight in the provinces, though some do business without a licence. *Sarrafs* are favoured by some merchants in preference to the impersonal atmosphere of the modern banks, which, by their readiness to take greater risks, they to some extent complement. British banks established branches in Iraq before the First War; there are three in operation: the Ottoman, the Eastern, and the British Bank of the Middle East (originally the Imperial Bank of Persia). Other banks include the Commercial Bank of Iraq, the Arab Bank, registered in Jordan, the Federal Bank of Lebanon, the National Bank of Pakistan and the Banque Nationale pour le Commerce et l'Industrie (Afrique), registered in Algiers. The Banca di Roma discontinued operations in 1941 and two Jewish banks in 1950. In 1941 the government founded its own commercial bank, the Rafidain. Most of the foreign commercial banks have branches in Basra and Mosul and some also in Kirkuk, Arbil or 'Amara, while the Rafidain Bank has one in every provincial headquarters. The banks can meet all reasonable demands for short term credit because they maintain a high degree of liquidity; they hold a large proportion of their assets either as cash on their own premises or with the Central Bank, or else as deposits and investments abroad. There are two Iraqi insurance companies, and a number of foreign companies are represented. The Jewish exodus cost Iraq an important part of her banking and commercial community, but the credit shortage and check to commerce that immediately resulted were overcome fairly quickly in the expanding economy.

COMMUNICATIONS

IN A PERIOD of capital development and growing trade her communications are more than ever important to Iraq. The routes and the centres they serve have not themselves changed greatly since Ottoman days. The chief commercial cities, all on the great rivers, are still Basra, Baghdad and Mosul, the centres of collection and distribution for the south, centre and north; Basra is in particular a centre of the date, and Mosul of the wool trade. From these cities the foreign trade routes spring: from Baghdad by land to the Mediterranean coast and Persia, and from Mosul to north-east Syria and Turkey, while from Basra, her commercial port, Iraq has fortunate access through the Persian Gulf to the sea. These, and particularly the sea route from Basra, are still the channels of foreign trade, although air transport now provides an alternative for mail and passengers; but on the land routes motor vehicles have practically supplanted animals, and the road to Turkey has been duplicated by a railway.

Within the country itself the direction of movement has hardly changed. The main local markets, linked with the great centres, are still Arbil, Kirkuk, Sulaimaniya, Hilla, Karbala and Najaf. Najaf, Karbala, Samarra and Kadhimain are still the principal centres of the great Shi'i pilgrim traffic, especially from Persia, while Sulaimaniya and Arbil have become collecting points for Kurdish tobacco and Kirkuk the railhead for supplying Iraq's largest oilfield. The means of transport have, however, changed considerably. By tradition it has been provided primarily by the Tigris and Euphrates along which agriculture and urban settlement have mostly lain, and by the tributaries of the former. Merchandise was shipped on them by raft or boat, while animal transport linked them with inland centres, and the inland centres with one another. In the absence of vehicles roads were unnecessary. There were a few bridges across lesser rivers, the larger being crossed by ferry. River steamers have been in use since the middle of the nineteenth century, extensively between the wars, but river and animal transport are giving way to railways and, as roads are built, to motor vehicles.

Before the First War Iraq was closely connected in the western mind with railways, for she was to provide the terminus of the Bagdadbahn; but only eighty miles of that much-negotiated line were completed before the British occupation, and it was, as we have seen, essentially to the British army that Iraq owed the nucleus of her railway system. At the end of the Mandate her State-operated railways consisted of a standard gauge line from Baghdad to Baiji on the Upper Tigris (the old German line with extensions), and a metre gauge line from Baghdad to Basra along the Euphrates and from Baghdad to Jalula on the Diyala, where it branched, eastwards to Khanaqin on the Persian frontier and northwards to Kirkuk. In 1939 the Bagdadbahn was completed by carrying the Baghdad-Baiji line through Mosul to Tall Kochek on the Syrian frontier, which had recently been joined by rail to Istanbul and Western Europe. After the Second War the Baghdad-Kirkuk line was brought forward to Arbil, with an extension to Mosul possibly to follow.

The railways have become the main arteries of Iraq's communications, arteries which have functioned well but have now become too constricted for her new economic needs. The first shortcoming is the lack of adequate connexion between the three lines from Baghdad to Basra, Arbil and Mosul. The Baghdad termini of the first two are on opposite banks of the Tigris and it was only in 1950 that they were joined by a railway bridge across the river; previously wagons were ferried across, with inevitable delay and flood-season difficulty. The Basra and Mosul lines have their Baghdad termini within a few yards of one another but are of different gauges; consequently all goods passing between Mosul and the port must be transhipped. The metre gauge lines were designed for eventual conversion to standard gauge but the funds are only now available to effect this. A counter proposal has, however, been adopted: to give Iraq two complete rail systems from north to south by extending the metre gauge line from Arbil to Mosul and laying a new standard gauge line from Baghdad to Basra, preferably through Kut. This will be an important contribution to national development, for a second shortcoming of the railway system has been the lack of double tracks, with existing embankments too narrow to permit of them. Heavy traffic in either direction can disrupt the whole system and injure merchandise through delay. A third shortcoming, the omission of important areas from the arterial system, will be largely met by the line through Kut and the extension from Arbil to Mosul. Iraq's new wealth will also rectify the mechanical deficiencies of the system. Finances have never before permitted adequate replacement of the original track, locomotives and rolling stock inherited from the British army. There is a suggestion that steam should eventually be replaced by Diesel traction, with which experiments are in progress.

Road transport can both supplement the arterial railways and

connect them with outlying areas. Motor vehicles were introduced
in increasing numbers after the First War—there are now some
18,000 private cars, 6,000 taxis, 3,000 buses and 11,000 lorries—
and roads and bridges have been constructed to carry them. The
most impressive early achievement, completed in 1931, was the
'road through Kurdistan'; it joins Arbil, through the Rowanduz
Gorge, to the Persian frontier, there to meet roads from Urmia
and Tabriz, but has proved more valuable for domestic communications than for foreign trade. Apart from this the most
important of existing routes are those from Baghdad to Mosul
through Kirkuk and Arbil; from Kirkuk to Sulaimaniya, and
thence to Halabja, Panjwin, Choarta; from Baghdad along the
Tigris to Mosul and thence to 'Amadiya, Zakho, 'Aqra; from
Baghdad to Basra along both the Euphrates and Tigris; from
Baghdad to Karbala and Najaf and from both those towns to
Hilla. The main routes to neighbouring countries are from
Baghdad through Khanaqin to Tehran; from Baghdad through
Rutba to 'Amman, Damascus and Beirut; and from Mosul
through Tall Kochek and north-east Syria to Turkey.

The existing road system is inadequate for Iraq's requirements,
inadequacy being, like so many others, the result of slender
resources. In 1950, when the Development Board began its
operations, there were some 5,000 miles of road of which only
1,500 miles were metalled and surfaced; the earth roads which
constituted the remainder became impassable in wet weather.
Sections even of surfaced road, laid, without bridges, across the
beds of seasonal water courses, could not be used when these
were in spate. Except in the immediate vicinity of Basra there
were no all-weather roads in the south, where road-making
material is not locally available. Lacking a railway, the lower
Tigris region had consequently no certain access to either Baghdad
or Basra. Throughout the country many smaller centres were
linked with the larger still only by foot, beast or marsh craft.
Where roads existed the surface was often ill-suited to motor
vehicles; even the well-constructed roads of the north were not
all well maintained.

The programme of the Development Board has taken account
of these inadequacies and in the first and second development
budgets the sums of £27 million out of £155 million and £87
million out of £500 million have respectively been allocated to
road and bridge making. Most of the major roads are being given

all-weather surfaces, and existing surfaced roads will later be strengthened to bear modern traffic. A new road is projected to connect the administrative headquarters situated along the eastern frontier. Earth feeder roads will give access to smaller rural centres and approach roads are being laid to the sites of dams and other development projects. New construction, never lacking in difficulties, has, like the railways, suffered from flooding, particularly in 1954; the solution to Iraq's problems of communication in fact depends partly on water control. It has also suffered at times from faulty methods, which can be remedied only through a detailed study of local conditions.

With these improvements and extensions road transport will develop rapidly. Freight is already carried regularly on the better inter-urban and on the international roads. Passenger transport is best organised within some of the large towns: in Baghdad, Basra, Mosul and Hilla the municipality, and in Kirkuk private enterprise, provide regular bus services, taxis are numerous and a few horse-drawn carriages still ply for hire. Elsewhere and between the towns passenger services are irregular. On the international routes there is a heavy pilgrim traffic with Persia and several companies run regular passenger services across the desert to Damascus; of these the most highly organised is the Nairn Company, which runs an air-conditioned pullman-coach service. As road facilities increase so will the need for co-ordination between road and rail transport, if resources are to be exploited economically. The government is in consequence studying the creation of a Communications Board to co-ordinate all forms of transport, prevent their unnecessary duplication and ensure that they best serve the needs of production, marketing, administration and defence.

Until national development multiplied the demands upon it, the efficient Basra port organisation was fully competent to deal with Iraq's expanding trade. The port, as we have seen, was created, like the railway system, by the British army during the First War; by an agreement of 1930 both were transferred from the ownership of the British Government to the legal ownership of the Iraqi Government and the beneficial ownership of a Port Trust and Railways Corporation respectively, which were to administer them and arrange their finances. After the Second War both became the full property of the Iraqi Government and their direction passed entirely from British to Iraqi hands.

Both have remained autonomous administrations, with independent budgets. By reasonable charges on shipping the port has managed throughout to meet its running expenses. These include half a million pounds a year for dredging, which is required continuously to keep the channel clear, for an outer and inner bar formed of deposited silt offer natural obstacles to shipping; dredging costs will be lightened by the recent completion of a new channel across the outer bar. The Port Authority extends from the outer bar to a point seventeen miles up the Shatt al-'Arab from Basra; it consequently handles shipping not only for Basra (up to twenty-eight feet draught) and the recently built Iraqi oil port at Fao (up to thirty-three feet draught) but also for the Persian port of Khurramshahr (formerly Muhammara) and oil port of 'Abadan (up to thirty-two feet draught). In 1951, indeed, it was handling five or six times as much traffic for 'Abadan as for Basra and the closure of 'Abadan during the Anglo-Iranian oil dispute involved it in heavy loss. The port of Basra itself, in consequence of extensions made during the Second War, now contains nearly a mile of jetty, sufficient for ten large vessels. In 1956 some 450 ocean-going merchant vessels docked at Basra and 500 oil tankers at Fao. With the growing burden upon Iraq's single commercial port, the Development Board has allocated funds for the construction of another to supplement it, at Umm Qasr, on an inlet of the Persian Gulf immediately west of the mouth of the Shatt al-'Arab; during the Second War it was in fact used for this purpose, but its installations and link line to Basra have since been dismantled. With the increase in the country's trade the establishment of an Iraqi shipping line is under consideration.

Since the development of air traffic in the late 1920's Iraq has been a staging post on the air route to India and the Far East and has remained so despite the longer stages of which modern aircraft are capable. Airports were constructed in the early 1930's at Basra and Baghdad; both are being provided with the 2,500-metre runways, the navigation aids, the communications system and the meteorological service which will qualify them as Class B standard airports of the International Civil Aviation Organisation. One or other of them is used by most of the great international airlines as well as by those of Middle Eastern countries. A State-owned air-line—Iraqi Airways—was established in 1945 and now runs regular passenger and mail services to the Persian Gulf,

Tehran, Damascus, Beirut, Cairo and, by alternative routes, to London. In the pilgrim season it organises special flights to Jidda. It also maintains regular services between Baghdad and Basra, Mosul and Kirkuk. Its administration is integrated with that of the State Railways, the British Overseas Airways Corporation acting as technical adviser.

The telecommunication system has been greatly expanded since the Second War. At least thirty towns and smaller centres have interconnected telephone exchanges, six of which are automatic. The intention is to instal automatic exchanges in all the principal towns and manual exchanges in all smaller towns and considerable villages. Iraq is linked by telephone with Syria, Jordan, Turkey and Persia; by radio telephone with Europe and America, and with Pakistan, Libya, Egypt, Lebanon, Sa'udi Arabia, Kuwait and Bahrain; and by wireless telegraph with Europe, America, Japan, India, Egypt, Lebanon, Kuwait and Turkey. She is a member of the Universal Postal Union, and has begun to commemorate the achievements of her development programme in specially designed postage stamps.

MONEY

THE UNIT of Iraqi currency is the dinar (ID in abbreviation), which is based on and equal in value to the pound sterling. It is divided into a thousand sub-units, each called a fils. Iraq adopted this system of currency in 1932 in place of the Indian currency introduced in 1915–18 under the British occupation; at the same time she left the Indian monetary area. Until 1949 the new currency was completely covered by a sterling reserve fund in London and was issued and administered by a Currency Board, also sitting in London. In that year a National Bank of Iraq (the name was altered in 1956 to Central Bank of Iraq) took over the functions of the Board, in accordance with a law which further provided that the currency should be completely covered by a reserve composed not less than 70 per cent of gold and foreign currencies and not more than 30 per cent of Iraqi Government securities. In fact total foreign exchange reserves maintained have been more than currency issued, and, in consequence of increasing oil revenues, have continued to grow. Iraq has at present a gold reserve equivalent to £7 million.

Apart from the issue and administration of the currency the

E*

functions of the Bank are to control and co-ordinate banking operations and foreign exchange, to keep the accounts of the government and of para-governmental departments and to make loans to the same bodies. In the absence of a money and a capital market, the Bank's means of controlling the money supply, in which the possession of foreign exchange has been a main factor, have been restricted. The large commercial banks (including the governmental Rafidain Bank) are limited in the amount of the deposits which they may hold abroad; the liquidity resulting from their foreign exchange assets is nevertheless sufficient to make them less reliant on the Central Bank for rediscounting bills or for making advances.

Most of Iraq's foreign trade is carried out in sterling. In this she preserved before the Second War a rather precarious balance; but her wartime supply of goods and services permitted an accumulation which in 1947 stood at £57 million, declined in 1949 to £43 million and has subsequently increased to £116·5 million in 1956. From 1947 to 1952 a part—initially four-fifths—of her total balance was frozen by agreement with Great Britain, and in 1948, by reason of a heavy trade deficit, the war in Palestine and the closing of the oil pipeline to Haifa, she was approaching the end of her free balance. She was saved by releases from the frozen account and improvements in her economy, and in 1952 all restrictions on her sterling balances were removed. The balance of her more limited dealings with the dollar area, on the other hand, has since the Second War been increasingly adverse and has been met by releases from the sterling area pool of dollars.

STATE FINANCE

THE IRAQI Government, until its recently acquired prosperity, has been poor but solvent. Its liabilities, apart from the running expenses of the State, have included several debts taken over with the Kingdom itself; these, which were discharged over varying periods, comprised a share of the Ottoman Debt, assigned to it under the Peace Treaty with Turkey, and liabilities incurred in taking over Basra port, the railways and various public works from the British Government. A second responsibility was that of economic development. To finance major irrigation and other works, the government established an independent Capital

Works Budget in the early 1930's, which received the oil revenues and the revenues of the Iraqi Currency Board. The Ordinary Budget could normally be balanced by rigid economy; but in emergencies its deficits were met from the Capital Works Budget. Recourse for this purpose to foreign and domestic loans was thus avoided, but at the expense of national development. Such emergencies arose in 1930–31, when the world depression brought down the price of agricultural products, and in the middle 1930's, when operations called for by tribal risings were a drain on the treasury. After the Second War expenditure increased with an expansion of the administrative machinery and public services, the initiation of a programme of public works and the heavy cost of the Palestine War; at the same time revenue was reduced, as we have seen, by bad harvests and the closure of the Haifa pipeline. In the fiscal years ending in 1948, 1949 and 1950 there were small deficits in the Ordinary Budget and in the year 1946–7 in the Capital Works Budget; the greatest overall deficit, occurring in the year 1948–9, amounted to ID 4 million or 15 per cent of the revenues. The situation was restored by more drastic fiscal measures and re-established on a highly satisfactory basis by the oil agreement of 1952. With the creation of the Development Board in 1950 the Capital Works Budget as such has ceased to exist; instead the Development Board has its own budget, approved independently by Parliament. The new Development Budget is fed by 70 per cent of the oil revenues. The Ordinary Budget has received the remainder and has otherwise been supplied mainly by domestic taxation.

In 1955–56 the tax revenue amounted to some ID 33 million out of a total ordinary revenue of ID 40 million. Of this sum some ID 2·5 million was derived from taxes on agronomy, ID 19 million from import duties, ID 5·5 million from excise and ID 2 million from income tax. Total oil revenues for 1956, reduced by the interruption of pumping, were ID 69 million out of an expected ID 80 million. The national income for the same year has been estimated at some ID 300 million.

The most striking feature of the State income has been the small proportion of it which accrues from direct taxation and in particular from agronomy. The only agronomic taxes which fall directly on production are those on date palms and per head of camels, buffaloes, sheep and goats. The Iraqi kingdom inherited from the Ottoman régime a system of agricultural taxation which

differed with the district and the crop and was levied variously
on the produce, the area cultivated, the number of date palms
and the power applied to lifting water for irrigation. The government wished to replace these complications with a uniform
assessment based on measurement but, lacking a cadastral survey
on which to base it, substituted in 1931 three levies: a land rent
supposed to equal 5 per cent of the crop, a water tax varying from
2 to 10 per cent according to the method of irrigation, and the
istihlak (consumption) tax consisting of 10 per cent or $12\frac{1}{2}$ per cent
of produce brought to market centres. Rent and water tax were,
as we have seen, compounded in 1939, except in the case of state
lands leased regularly by the government. The *istihlak* tax falls
rather on the purchaser than the produce. The influence of the
big landowners has been exercised in the past to keep agricultural
taxation low; but projects for fiscal reform at their expense have
reached at any rate the stage of practical discussion. In 1953 the
Jamali Government considered the introduction of a land tax
based on area and productivity. It was unable to do so, but
discussion of the tax, on alternative bases, continued.

The most important of the direct taxes are the income and
property taxes, both of Ottoman origin. The former, whose rates
are progressive, is imposed on the profits of industry, commerce
and the professions but not of agronomy. The property tax is a
10 per cent levy on the annual revenue assessed for houses, shops,
factories and other commercial buildings and sites.

Tax evasion is no less practised than elsewhere; it is believed that
in the case of the *istihlak* tax it amounts to thirty or forty per cent,
and that the income tax is fully discharged only by the more
modern companies and by salaried employees. Failing a more
systematic collection of taxes and the developed public spirit
which must await further social and political development, the
exchequer is perhaps in practice served better by indirect than
direct taxation, whatever criticism it may provoke for penalising
the smaller incomes. This it does by taxing such basic requirements as sugar, tea, textiles, matches, cigarettes and spirits—
as indeed it must in order to be effective. The smaller fixed salaries,
unable to evade income tax, are thus between two fires. Apart
from these personal and household commodities the main customs
revenue comes from motor vehicles, rubber and paper and excise
revenue from motor spirit and alcohol. Remaining sources of
revenue are the post and telegraph services and the tobacco

monopoly; the government is the sole purchaser of the crop and takes three-quarters of the profit.

In 1958, with the financial demands of the federation with Jordan and the realisation that continuous outlay on capital projects was likely to involve the country in greater day-to-day expenditure than it could meet from existing sources, draft laws were being prepared—with what prospect of success it was impossible to say—for increasing the tax revenue. This was to be effected by imposing graduated death duties and a graduated land tax and by strengthening the machinery for income tax collection.

Between the two wars the annual revenue of the Ordinary Budget hardly exceeded some four or five million dinars; and despite an increase during and after the Second War it is only in the last five years that the government could exceed the bounds of a disheartening austerity. By 1955–6 expenditure in the Ordinary Budget had increased to ID 55 million. The main ordinary expenditure has always been on the army and the police, accounting for well over a third of most budgets; that on agronomy, minor works of irrigation, public works, health and social services has together rarely claimed more than 5 to 8 per cent of the whole, and often less. Education has been more favoured, rising from 3 to 5 per cent under the Mandate and afterwards maintaining itself at 10 per cent or higher. All these services are now benefiting from the development budget.

COST OF LIVING

IT IS only since the Second War that the cost of living has been a serious concern to the population of the towns. During this period the countryside has also had its economic problems, but they were the product of rather different factors. The rural population, indeed, itself commanded a number of the basic necessities, and its needs were inevitably so limited that it was unaffected by some of the severest stringencies of urban life. Tea, sugar and cotton textiles were outside its control; but its bread was more directly assured and it was free of house rent.

During the ten years that preceded the war and even the first months of the war itself, the cost of urban living remained fairly constant and reasonably in accord even with fixed salaries. But in 1941 the effect of wartime conditions was felt. Imports diminished with the scarcity of shipping, Iraqi grain and livestock were bought in large quantities to meet deficiencies elsewhere in the Middle East, and ever more food was consumed by the growing British forces, whose expenditure also increased, so that between 1939 and 1944 the circulation of money multiplied eightfold. Soaring prices were eventually checked by price control and by rationing basic commodities; in January 1945 the cost of living index for unskilled labour, the first published in Iraq, stood at 618, on the basis of 100 for 1939. Workmen, however, like farmers, business men and contractors, profited from wartime conditions; for local products, labour and services commanded high prices no less than imports, and the requirements of the British forces were enormous. The mere fact of shortages brought wealth to many. The victims were those with nothing to sell—the untrained, the unlucky, the unenterprising, and above all junior civil servants and the lower educated class in general.

In 1947 and 1948 the urban cost of living again rose in consequence of the two exceptionally bad grain harvests. In a year the cost of grain doubled and the cost of living index rose by nearly half, to the figure, unequalled before or since, of 763. This time there were no compensating benefits for workmen, who suffered with the salaried classes. In 1948 they were becoming desperate and there were food riots in Baghdad and several of the larger provincial towns; the situation was relieved by the import of grain and control of the bakeries and was finally restored by two good crops.

Food prices were only an intermittent anxiety, and the price of imports dropped at the end of the war as supply became normal. It is the price of houses and the level of rent which have been the major post-war problem of family economy. Here supply, depending on the limited availability of land and labour, could not be increased to satisfy the keen and growing demand. Rent rose proportionately and has become a major drain on income, of which it may sometimes claim as much as half. Even more than increases in pay—which may be followed immediately by an increase in prices—it is the provision of cheap accommodation which will balance the townsman's budget. It is to this end that the government and the oil and other industrial companies have introduced their very considerable housing programme.

It has still to be seen whether the expenditure of large sums of money on a development programme which does not immediately increase production will lead to inflation. Its extent, if it occurred, would be limited. It would be likely to concern directly certain materials and categories of labour required for development, and indirectly the commodities and services for which higher wages and profits stimulate a larger demand; these would include particularly land, locally grown foodstuffs, and building material and labour, for which private enterprise would probably compete with the State. Even though confined to this field, inflation would cause hardship and unrest, and it might become necessary to regulate the progress of development in order to check it. So far the wages of certain skilled occupations have risen steeply, but the general rise in prices has not been alarming. Meanwhile expert committees are giving the situation careful study.

NATIONAL DEVELOPMENT

NATIONAL DEVELOPMENT, as we have seen, had been in the mind of governments and the public since the foundation of the Kingdom. A special budget was early instituted to finance it; and although its purpose was partly frustrated by events it expressed a statesmanlike attitude to the country's oil resources, as a treasure not to be dissipated for immediate benefit but to be invested for future generations. The same attitude in 1950 created the Development Board, whose functions, laid down by law, were to draw up and, after parliamentary approval, execute a general economic and financial plan for developing the country's resources and raising its standard of living. The plan was to include, but not be limited to, projects for water conservancy, flood control, irrigation, drainage, industry and mining, and for the improvement of communications by river, land and air. Once completed the projects were to be handed over to the appropriate ministries for administration and maintenance. It was finally determined that the independent budget of the Board should receive 70 per cent of the government's oil revenues; these, which stood at some ID 2 million a year immediately before the second war and ID 6 million in 1950, were by the time of the Suez crisis approaching ID 80 million. The government's determination to conserve present wealth for future well-being was the more to its credit in the circumstances that then prevailed. At a time of some political tension, when the feelings of the politically conscious classes were exacerbated by their economic conditions, it was tempting to gain easy popularity both with them and with the country at large by using the vastly increased oil revenues mainly for immediate measures of welfare and alleviation. Instead the government adopted the position that the life of the country must rest not on its oil revenues, which could be relied on to continue neither indefinitely nor undiminished, but on its own natural economy which oil revenues must be used primarily and urgently to develop.

The Board set about its task systematically and comprehensively. On the recommendation of expert reports projects for water control, irrigation, afforestation, communications and an oil refinery were already in the process of planning or execution, and new crops and industries were under study. At the request of the government the International Bank for Reconstruction and Development combined these and supplementary projects in a coherent plan covering the whole economic and social field; it was on this that the first six-year plan of the Development Board (1951–56) was based. Various aspects of the programme were in the following years made the subject of detailed surveys; they included water control and utilisation, subterranean water, mineral resources, power resources, industrial development, the utilisation of natural gas, and various specific agricultural and industrial projects. We have already considered the progress that has been made, on the basis of these expert studies, in the various fields of economic development. Nor were the integration and wider implications of the programme ignored. In 1954 a Danish financial and economic mission under Dr Iversen presented a study of the monetary problems it posed and Lord Salter was invited to prepare a report on the development policy and plan as a whole, the timing and balance of the different projects, their co-ordination with each other and with the action of other authorities, the impact of each upon the others and upon the general economy of Iraq, and such modification in the administrative machinery of the Board and the departments of government as was needed to ensure their successful execution. The second six-year plan of the Board (1955–60), which replaced the first before its course was fully run, took account of this further research and analysis. In its diverse planning the Board has the benefit of an efficient statistical organisation established within the Ministry of Economics, which, working systematically and with modern methods, provides detailed and accurate information over a rapidly increasing field of the national economy. In particular, a series of censuses and inquiries has been completed, on agriculture and livestock, industry, the oil industry, the wholesale and retail trade, housing, family budgets and traffic; and in 1957, after an interval of ten years, Iraq had her second population census.

For the two six-year plans of the Development Board the total budget was some ID 155 and 500 million respectively. The percentage of the total budget allocated in each case to the major aspects of development was approximately as follows: water control, irrigation and drainage 34 per cent and 31 per cent; communications 20 per cent and 25 per cent; buildings (including schools and hospitals) 12 per cent and 19 per cent; agronomic development 8 per cent and 3 per cent; industry, mining and electrification 20 per cent and 13 per cent. Even in terms of the country's crying need most of these are large sums, and they are likely to become progressively larger. In her campaign for national development Iraq seems assured, indeed, of all that money can buy; the fundamental question is how great its power in fact is, how much the ability to spend it depends on other factors it cannot itself control, and beyond what point money in itself becomes worthless as an instrument of development.

Most of the complementary factors of development have come already to our attention. The first is the existence of an administration which is capable of planning and co-ordinating with precision and executing its plans with reliability and initiative. The development of agronomy must comprise in an integrated whole the control and distribution of water, research and experiment, agricultural guidance and basic education, a generous yet vigilant supply of capital, the improvement of communications and marketing facilities and provision for health (to which new irrigation may bring a new threat), the education of the young, community development and perhaps the promotion of local government in the villages. Industrial development demands an equal co-ordination of training, communications, marketing and, especially when planned at some distance from existing centres, of welfare, in which housing will play an important part. In a country with little tradition of self-reliant peasantry or private co-operation most if not all of these tasks will fall upon the State.

The State undertook its programme of development with an administrative machine which was adequate for the burden neither in scale nor in organisation. Just as agriculture lacked its trained estate managers, industry its managers and technicians, and engineering its foremen, so the administration has lacked a range of executive officials to whom the makers of policy could commit its implementation. Ministries have also been denied the permanent secretariat which has elsewhere been found useful in co-ordinating the various departments on a Minister's behalf. The large measure of centralisation which has tended—and not without reason—to characterise the administration, has therefore constituted a burden upon the Minister himself, competing with other duties for his limited time. The administration has, moreover, been static, serving well enough—and very much better than in many countries—for the routine of government, but temperamentally unsuited to execute a dynamic policy of development. Nor has this fact been fully appreciated. The makers of policy, often men of ability and imagination, have not always realised that the fulfilment of their policies requires more than decisions and general directives; that execution must be planned in pedestrian detail and the executive apparatus equally planned; that creation does not automatically follow the word.

The need for psychological adjustment to an era of development is natural in a country where large-scale material development is a new conception; and the adjustment has been complicated by a certain social outlook and the type of education it engendered. This we shall later discuss in some detail (pp. 176-177); briefly, it has tended to reproduce in the educated individual the divorce of intellect from practice which characterised the administration itself. The attitude is, however, changing and responsible executives are being trained in increasing numbers.

A second limiting factor on the efficacy of mere money is the supply of manpower for the development programme—not merely of the qualified engineers, technicians and skilled workmen, whose shortage the government is striving to remedy, but also of unskilled labour. Taken throughout the country the number of unemployed and under-employed is possibly sufficient to provide the unskilled force required; but this simple equation presupposes a mobility of labour which does not exist and a readiness for full employment which may not exist either. If the programme itself is not to be interrupted and the general economy to be dislocated, there must be an economical marshalling of human resources in space and time such as to prevent any disproportionate rise in wages. An alternative would be to import labour or encourage immigration from neighbouring countries; this presents many problems, but has been seriously considered since the federation with Jordan.

Unless the rural standard of living is quickly raised, agriculture is likely to be the first loser in a competition for labour; even before the demands of the development programme were felt there was a steady drift from the estates of the less enlightened landlords to the towns. The exodus may to some extent rectify under-employment and any vacuum created may to some extent be made good by mechanisation. But in that case rural development, while bringing economic gain, would have failed in its social purpose, to create a prosperous class of small farmers; the very provision of the irrigation works and other instruments of betterment, by seducing cultivators to construction, would have denuded the country-side of the very people they were designed to benefit.

For a third factor of successful development is the participation and support of the population. The purpose of the programme, as laid down by law, is not only to develop the resources of Iraq but also to raise the standard of living of her people. Much of the vast work of construction will inevitably be slow in its effect and may meanwhile bring hardship rather than benefit. Changes of locality, of working method, of everyday life may produce psychological stresses and material straits. The uneven profit and social fluidity of a period of development may arouse envy and resentment. Those who do not profit at the outset may suffer from rising prices. Improved communications and increased movement of individuals may infect virgin areas with restlessness and discontent. If the programme is carried successfully to its conclusion initial vexations will be forgotten in the ultimate improvement of living; even so it would be worth winning public confidence from the start. The obstacles to success, and particularly the social and psychological obstacles, are enough to tax the capacity of any government. It is perhaps only on a wave of popular enthusiasm that they can be overpassed and the painful process of trial and error be transformed into an epic of national achievement.

OIL

IRAQ RANKS sixth among oil producing countries. Her production is exceeded in the Arab Middle East only by Kuwait and Sa'udi Arabia; it is one-twelfth of that of the United States, the leading producer, and approximately a third of the reported Russian production. Her oil reserves, as estimated in 1953 were 10·1 per cent of the world total. With her growing domestic needs for re-fined petroleum products and a newly acquired capacity to manufacture them she is herself absorbing more of her rapidly increasing output; but by far the greater part of it is exported, by tanker from the southern fields and by desert pipeline from the northern. It is its sale in western markets which is providing the financial basis of economic development: it accounted in 1957–58 for some 8 per cent of British and 34 per cent of French total oil requirements.

The Iraqi State has entrusted the development of the oil resources to four companies, each operating within a fixed con-cessionary area. Three of these companies, the Iraq, Mosul and Basrah Petroleum Companies, fall within the Iraq Petroleum (formerly Turkish Petroleum) group, whose shares are held by Anglo-Saxon Petroleum Company Limited (Royal Dutch Shell), BP Exploration Company Limited (BP, formerly Anglo-Iranian) and Compagnie Française des Pétroles, each with 23·75 per cent, Standard Oil Company (New Jersey) and Socony Mobil Oil Company Inc., each with 11·875 per cent, and Participations and Explorations Corporation (the Gulbenkian interest) with 5 per cent. The concessionary area of the Iraq Petroleum Company (IPC) covers that part of the Ottoman vilayets of Mosul and Baghdad which lies east of the Tigris, excluding the Transferred Territories indicated below; of Mosul Petroleum Company (MPC) that part of Iraq which lies west of the Tigris and north of latitude 33; of Basrah Petroleum Company (BPC) the remainder of Iraq. The concessions of the three companies, all valid for seventy-five years, date respectively from 1925, 1932 and 1938. MPC, which was formed in 1937 as Mosul Holdings Limited, took over the existing concession of BOD (British Oil Development) Limited, an independent company with British, Italian, German, Dutch, French-Swiss and Iraqi participation. The fourth concessionary area is that of Khanaqin Oil Company (KOC), a subsidiary of BP; it covers small areas in the east of

Iraq, adjacent to the Persian frontier, and was originally part of the Anglo-Iranian concession in Persia, but was transferred to the Ottoman Empire in 1913 on the understanding that existing concessionary arrangements should be honoured. These were confirmed by the Iraqi Government in 1925.

It was in this frontier area that oil was first struck significantly, at Naftkhana in 1923. The field was developed by KOC and its oil was refined at Alwand nearby for the country's internal consumption. It is from the other concessionary areas, and particularly from that of IPC, that crude oil has been produced for export. IPC struck oil in 1927 at Kirkuk, and by the end of 1934 was exporting it through two 12-inch pipelines to Tripoli (Lebanon) and Haifa (Palestine) on the Mediterranean coast. These were after 1945 to have been supplemented by two 16-inch pipelines; but the Palestine war interrupted work on the new line to Haifa and the existing Haifa line was disconnected at the Palestine frontier and has remained so. The 16-inch line to Tripoli was inaugurated in 1949 and was supplemented in 1952 by a 30/32-inch pipeline to Banyas in Syria, which follows the course of the Tripoli lines as far as Homs. The annual capacity of the 12-inch line is approximately two million, of the 16-inch four million, and of the 30/32-inch seventeen million tons. The Tripoli lines are 534 miles long, the Banyas line 555 miles; the motive force for the oil is provided in pump stations which are situated at intervals of some seventy miles across the Syrian desert. Oil was first exported from the BPC area at the end of 1951; it was piped from the Zubair field near Basra to an oil port which had been constructed seventy miles away at Fao, at the mouth of the Shatt al-'Arab. In 1958 BPC announced its intention of building a deep-water oil terminal at the head of the Persian Gulf. The MPC field at 'Ain Zala, north-west of Mosul, has exported since 1952; it is linked to the IPC pipeline system which connects Kirkuk with the Mediterranean coast.

The annual oil exports of Iraq have risen from approximately four million tons in the 1930's to nearly thirty-three million tons in 1955. Sabotage of the Syrian pump installations during the Suez crisis interrupted the export of IPC and MPC oil for a period of four months; it was only in 1958 that it returned to normal.

The search for oil has meanwhile continued vigorously in all parts of the country, assisted by the development of geophysical and other scientific methods of exploration. In consequence new oil-bearing structures have been discovered: the important Rumaila field near Basra (BPC), Bai Hasan and Jambur in the Kirkuk area (IPC) and Butma near 'Ain Zala (MPC). Exploration is of some urgency in view of the pressure decline at Kirkuk and particularly at Zubair and 'Ain Zala, which makes it necessary to discover new reserves; meanwhile it is being countered by artificial methods. In the case of MPC the producing structures are, moreover, of very limited capacity and it has been difficult to maintain the minimum level of production laid down in its concession.

The financial basis of the concessions has undergone considerable modification. They originally provided that the government should receive from the four companies a royalty of four shillings (gold) per ton of crude oil, and in the case of MPC and BPC should also be entitled in kind to twenty per cent of all oil produced. In 1950 a new agreement was made with the three companies of the IPC group by which the payment per ton was increased to six shillings gold. In a further agreement, ratified in February 1952 and made retroactive to the beginning of 1951, the system of royalty payment was in effect abandoned. Instead the government was to receive half the companies' profits from their operations in Iraq, before deduction for foreign taxes; its half share was to include up to $12\frac{1}{2}$ per cent in kind of all oil produced for export, which it could sell to the companies or to whomever it chose. Its revenues were to be doubly guaranteed: they were in no circumstances, except those of *force majeure*, to be less than a quarter of the seaboard value of oil exported by IPC and MPC plus a third of the seaboard value of oil exported by BPC; they were to amount in any case to at least £25 million sterling. If oil production were suspended by *force majeure* the government would receive a minimum annual revenue of £5 million sterling for two years. The companies further undertook to produce between them minimum quantities of crude oil which by the beginning of 1956 would amount to thirty million tons; this figure was in fact exceeded. At the same time the government made a simultaneous agreement with KOC, by which crude oil not required for domestic refining would be exported on a similar basis of profit-sharing; a minimum of two million tons was to be exported annually and export was to begin by 1959.

Adjustments in the government's favour have since been made within the terms of the 1952 agreement with the IPC group;

and in the course of discussions in July 1958 the companies expressed their willingness in principle to consider modification of the original agreement to provide for surrender of portions of the concession area, and indicated that the increased capacity planned by the end of 1961 would be capable of handling a production equal to almost twice the expected offtake in 1958. In an exchange of letters subsequent to the 1952 agreement the same companies had undertaken, in the case of any neighbouring country receiving more per ton of oil than Iraq, to examine the situation with the government; in the light of this undertaking the government was in 1958 studying the practical results of more recent agreements in the area.

In 1952 the government assumed control of oil refining and the distribution of refined products, of which rather more than half a million tons a year were then being consumed, a quantity which has subsequently almost doubled. Until its closure in 1951 the southern areas of Iraq had been supplied by the Anglo-Iranian refinery at 'Abadan, the northern and central areas by the KOC refinery at Alwand; the latter did not, however, produce lubricating oil or aviation spirit. In 1951, to replace the imports from 'Abadan, the production of Alwand had been increased to nearly half a million tons a year and was supplemented with supplies from IPC at Kirkuk and from a small refinery hastily constructed at Basra. Marketing had been undertaken by the Rafidain Oil Company (ROC), another Anglo-Iranian subsidiary. By an agreement concluded in December 1951 with the two companies the government bought their refining and distributing establishments, retaining KOC for ten years as its agent for distribution and for operating the Alwand refinery. In 1952 the Government Oil Refineries Administration (GORA) was established and has since been responsible for refining and distribution. In 1955 it brought a State refinery into production at Daura, near Baghdad, with an output of a million tons of refined products a year, which it is planned to increase. Daura refinery is supplied with crude oil from Northern Iraq, in accordance with a clause of the 1952 agreement with the IPC group. A lubricating oil plant has recently (1957) been added to it, designed to meet all the country's requirements. It includes a bitumen plant, and GORA operates another at Qaiyara, south of Mosul.

These developments and others we have noticed bring the

Iraqi oil industry into an ever more integral relationship with the national economy. It can now supply the fuel for transportation and for mechanised agriculture and industry, and its conversion into electric power will lie at the base of the large modern industries which are being planned. For two of the most important of them—the manufacture of sulphur and petrochemicals—it will also provide the raw materials. As it develops economically the country will depend increasingly on its oil resources, quite apart from the revenues they earn.

Even before the present programme of national development the interdependence was very great. The oil industry has in recent years been spending sums in Iraq which amounted to half the value of her non-petroleum exports. Part of its outlay has been on wages; it employs a sixth of the industrial labour and is the largest single employer. The rest has been in payment for locally grown food-stuffs, the products of domestic industry, foreign goods imported by Iraqi commercial firms and services provided by the State or by private individuals. It has made extensive use of the communications system: the railways and airlines, the Port organisation and the posts and telegraphs. It has been able to make mutually satisfactory arrangements with the Ministry of Education for teaching its employees' children in remote stations. It has relied very considerably on Iraqi building and engineering contractors. And its employees, adopting a standard of living consonant with their substantial pay, have made similar demands, which the domestic market and public services have been able, sometimes by *ad hoc* expansion, to satisfy. To meet the needs of itself and its employees it has in some cases deliberately encouraged domestic enterprises, where none existed, by offering premises, technical advice or training and a guaranteed order.

In return for the co-operation it has enjoyed from the government and public it has been able to offer direct or indirect services which linked it more closely with the country's economy. Roads and bridges built for its own operations have been open to public transport. Medical facilities have been offered outside the circle of its own employees. It has often served the country, particularly the provincial administration, with its technical assistance. At Kirkuk it long supplied the municipality with water and electricity. It helped, in fact, to supply the country's needs until, with increased wealth and technical experience, the country could meet them itself.

One of its most important contributions was indirect. At a time when there were no modern industrial establishments outside the oilfields, the railways and the Port, these organisations set an example of good wages and working conditions on the one hand and of good workmanship on the other. Subsidised canteens, shopping facilities, medical treatment—the IPC hospital in Kirkuk is one of the best in the Middle East—sickness benefits, leave, end of service gratuities, transport to work, clubs, cinemas and sports grounds, housing estates and subsidised building societies, savings schemes, joint consultative practice, evening classes—all these were to have their influence when modern industry developed after the Second War and in its turn sought to promote health and satisfaction among its employees. The standard of performance was no less important. The nature of the work demanded accuracy and care, sometimes to an extreme degree, and regularity and reliability, qualities which were latent in the Iraqi workman but not necessarily developed by the traditional economy. They have been encouraged not only in employees but also in associated contractors' organisations and, because of retirement and the natural turnover in labour, in the working population outside. Thrift has also been fostered, a quality of high importance to the national economy which has blossomed readily in conditions of good pay and security.

In many of these spheres the oil industry has served as a testing ground for the country as a whole, producing at least tentative answers to questions which were later to have wider application. How can the intense individualism of the working man, and his tradition of personal relations with an employer, be reconciled with the demands of a large and highly organised industry? In providing him with healthy accommodation is it possible to avoid establishing residential estates which, in the social tradition of the country, may become isolated and self-conscious communities, connected only indirectly with the main body of society? One of the problems of the industry has been fundamental to the whole modern economy of Iraq. In a country which lacks mechanical and modern administrative tradition, and the combination of education with practical work, how quickly can the population be trained to man the diverse undertakings of its new development? To this the oil industry has been able to give the country an encouraging answer, provided that there is unconditional insistence on high standards, that those under training

are educated out of social prejudice, and that a firm general
foundation is laid for more specialised instruction. Apart from its
production of highly skilled artisans and efficient office staff, it is
having some success in creating within its own field just those
classes that the country in general lacks: educated foremen and
technicians and, on a higher level, administrators with sound
practical instincts and experience.

Chapter 7

The Machinery of State

A S IN HER economy, so in her administration, security forces, education and public services, Iraq has advanced far since the First World War. Law and order have been universally established, the remotest regions brought under administrative control, a modern army created; and the government has increasingly accepted responsibility for the physical and intellectual well-being of the people. In recent years the programme of national development has imposed new and heavy burdens on the whole State machine, and the process of expansion and adaptation will long continue.

ADMINISTRATION

IN ACCORDANCE with Iraq's system of cabinet government, the departments of the administration, staffed by permanent civil servants, are grouped in ministries. Before the federation with Jordan the ministries were those of the Interior, Justice, Finance, Communications and Works, Economics, Agriculture, Development, Education, Social Affairs, Health, Defence, Guidance and Information, and Foreign Affairs. Most of them had existed since the foundation of the Iraqi Kingdom in the 1920's, though some of them had at various times been subordinate departments of other ministries. The Ministries of Economics and Social Affairs were created in 1939, the Ministry of Development in 1953, the Ministry of Guidance and Information, after a brief earlier existence, in 1958. A former Ministry of Auqaf (religious foundations) was merged in the Prime Minister's office in 1929 and a Ministry of Supply was formed during the Second War and disbanded at the end of it. After the federation the Ministries of Defence and Foreign Affairs were absorbed into the federal cabinet.

The administrative authority of the departments of state is

exercised throughout the country by means of a provincial organisation. Iraq is divided into fourteen provinces (*liwas*), these into *qadhas* and the *qadhas* into *nahiyas*, administered respectively by *mutasarrifs*, *qa'immaqams* and *mudirs*. The *liwas* are those of Mosul, Arbil, Sulaimaniya, Kirkuk, Diyala, Baghdad, Dulaim, Karbala, Hilla, Kut, 'Amara, Basra, Muntafiq and Diwaniya. The *mutasarrif* is responsible directly to the Ministry of Interior for the administration of his *liwa* and also respresents the particular interests of other ministries. Some of these maintain heads of departments in the *liwas*, who attend the *mutasarrif's* administrative and general councils, either as permanent members or as co-opted members when necessary; both councils also include elected members. To finance its operations the *liwa* administration is entitled to a share of the property and *istihlak* taxes of the area. For specific projects it may receive grants from the Treasury and may also, with governmental approval, float loans for purposes of development. The administration of a municipality is supervised by a *ra'is baladiya* (mayor), who is appointed by and responsible to the Minister of Interior and presides over an elected council. The system of *liwa* and municipal councils, like the administrative divisions themselves, was modelled fairly closely on Ottoman organisation, with, however, the abolition of the three *vilayets* which constituted the largest Ottoman administrative units.

In the administrative services themselves it was natural that the Iraqi Government should adopt and adapt familiar Ottoman procedures; it was, however, a cramping legacy. The administration, as we have seen (p. 146), while adequate for the routine of State, has required development to suit it to the country's integrated and delicately adjusted economic programme. Nor has its operation been assisted by traditional social loyalties, which could not be expected suddenly to change, nor by the tastes and outlook implanted by the prevailing educational system; the rapid expansion of education, indeed, which was effected partly to staff the administrative apparatus—there are now some 14,000 permanent civil servants where there were less than 8,000 at the end of the Mandate—has at times been in danger of supplying the required capacities in inverse proportion to numbers. Nor have salary rates and conditions of service been such as to stimulate endeavour. Salaries were kept low and even at times reduced because of the financial difficulties of the State, and did not, after the Second War, keep pace with rising prices. Tenure of office was insecure; officials were not infrequently retired for the same financial reasons or because ministerial changes brought a redistribution of posts. Austere living conditions in the outlying areas reinforced the townsman's reluctance to serve outside the larger centres. If young men continued to seek a civil service appointment as the summit of their aspirations it was partly because of the social prestige with which it was invested—another Ottoman legacy—and partly because a country of mainly agricultural economy offered only limited alternative employment to the educated.

The government has recently been engaged in the most serious of repeated attempts to conform the civil service to modern needs. On the one hand, in 1957, it retired or suspended nearly 300 officials judged to be of inferior quality. It has, on the other, sought expert advice in removing the material causes of shortcomings. The resulting reports on various branches of the service agreed on certain general requirements, the most fundamental being that a modern organisation and modern procedures will be efficiently operated only by officials who are properly trained and assured of reasonable pay, security, conditions of work and reward for merit. It was recommended in particular that appointment should be by competitive examination and salary be determined by reference to duties and responsibilities, not by formal scholastic qualifications; that posts should be created only for reasons of administrative necessity; that pay and conditions should be standardised throughout the various branches of the service and a central personnel agency be established to administer them all.

The government reacted swiftly to these recommendations. A new and comprehensive civil service law was passed in 1956 which incorporated a number of the most important of them. It provided in particular for a Public Service Board, which was established in 1957; the power to appoint officials is transferred to its direct authority from that of the ministries, promotions are subject to its approval and its decision is final in cases of complaint. It has instituted a system of examination for candidates and applied strict standards. Its members are men of integrity; an interested and realistic public prays that it may have strength to resist the social pressures to which it may be subjected. At the same time, officials' salaries have been raised, in some cases by as much as half; of equal importance, various official agencies are building houses in large numbers for government servants to rent at reasonable prices, and instituting building societies for those who wish to buy their own.

The new civil service law provides for training courses in the various ministries and various centralised training schemes are under discussion, including the establishment of a Civil Service Institute. Meanwhile a number of young men are being trained in American schools of public administration and appointed to key positions on their return. Much good will also come from the young men with engineering qualifications who are returning in increasing numbers from foreign institutions to assume positions in the more technical departments.

LAW AND ORDER

THE LAW of Iraq had already been determined in its essentials before the Kingdom was established. The British administration and mandatory period retained the Ottoman Civil and Commercial Codes and replaced the Ottoman Penal Code (based, like the others, on French law) with another, which has remained in force. New commercial and civil codes were introduced after the Second War.

Tribesmen can alternatively have recourse to traditional tribal justice. The tribes have a severe code of ethics and custom which differs vastly from the normal law of the State; in certain cases of family honour, for example, particularly where a woman of the family is concerned, tribal morality may not merely condone but demand murder, in which case severe punishment imposed by the State would be considered injustice. The British administration, drawing on Indian experience, promulgated regulations by which tribal disputes, whether civil or criminal in terms of the State law, could be referred to tribal arbitration. They have remained in force, with some amendment, to the present day, but continue to arouse controversy. Provincial administrators, as well as the tribes themselves, have usually favoured their application, while urban officials and politicians have opposed them, partly in the interest of administrative uniformity and national unity, partly because of the evasion which the regulations have permitted. The quickened pace of economic development is likely to hasten the disintegration of tribal society until it can have no reasonable claim to special procedures.

The constitution provides for three classes of law-courts: civil, religious and special. There are civil courts in every considerable town, with jurisdiction in all civil, commercial and criminal matters. There is a Court of First Instance in every *liwa*, and above them Courts of Appeal. Cases are decided by judges; trial by jury is not practised in Iraq.

Matters of personal status, such as marriage, dowries, divorce and inheritance, continued after the First War to be decided by the major religious communities according to their own religious law in their own religious courts, a right that was guaranteed them in the constitution. An innovation was that Shi'is were no longer compelled to submit cases of this sort to Sunni religious courts.

The special courts, apart from courts martial and those dealing with tribal and land cases, are the High Court and the *Diwan Khass* (Special Bench). They are convened *ad hoc*, the High Court by royal decree and the *Diwan Khass* at the request of a cabinet minister. The function of the High Court is first to try cabinet ministers for political offences relating to their public duties and judges of the Appeal Courts for offences in connexion with theirs; and second to examine questions relating to the interpretation of laws and their conformity with the constitution. The *Diwan Khass* is convoked to interpret laws or regulations in circumstances which fall outside the scope of the High Court.

There has been no dearth of litigation in the Iraqi Kingdom and lawyers have increased from the small group in Ottoman days to over a thousand at the present time, of whom two-thirds reside in the capital. The professions of barrister and solicitor are not differentiated. The training of lawyers has normally been confined to the standard four years' course at the essentially vocational Baghdad Law College, graduates of which have been entitled immediately to plead in minor courts and, after a fixed period, in higher courts. Many publicists and politicians have had this training and a number of them have been practising lawyers. Lawyers have been in the forefront of the nationalist movement, of which the Law College was both the main incubator and citadel.

Iraqi justice has had on the whole a creditable history. Its exponents have for the most part been men of intelligence and integrity. The independence of the judiciary is laid down in the constitution; and if at times political pressures and loyalties have had their effect, this was not surprising in a group of societies which were still evolving towards nationhood and political maturity. And if leading citizens have at times regarded themselves as less accountable for their actions than ordinary men, they have perhaps themselves been the greatest victims of the privilege they claimed, for a belief in that privilege has aggravated public resentment against the old order of government. Other aspects of national justice which have incurred the resentment of the educated classes are the extension of criminal jurisdiction to cover political belief and the summary trial by court martial to which, in times of crisis, conviction for political offences has been due. Governments may consider themselves justified in taking swift, stern action to ensure domestic security; but if such action were ultimately to excite distrust of the judicial system, its result might be to damage security still more disastrously.

The efficient police force which was built up in mandatory and independent Iraq owed nothing to the shabby, if tough, gendarmerie and urban police force of the preceding régime. A completely new force was created, which was soon committed to Iraqi command, although British advice and inspection continued until after the Second World War. Its numbers increased from some 3,000 at the genesis of the Iraqi Kingdom to some 8,000 at the end of the Mandate, and now stand at over 20,000. It is organised separately for service in the towns (where, among other functions, it is slowly bringing the unruly traffic under control), in the rural areas, in the desert (where it is equipped with armoured cars and camels), in the oilfields, on the railways and for customs duties. It includes a mobile, militarised force of some 5,000, in which a mechanised regiment is incorporated. Criminal investigation is scientifically organised. There is a Police Training College in Baghdad and missions of police officers have been sent regularly for specialised training in Great Britain.

The police are in general a disciplined, well-officered and loyal body and, considering the low pay of the subordinate ranks— that of the officers has recently been increased—of surprising integrity. Their energy, bravery and, at times, military skill have established security throughout the State, even in tribal and formerly bandit-infested areas. Crime still exists and, as long as tribal morality maintains its hold, will exist in a violent form; but it is increasingly difficult for the criminal to escape arrest and trial.

DEFENCE

THE IRAQI ARMY was created almost simultaneously with the Kingdom itself and there were material reasons for its creation. In the early life of the Iraqi State the good neighbourliness of adjoining countries and their sometimes unruly subjects was by no means assured, while within the country the turbulence of Arab tribes and Kurdish confederations might be supposed to threaten the existence of the State from within. These organised communities, which were moved by no feeling of loyalty and sometimes by positive ill will towards it, could put well-armed forces into the field; the State could be guaranteed survival only by the command of stronger forces. At the outset these were provided by the British Government, a situation which was agreeable neither to that government itself nor to nationalist sentiment in Iraq.

On the British side imperial interests demanded that Iraq should be protected from outside attack and from disruption within; but British public opinion was strongly opposed to maintaining sufficient forces there to ensure such protection. The solution adopted was to keep British forces in the country at a minimum and to make Iraq as far as possible responsible for her own defence. Within four years of the conclusion of the first (1922) treaty she was to accept full responsibility for the maintenance of internal order and, subject to military assistance from her British ally, also for her defence against external aggression; the responsibility was confirmed by the treaty of 1930, which remained in force until 1955.

To Iraqi nationalism the possession of a strong army of its own has always been a symbol of national dignity and independence. This was the more natural in that it achieved its most vigorous early expression in the person of army officers, who had been prominent in the Arab Revolt, played a significant part in opposing the consolidation of British authority in Iraq, and initially provided the main support for the monarchy. It was inevitable that Iraqi nationalism should contain a strong military element, though—with obvious exceptions—the parallel civilian element has usually been strong enough to preserve a balance between the two.

For these various reasons the government was seriously concerned in the initial formation of the Army and its subsequent

F

maintenance and improvement; in the latter it was encouraged by the personal interest of King Faisal and King Ghazi and by the influence of Army leaders on the cabinets of the time. The provisional Iraqi government of 1920 contained a Ministry of Defence and the Army was formally instituted in January 1921, even before King Faisal's accession. In the same year General Nuri al-Sa'id was appointed its first Chief of Staff. By the 1922 treaty the government undertook to devote not less than a quarter of its annual revenue to defence; in the event, the defence budget has consistently accounted for an even higher proportion. By 1925 there were six infantry battalions, three cavalry regiments and two batteries of artillery, and ten years later two infantry divisions, each of three brigades, and a special frontier brigade. In 1938 a third and in 1940 a fourth division were added. As organised in 1958 the Army consists of two motorised infantry divisions and a mountain division with pack transport; as tanks are received an armoured division is being formed. More fortunate than in the past, the Army is now manned and equipped up to strength. An Air Force was formed in 1930, as a dependent service under the command of the Chief of Staff. It now consists of four fighter squadrons and a squadron each for transport and general duties and for aerial photography. In 1955 the Royal Air Force bases which were maintained at Habbaniya and Shu'aiba under the terms of the Anglo-Iraqi Treaty of 1930 passed under Iraqi command (p. 225).

Until 1935 the Army depended on voluntary enlistment. Nationalists had from the first wished to introduce conscription as a means of increasing the country's military strength and as an expression of national solidarity. They encountered strong opposition, however, from the Kurdish and Shi'i communities, while to the general public conscription recalled hated Ottoman practice. In 1934 a National Service Law was finally passed and came into effect the following year. It made every adult male liable for military training of eighteen months to two years, according to the arm, followed by reserve service to make a total of ten years. Exemption might be granted from all but three months of the initial training (one month in the case of technicians) on payment of a fee; and in the case of graduates of secondary and higher schools the period of training was reduced to six months. Those who can afford the fee have continued to enjoy exemption; but the steady extension of governmental authority over tribal areas has made conscription more effective in its application. The Army's care and treatment of its recruits is good and regularly produces a marked improvement in their physique. Conscription is in fact regarded by the government as serving not only a military and political but also a social purpose, of raising the standards and degree of awareness of the population. Since the Second War fundamental education has formed part of army as also of police training.

The Anglo-Iraqi treaties provided that Great Britain should supply the Iraqi forces with arms, ammunition, equipment and aircraft of the latest available pattern. These have, in fact, been delivered to the limit of British capacity though not always of Iraqi aspiration; this discrepancy had its effect on the relations of the two countries before the Second War, when the Axis Powers were seeking Iraqi favour. In 1936–37 Iraq placed orders for arms in Italy, Germany and Czechoslovakia, but with little result. In 1954 the United States agreed to supply arms and equipment and have recently increased deliveries under the Eisenhower Doctrine, in some cases providing American material, in others paying for the delivery of British. At present Great Britain supplies most of the fighting equipment and all the aircraft, the United States special types of weapon and most of the motor transport. With the increased supply in recent years the Army has been fully equipped by western standards and it is now receiving intensive training in the use of its new material.

Since 1924 Iraq has been in a position to train her officers; in that year the Royal Military Academy was established, to be followed in 1928 by a Staff College. In accordance with the successive Anglo-Iraqi treaties Army officers have gone to Great Britain for specialised training and Air Force officers, until after the Second War, for all their training; some now receive their basic flying instruction in an Iraqi Air Force College and only their final training in Great Britain. The treaties further provided for the attachment of British officers to the Iraqi forces in an advisory capacity and there was a British Military Mission in the country until after the Second War. It has now been withdrawn, but individual British officers are still on loan as instructors or advisers. A United States group is responsible for the delivery of American equipment and for training Iraqis in its use.

HEALTH

THE BURDEN of disease that the Iraqi Kingdom inherited was the product of man rather than of nature. Nature had given the greater part of the country a desert climate whose dry extremes, trying but not normally dangerous to man, were inimical to some of his smaller enemies. Man, however, had created for himself such a material and social environment that the physical condition of the bulk of the population was deplorable and the infant mortality among the highest in the world. Stagnant water left by irrigation bred the mosquitoes and snails that carried malaria and bilharzia. The lack of sanitation promoted the conditions for dysentery, enteritis, hookworm and typhoid and multiplied the flies which carried not only intestinal diseases but also diseases of the eye. Crowded conditions in town and village alike and ignorance of the simplest rules of hygiene encouraged tuberculosis and typhus. Venereal diseases were widespread. Most of these sicknesses were endemic; they took a high and regular toll of life and in the chronic form which some of them assumed led to permanent enfeeblement. Equally debilitating was malnutrition born of poverty, an enemy of vigorous labour and an invitation to disease. To the general ill health of the country the heavy pilgrim traffic added the peril of epidemic, in particular of cholera, plague and smallpox. With such conditions of self-perpetuating misery the Ottoman administration had been ill adapted to deal, and it was on the slightest of foundations that the British administration and later the Iraqi Government had, with limited resources, to build.

Rapid progress has nevertheless been made. The health services have established a network over the country. Simple conditions are now treated in some five hundred dispensaries. For more complicated cases there are a hundred hospitals, which provide roughly one bed for every thousand people. Every considerable town has at least one general hospital, in addition to which specialised hospitals exist for maternity and child welfare, for infectious, chest, eye, venereal and mental diseases and for leprosy. The army, police, railways, Port of Basra, Ministry of Education and the oil companies maintain their own medical services and hospitals and there are in addition an American Mission hospital and a number of private Iraqi hospitals and nursing homes. The two six-year plans of the Development Board together allocated fifteen million dinars to hospitals and health institutes. These are to include a modern medical centre in Baghdad, comprising a hospital with a thousand beds and new buildings for the various branches of medical teaching. Of these the Medical College and the School (later College) of Pharmacy were founded during the Mandate, and the Nursing School and College of Dentistry were added subsequently. There are now nearly a thousand doctors, of whom four-fifths are employed by the State, and some two hundred dental practitioners. European and American specialists have regularly been employed as lecturers in the teaching institutes and as advisers in the Health Department. This department, which ranked as a full ministry in the first Iraqi cabinet, became so again in 1952, after thirty years of subordination. Apart from the curative services there has been considerable success in preventing disease. Strict quarantine and the use of vaccines and other methods of control have proved an effective check to epidemics; smallpox and typhus have been controlled in this way and cholera and plague have not occurred since the 1930's. Of the endemic diseases malaria has been eliminated from a number of areas and measures are being systematically planned against *bejel* (a non-venereal form of syphilis), bilharzia, hookworm and tuberculosis.

Despite these considerable advances many problems remain and their solution is important not only for individual well-being but also for the development of the national economy. The infant mortality rate is in the towns nearly three times, and in the remoter areas perhaps seven or eight times, that of highly developed countries. Hookworm, ascariasis, trachoma, *bejel* and tuberculosis are still common. In particular a large part of the agricultural population, the pillar of the country's natural production, remains debilitated by disease and malnutrition. In the south the incidence of bilharzia is estimated at thirty per cent on an average, and much higher in the riverain and marsh areas. In the north malaria, which kills as well as weakens, is a relentless enemy; some quarter of a million cases are treated a year. The development programme is likely to increase the danger of malaria and to extend bilharzia to the north unless preventive measures accompany the new projects of irrigation; in the absence of close co-operation between irrigation and medical services the experience of other countries, and to a limited extent of Iraq herself, has been tragic. Among the industrial population the working conditions in some of the more primitive concerns are at times such—injuries apart—as to produce bad eyesight, anaemia, tuberculosis and dermatitis. Working conditions are indeed regulated by law but, failing a gigantic inspectorate, this is difficult to enforce in the labyrinth of small workshop industries. In most modern industries the health of employees is good, for working conditions are satisfactory, there is adequate protection against any occupational hazards and some establishments provide medical facilities.

There is no lack of appreciation of the many problems and in some cases their solutions have been studied in detail. The wish to solve them is there. But to remedy the evil inheritance quickly would try the capacity of any country and hitherto, as in so many fields, Iraq has been impeded by lack of funds: less than seven per cent of a meagre budget could usually be devoted to public health. Now that ample resources exist they have still a limited value until enough human instruments can be trained and the physical and psychological environment is such as to facilitate their efforts. This, as so often in modern Iraq, is the difficulty: not so much to build imposing hospitals and institutions as adequately to staff, equip and administer what exists; not so much to install in the capital the whole varied apparatus of modern specialisation as to extend and improve the basic medical services, inculcate simple hygiene and promote the material foundation of good health in the country as a whole.

The country requires a larger medical staff of every type, and one that is more widely distributed. There is a lack of doctors, with at present only one to every 8,000 persons; the present teaching organisation, itself of high quality, is to be increased to train what will be a sufficient number of them, provided that they are supplemented with trained health officers and that half of them do not, as at present, practise in the capital. There is a lack of nursing staff, particularly of female nurses; there would be an immediate increase in numbers and in quality if Muslim families of substance would allow their daughters to serve. There is a lack of trained midwives, especially in the rural districts, and of trained staff for the rural dispensaries; on these the well-being of the agricultural population must directly depend. The preventive services are in even greater need of staff than the curative, for they have taken much longer to develop. This is not a specialisation which has appealed to doctors, partly perhaps for financial reasons, partly because it has not formed as important an element in the ordinary training of doctors and nurses as the state of the country's health might seem to demand. More specialists in public health are now being trained, even so in not yet adequate numbers, and a sanitary corps is in process of organisation. Above all there is, in every field, a lack of experienced administrators. It may be said in general that what money can buy is being purchased already; and the State is striving valiantly, within the limits of its capacity, to provide the rest.

But its capacity, here as elsewhere, is restricted by social and economic factors. The doctor's task is still aggravated by bad sanitation, overcrowding, malnutrition and ignorance. The development programme provides for a supply of pure drinking water throughout the country, for town drainage and for housing projects in country as well as town; and in the multitude of small villages in which the government cannot undertake work directly its new organisation for rural development will suggest methods of self-help and offer material and advice towards carrying them out. Over a longer period it is hoped that peasant resettlement, the more abundant irrigation of existing cultivation and improvements in agricultural method will raise rural incomes, break the vicious circle of poverty and ill health and generate the independence and self-respect on which pride of community must ultimately rest. In those circumstances fundamental education, diffused from schools, dispensaries and community centres, will have some chance of success; and the peasant will acquire, beside new techniques of agriculture, a sense of personal and community hygiene. In the towns the environment is evolving more quickly. The administration is closer, poverty less acute and material conditions more rapidly improving; modern industry, as it attracts labour from the traditional working environment, will assist the process. In the towns, moreover, education comes more easily to children and adults alike and the force of example—not least in army, police and organised industry—is stronger and more persistent.

LABOUR AND SOCIAL SECURITY

THE MODE of agricultural and industrial activity in Iraq is an impediment alike to labour organisation and to governmental control of labour conditions. The peasantry consists predominantly of sharecroppers living and working within a tribal framework, and industrial workers are mostly divided in ones and twos among the thousands of tiny workshops and craftsmen's booths which still constitute the greater part of the national industry. Conditions of work and employment have been to some extent controlled by law since 1936; but the law specifically excludes agricultural operations, and in industry the State apparatus can be expected to enforce it consistently only among the larger concerns, though the Department of Labour and Social Security is active and, with its small body of inspectors, achieves what it can. The Labour Law and its accompanying regulations provide for safe and sanitary working conditions, rest periods, indemnity on discharge, compensation for death, injury or disease, and paid sick and confinement leave, and impose limitations on night work and the employment of children. In 1954 regulations were enacted for the settlement of disputes.

Clearer definition of the rights, obligations and organisation of trade unions is under consideration. The Labour Law admits the right of workers 'to establish special associations for themselves, in order to care for their special interests, to spread the spirit of co-operation and assistance between them, to endeavour to effect improvements by educational, cultural, hygienic, social and moral means and to develop the industries in Iraq.' Such associations 'may also offer guidance facilitating the application' of the Labour Law. At the same time an association is subject to government inspection, and may be dissolved if its activities impair the security of the State or prejudice the proper performance of the work. Trade Unions were first legally recognised in 1944; associations had been formed unofficially since 1924, but none of them was very active or effective. In 1944 and subsequent years many were formed, some receiving official recognition. Their inexperience exposed them to communist infiltration, which was partly responsible for the wave of strikes that ensued among workers in all the considerable enterprises—railways, the Port, posts and telegraphs, oilfields, cigarette factories; it ended in consequence of the martial law which was imposed at the time of the Palestine War, and of the government's drive against communism. In the course of their conflict with the government a number of unions were closed; but strike action not infrequently resulted in higher wages and improved conditions of employment, for which communism often secured the credit. Since 1948 several of the strongest unions have disintegrated; others are still in operation, but less numerous and active than before.

In the absence of effective union organisation wages have not been determined by collective bargaining but by individual contract. The Labour Law authorises the government to prescribe minimum wages for any trade; a minimum daily wage for unskilled labour was laid down in 1954 and was increased in 1957.

In 1956 a Law of Social Security was enacted. It provides for contributions from employer, employee and the government and, in return, for benefits to the employee in old age and disablement, marriage, maternity, sickness, unemployment or the death of a dependant, and to his dependants in the event of his own death. The law has been applied experimentally and successfully to employees of official and para-statal departments and of the oil companies, and to those of specified enterprises employing thirty or more persons in five of Iraq's provinces; it is to be extended over the rest of the country. The Labour Law had already provided for indemnity on discharge, and government officials draw pensions on retirement. As a means to further security an experiment is being made with labour exchanges. A bill is in preparation to assist orphans, widows, the disabled and the dependants of prisoners. A notable work of welfare is performed by Iraq's numerous philanthropic societies, including several organised by women; these are financed by public subscription, religious endowment and government grant. Their activities include the maintenance of orphanages and homes for the disabled; of these, three of the most notable are the orphanage of the Red Crescent Society, the Ramzi School for retarded children and the Queen Huzaima Institute for the Blind.

TOWN AND COUNTRY DEVELOPMENT

SINCE THE foundation of the Kingdom the face of urban Iraq has been transformed—and since the Second War with an astonishing rapidity. Broad main streets have been driven through the traditional maze of crowded houses and twisting, narrow lanes, and attractive suburbs have appeared, laid out with shady boulevards and public gardens. In an increasing number of towns streets are well lit, well paved, and well kept, and in riverain towns wide new bridges have been built where previously, if bridges existed, they were unsuitable for modern traffic. The lack

F*

of proper drainage has hitherto been an obstacle to cleanliness
and public health, particularly in Baghdad, where the level of
sub-soil water is high. A comprehensive sewage project is in
hand for the capital, and the example will be followed elsewhere.
The larger municipalities have modern water systems and all
will have them shortly. In most towns old-fashioned features
survive, nor are they all deplorable or unsuited to the physical
conditions of the country; but the growing civic pride of Iraq is
modern in sympathy, and they are in the long run doomed. The
most systematic change is taking place in the three largest cities,
Baghdad, Basra and Mosul, which are being completely replanned
under expert foreign advice.

Urban architecture has equally changed. With the economic
and administrative development of the country the number of
public buildings has steadily increased. Between the wars most
of them were neither very imposing in their proportions nor
determinate in their style; an exception might be made in the case
of King Faisal's mausoleum in Baghdad and the Port Building in
Basra, both of neo-Islamic design. In recent years large and sometimes impressive buildings have appeared in a number of towns,
which include banks, hotels and other commercial premises,
schools, colleges and hospitals, and in Baghdad a vast central
railway station, a new Royal Palace and a Parliament building.
The new university (p. 180) will offer an unprecedented
opportunity for distinguished building, and there is to be
a sports stadium designed by an architect of international
repute.

Domestic architecture has inevitably been influenced by the
migration to the suburbs and by the change in taste and social
habit which has provoked it. Married children have tended to
leave their parents' house for independent dwellings of their own
and it is of these that the suburbs largely consist; they vary from
mansions to the workman's tiny unit in a terrace. Most of the
smaller are single-storied or have one full story and one or two
rooms above; all are flat-roofed to permit outdoor sleeping in
summer, though among the wealthier air-cooling now obviates
the need. The larger houses have gardens, in which their owners
often take pride. The design has varied through the years. The
workman's house tends to preserve the traditional inner court-
yard, on which the house is designed to look. For some time
middle-class houses retained it in the form of a central hall, but

this is now passing away. Between the wars houses were planned with little regard to comfort or the climate, being in the latter respect often inferior to those of Ottoman design. In recent years architects who have these considerations in mind have been employed both by private individuals and by the government for its housing estates.

Since the Second War Iraq has faced an acute housing problem, of far greater dimensions than private enterprise can solve. Family division, the natural increase of the population and the steady migration from country to town have enormously increased the demand for houses, and during the war shortage of materials restricted the natural supply. Post war competition for land and labour have raised prices to a level which threatens the living standard of the public (p. 142). Various government departments have undertaken measures of alleviation, which are now being co-ordinated in a single national programme. For working men and junior officials housing estates are being built, the houses to be rented or purchased over a period; in addition the larger industrial concerns have been encouraged to follow the example already set by the Port, railways and oil companies and make provision for their labour. For others governmental banks (particularly the specialised Real Estate Bank) and departments— as again the oil companies—have instituted building societies, through which families can have houses built to their own design and pay for them in instalments. Under legislation which permits it to control a proportion of the privately registered land situated around towns, the government has been able to offer building sites at low cost. Provision is also being made for the peasants who have drifted from the land and formed slums of village-like huts in and around the cities, especially Baghdad (p. 186); land is to be levelled, streets, water, electricity and sewage facilities to be installed and the foundations laid for houses which the owners will build themselves. A condition for the success of these enterprises is the training of sufficient skilled workmen and the development of suitable building materials, both of which are being seriously undertaken.

Many of Iraq's nine thousand villages have been little affected by the developments of the last forty years. The country's programme of road-building will now make them more accessible and they are to be supplied with pure water and eventually with electricity. Given these essentials, it is proposed to provide them also with materials and expert guidance which will enable them to make their own material improvements.

In town and country the provision of dwellings and utilities is part of a larger programme of community planning, a conception which was absent in the vigorous but unco-ordinated development of the past. The programme, still in its earliest stages, is concerned not only with the physical environment of the community, but also with its health, child welfare, literacy and social education, and, in the rural areas, with agricultural guidance and assistance, co-operative institutions and the establishment of village industries. These services are to radiate from community centres; a few of these have already been built, and the first group of social workers and instructors for urban and rural areas has finished its training. It is proposed, moreover, to accustom villagers better to organise their communal affairs by instituting elected councils which will encourage considerable local initiative; the election of village headmen—previously appointed by the government—has already begun. The courage with which these broader programmes have been introduced in a country whose housing requirements alone must take some twenty-five years to fulfil is highly commendable; their success will depend on a simultaneous development of the administrative machine and on regional initiative, which itself will depend—for the process is circular— on their success.

EDUCATION

To IRAQ in her national evolution education has appeared as a talisman of transmutation and success. It had traditionally been revered as a preserving force in Islamic society, the means to the good Muslim life and, among the ignorant, as of magical virtue as well, giving power over nature and the supernatural to man's good. When Iraq met the new world of the west, in remote and limited contact before the First War and face to face during and after it, it was in a new education that the key to the new situation was sought, to the problem of relationship with the western world, of the horizons that the new contact had revealed and the functioning of the newly created State. The new Iraq was poor, weak and divided, most of her population conservative and ignorant, her material advance dependent on foreign skill. Western education would create an enlightened and progressive society

capable of directing her destinies through modern organisations
and democratic institutions. It would implant a sense of solidarity
and civic responsibility among her diverse communities and unite
them against foreign interference. And on a personal level it
would offer every young Iraqi riches and influence.

Successive governments have pursued these aims with faith and
determination. In their favour was the enthusiastic support of
the educated classes and their political leaders; against them the
apathy of the rural population and sometimes the hostility of its
potentates, the poverty which dogged the independent Kingdom
as well as the mandatory regime, and the tenuous Ottoman
foundation on which to build. Upon a traditional layer of elementary *mullas'* schools and more advanced mosque schools the
Ottoman Government had imposed a system of western education consisting of primary and secondary schools, one or two
industrial schools, a law school and a school of civil administration,
with an independent system of military instruction. The sums
spent on it were small, the organisation weak, the standard of
teaching low and the students few.

After the First War the situation rapidly improved. National
education, which was from 1921 under Iraqi control, received
budgetary allocations increasing to an average of rather over
10 per cent. From 1920 to the present day State primary schools
have increased from 88 to 1,700, their teachers from 500 to
10,000, their pupils from 8,000 to 333,000, and the number of
State intermediate and secondary schools and their teachers
and pupils from 3 to 150, 30 to 2,000 and 100 to 45,000. On an
advanced level of education the Ottoman law school was quickly
revived as the Law College and has continued to train civil
servants and publicists as well as lawyers. Under the mandate a
Higher Teachers' Training College and a Medical College were
added, a College of Pharmacy in 1936, an Engineering College in
1942 and since the Second War Colleges of Commerce and
Economics, of Arts and Science, of Dentistry, and of Agriculture,
and a Higher Technical Institute for training technicians below
the grade of qualified engineer. There is in addition a College of
Islamic Law, with a special secondary school to provide preparatory training. Since 1939 the number of students in higher
institutions has risen from less than 1,000 to 5,500.

Female education has developed rapidly. There had been a
primary school for girls as early as 1898 and in 1920 five were

opened by the British administration, with rather less than 500 pupils. Primary schools for boys and girls were subsequently combined. By 1930 there were 7,000 girls as against 27,000 boys and the proportion has roughly remained. By the end of the Second War the same proportion was established in secondary education, which had first been opened to girls in 1929; male and female secondary schools are separate. It was in 1936 that the first higher institute—the Law College—admitted a female student and by 1947 all the colleges, including that of engineering, had become co-educational, with one exception. This is the Queen 'Aliya College, founded at the end of the Second War initially for girls whose families would not accept co-education. It offers arts and secretarial courses and in particular trains teachers of home economics, and workers and teachers for the expanding social services.

Apart from the Higher Teachers' Training College and the Queen 'Aliya College, which provide teachers for the secondary schools, there have been elementary teachers' training schools since the beginning of the Mandate. A Higher Physical Training Institute was founded in 1954.

Technical and other vocational training has long been under study; experiments in it have had, on the whole, indifferent success. At present, before the execution of new projects, there are technical schools and schools of domestic science in four of the main cities and a secondary school of agriculture and schools of nursing and midwifery in and around Baghdad, but the total number of students does not exceed 2,000. Specialised instruction of another kind is given in the Baghdad Institute of Fine Arts which gives instruction and trains teachers with considerable enthusiasm and success in music, painting, sculpture and drama.

In all these State-controlled schools and institutes instruction is free. In addition primary pupils and a large number of secondary pupils receive free books, while 20 per cent of the students in higher institutions are boarded and fed by the State. Students of vocational schools have their clothing also provided. Primary pupils are given free milk. There is an active department of school health, with its own clinics and hospital.

Primary education has been compulsory by law since 1940. Children may enter primary schools at the age of six and remain there for six years. Intermediate education lasts three and secondary two years; secondary pupils specialise by choice in arts or science. Until recent changes in procedure, leaving examinations at the end of the primary and intermediate grades and a Baccalaureate examination at the end of the secondary qualified for promotion to the grade above.

Under the Ottoman régime the education of the country was supplemented with higher education in Istanbul, and after the First War a regular system of educational missions was instituted. Students graduating from the Iraqi colleges with sufficiently high honours have been able to continue their studies abroad at the expense of the State, on condition of serving it for a fixed period on return. In all some two thousand have been sent abroad to gain ordinary university degrees, higher degrees or specialised training. Most students have been sent to the American University of Beirut, to Egypt, Great Britain or the United States, though in the later 1930's Germany was beginning to attract them as well as to influence Iraqi education at home. Since the Second War the United States has led by a large majority, followed by Great Britain; the government is anxious to improve the teaching of English so that more students can benefit from higher training in these countries. Apart from the official missions a number of students study abroad at their parents' expense. Of the subjects studied abroad engineering has always predominated, and since the Second War increasing attention has been paid to many branches of pure and applied science, including agriculture; the oil companies are assisting these advanced scientific studies by supporting fifty students a year in Great Britain. So systematic a programme of training is likely to win Iraq the scientific leadership of the Arab world.

In most fields of education the rate of expansion has been impressive in a country separated even now by barely forty years from Ottoman stagnation. In assessing its practical significance we must, however, consider the large part of the population it has not yet touched and its general nature and standards.

Despite their rapid multiplication, then, even the primary schools still receive in practice less than a quarter of the children of school age. Primary education is compulsory by law but the State has never yet been in a position to enforce it: first, because such universal provision has been beyond its capacity, if only for lack of teachers, secondly because enforcement would have imposed hardship on the many peasant parents who were too poor to dispense with their children's labour and would, in the case of the nomadic and semi-nomadic population, have been physically impossible. Landowners have on their side been sometimes accused of opposing the spread of education as inimical to their own control; certainly some are now turning to encouragement and even offering to build schools. Even among the children who attend primary schools there is a considerable wastage during the course of study; in most areas more than half of them drop out before the end of the six year period. In spite of educational expansion a majority of the population consequently differs little from its grandfathers in many aspects of its outlook and way of life: what change has occurred among them comes rather from listening to the radio, from hearing the newspapers read aloud and from growing contact with the towns, where the uneducated but informed margin is fairly wide.

In the second place Iraqi education has at all levels and of almost all kinds been hitherto markedly academic and abstract. Scientific subjects have been taught with little practical demonstration or experiment. Technical training has been comparatively neglected and when provided has not always been sufficiently related to industrial requirements. The tendency has been to produce theoretically qualified engineers rather than competent technicians. The education of the much more numerous arts students has been even further divorced from practical life. Handicrafts have occupied a minor place in the curricula and extracurricular pursuits have been few. Neither was encouraged by the traditional attitude of society, which considered education functionally and socially distinct from practical apprenticeship. Both of these were vocational. Education, if Islamic, qualified the student for traditional teaching and the religious law; if secular, for secular teaching, public service and the modern professions. The students themselves consider it to confer not only professional qualifications but also high social and political status in the community. It is held to be a serious business, with responsibilities and privileges; and many activities of the English schoolboy, highly valuable in developing character and interests but offering no measurable gain, would seem to them and their parents alike to be frivolous. There has been an exception in the case of sport. It was accepted as an aid to good health, held—in a keenly competitive form—an appeal for the students themselves, which was reinforced by western influences, and was promoted officially in the cause of nationalism. In the later 1930's it formed, with scouting, part of a para-military youth movement of fascist inspiration; and in the last few years both have had the advantage of earnest governmental promotion and an efficient organisation and are being extended to increasing numbers of students. Numerous sporting clubs cater for others.

Even the purely academic achievement has to some extent been frustrated by the method of teaching. The supply of schools and pupils outran the supply of fully trained teachers; and partly for this reason, partly in the interest of uniformity among diverse communities, partly from administrative tradition, a rigid centralisation was imposed; the content of virtually every lesson was laid down and examinations were confined to the facts presented in prescribed text-books. Traditional learning by rote had in consequence every encouragement to continue. The technique used formerly for the Qur'an, Arabic grammar and Islamic exegesis was transferred to modern subjects; the only change was to substitute for the authority of the teacher that of the impersonal text-book. Even the higher education in colleges has laid emphasis on text-books and dictated lectures. Iraqi students are by nature hard-working and intelligent, eager to learn and quick to think; but memorisation of facts and concentration on examinations have sometimes endangered the intellectual curiosity and the capacity for logical, critical and original thought which they possess to a high degree. It is nevertheless true that the enthusiasm of many teachers and the natural ability of many students have triumphed over the shortcomings of the system.

These characteristics of their education have influenced some young men in their approach to that world of politics which concerns them so passionately. Not all of them have had the opportunity of acquiring practical knowledge of their country, of the peoples and societies of which it is composed, of its economic life, of what policies are possible and impossible of fulfilment, of the time required for change and the conditions which must attend it. Without this anchor of experience they tend, in their devotion to a cause, to be impatient and uncompromising; and when, in addition, they lack the reinforcement of a vigorously independent logic, their political judgments are exposed to the onslaught of emotion and aspiration. Their convictions are moreover fortified by a sense of vocation, which arises from their lofty conception of student status. A minority in a still largely illiterate population, they do not consider themselves as under training for citizenship and politics but as already the fully forged instruments of national progress. It is in these terms that we must judge their apparent indiscipline at moments of public excitement. In recent years, indeed, not without political instigation and support, they have expressed academic and political grievances in frequent strikes and demonstrations, which have sometimes provoked governments to measures of expulsion, imprisonment or summary conscription in the army.

A shortcoming of modern education has perhaps lain in its providing no substitute for the universal philosophy of the Ottoman sultan-caliphate. Ottoman Islam was a complete and coherent system of government, law, administration, society, economics, religion, ethics, logic, science and even aesthetics; it was a whole civilisation, a form of emotion, thought and behaviour that was absorbed in the home, at school, in the mosque and in the work of the day. Modern education weakened its religious and philosophical fabric in Iraq, as the British forces in the First War destroyed its political structure, and economic evolution its social and economic framework; and it has been in danger of replacing them with borrowings from the west, severed from their own roots of centuries, sometimes incompatible with one another, and challenged by conscious or unconscious survival from the old Islamic system. From this may in part have arisen that spiritual malaise of which, in Iraq as elsewhere, there have been signs; and some of her young men have had recourse to a panacea presented from outside—the universal system of communism.

In a material instance education has also occasioned uncertainty and dissatisfaction. One purpose of its rapid promotion was to create the official and professional classes which the new State required. This it did; but when the initial demand was met it continued to produce, and in increasing numbers, secondary students and holders of a lawyer's licence far in excess of what the country could conveniently absorb. White-collar unemployment has been less serious than the fear of it, with all its social and political consequences; white-collar under-employment, on the other hand, has been considerable and its victims, for the very reason of their education, have been incapacitated for the manual work that existed in abundance.

Despite its many problems Iraq's modern system of education has played an essential role in the creation and consolidation of the State; without it, indeed, the State could hardly have existed at all.

Education gave it whole new classes of public servants, adequate in number and, until the new era of development, in training as well. It could not be expected in so short a time to engender a full public spirit and sense of democracy, but it has implanted a very considerable unity among dissident communities and, although it has not assisted all Iraqis to develop their potentialities, very many have been able to derive a complete education from the system even as it stood, and it has served many others as a foundation for personal study or further education abroad. These men and women are perhaps its most striking justification; and enough of them have by now been produced to exert an influence in education, administration and professional life. They are more highly qualified, more dynamic, more adaptable and resourceful, readier to accept practical responsibility with their authority. As educationists they can diagnose the country's educational needs and have the knowledge, experience and the administrative capacity required to meet them. Under their guidance an increasing number of students are graduating with excellent qualifications.

The demands of the country's development programme are, however, too extensive and too pressing to be met by natural evolution. The government and its educational advisers have recognised the immediate need for more administrators, managers and teachers of a new type, for more qualified engineers and still more technicians, foremen and trained artisans, and for a new outlook and new awareness on the part of the labouring classes in town and country if the nation's potentialities are to be exploited to the full.

We have noticed some of the steps taken to supply the more technical requirements; the ordinary educational system of the country is at the same time to be modified and developed. Primary education is to be expanded rapidly and its syllabus more related to practical needs; each school is intended eventually to have a small workshop attached to it in the towns and a small farm in the country, and crafts and elementary farming will be continued in the intermediate schools. The student's career on leaving the primary school will be determined as far as possible by aptitude. Those considered specially suited to an academic education will pass to the intermediate and secondary schools and on entering the latter will begin to specialise in arts or science; the most promising will graduate into the new University, which is expected to impose higher entrance qualifications than the present Baccalaureate certificate. Those considered more suited to practical training will be encouraged to enter agricultural or technical schools at intermediate and then, if capable, at secondary level. Graduates of the agricultural schools will, according to the level attained, become skilled farmers on land assigned them by the State, farm managers on governmental or private estates or technicians in the State agricultural organisation. The technical schools will supply skilled labour, foremen and technicians for industry, the ablest graduates first passing through a technical institute. There will be vocational education in domestic science for girls. In every type of school the method of teaching is to be improved and curricula and textbooks rationalised. In particular the preoccupation with examinations is to be discouraged. The government has started to abolish the school leaving examinations which automatically admitted the student to the next grade. The higher school will now control its own admissions, though whether they will be restricted and by what means has still to be decided. New schools of each type are already being built, facilities are being increased for training teachers and details of the new policy are under earnest discussion, together with proposals for encouraging extra-curricular and outdoor activities. The intention behind these proposals deserves the warmest approval; but it may be supposed that their execution will occasion some difficulty, for the State is seeking development in both quantity and quality, each in itself hard enough to accomplish rapidly with available resources.

The symbol and focal point of the country's educational aspirations is the Iraqi University. Hitherto the colleges which have provided the higher education of the country have operated separately though not independently, being attached to the Ministry of Education or another ministry which could intervene in their affairs. The University, in its constitution, organisation and outlook is to establish and maintain an intellectual tradition and standard throughout the country, to harmonise diversity, effect an economy of resources and ensure academic independence. The creation of a university has long been under discussion, one of its early advocates being the first King Faisal. In 1956 it was established by law. A distinguished Iraqi educationist has been appointed as its President, the purchase of land and design of buildings is in progress and a founding committee, although not yet joined by the foreign members who are to sit on it, is in course of deliberation. It will decide which colleges shall be admitted immediately to the University, what modifications others must undergo, what conditions students must satisfy for admission and what system of examination will be adopted; to ensure a proper standard the extensive employment of external examiners is being considered. The success of the University must depend very largely on an uncompromising determination to maintain high standards in the primary and secondary schools.

The system of State education, through which the overwhelming majority of educated Iraqis have passed, is supplemented by numerous private schools. These are bound by the government's educational syllabus and system of examinations. Otherwise there has never been any intervention in their internal affairs, even though some of them have received State subsidies. Over the last twenty years the number of pupils in private primary schools has remained constant, while in private secondary schools, like those of the State, the number has quadrupled. At present there are a quarter as many private as State secondary pupils, but only a twentieth as many primary pupils. Apart from the numerous kindergartens, private schools have been academic in their education and of three types: those established by Islamic organisations for Muslims, those established by Iraqi minority communities, with or without foreign assistance, for their own children, and foreign schools for any who wished to attend them. Of the last, two Catholic schools—Baghdad College, an American Jesuit secondary school for boys, founded in 1932, and the School of the Presentation, a French primary and secondary school for girls, founded in 1928— have educated members of some of the leading families, Muslim as well as Christian. A primary school organised by the British Council has in recent years become equally popular. The American Jesuits have in the last year founded the only private institute in the country for higher education; under the name Hikma University it is to provide courses in science, business administration and other subjects at an advanced level. The Technical Training Centre of the Iraq Petroleum Company has been mentioned elsewhere (p. 127).

In addition to its problems of educating the young, the Iraqi State has been confronted with an inheritance of public illiteracy and ignorance. Its campaign for literacy began before the end of the Mandate, when some two thousand pupils were being taught in thirty centres. In the period that followed facilities were rapidly extended, and there are now over five hundred centres, some for women, and thirty thousand pupils. Police and army recruits are given similar teaching. With the country's material development has come a vivid realisation of the need to provide fundamental education on the widest possible scale. It has an important place in the programme of community development (p. 172); it is hoped eventually to extend evening instruction to every centre of habitation in the country.

Within the functions of the Ministry of Education falls the sponsorship or control of the Iraq Academy and the Department of Antiquities. The Iraq Academy was founded in 1948 to maintain the purity of the Arabic language and adapt it to modern needs, to undertake research and publication on Arabic philology and literature and Islamic history and civilisation, and to preserve and publish rare Arabic works. Its members, who consist of distinguished Iraqi, Middle Eastern and foreign scholars, have made a material contribution to these ends and the Academy has within the limits of its resources given financial assistance to scholarship and research.

The Department of Antiquities was established in 1922 and was accompanied by an Antiquities Law; this gave the State control over all archaeological activity, which had hitherto been carried out by British, French, German and American parties without co-ordination or systematic and scientific supervision on the part of the government. Excavation has since been divided between foreign missions and the Department itself and their happy co-operation has made it possible to write or rewrite the early history of the country. The pre-Islamic museum in Baghdad, which was initially established in 1924 through the devotion of Gertrude Bell, contains one of the finest collections of its kind in the world; there are four other museums in Baghdad, and museums also in Samarra, Babylon and Mosul. One of the most striking features of the Department's success has been the creation of a competent body of Iraqi archaeologists, who, now independent of foreign direction, make it possible to maintain an internationally recognised programme of excavation, restoration and publication. Indeed, Iraq's remarkable archaeological richness and her unique place in pre-history are not only of vast interest in themselves and apt to invite friendly sympathy to the territory, but are a considerable economic asset as attracting the 'invisible exports' implicit in foreign excavation-parties and tourism.

Chapter 8

Society

THE SOCIAL PATTERN

SINCE the Second War Iraqi society has been evolving rapidly; in some of its main lineaments it has nevertheless changed little from Ottoman times. It is still a mosaic of discrete elements, some of them magnetised, as it were, by common characteristics into cohesion, others contained inertly by the external framework of the State. The post-war years have had a double effect: first, to introduce new pieces into the pattern and to change the size and importance of those that existed, and second, to soften and confuse their boundaries. It is still premature to speak of a single Iraqi society; but that unity is within measurable distance.

The factors of division are still numerous. They include regionalism; religion, mainly as between the different Muslim and Christian sects and the Jews; language, mainly as between Arabic and Kurdish, with the accompanying divergence of historical and cultural tradition; economic function; social habit; and education. These divisions, and particularly the last three, sometimes coincide, but more often intersect to form smaller groups whose separate identity is of some practical importance.

The most obvious distinction is that of tribe and city. The former comprises both nomadic herdsman and settled cultivator, whose difference was initially one of function. The vast majority of Iraqi peasants, whether Arab or Kurd, are of tribal origin and their tribal organisation and morality have largely survived their transformation from nomadic to sedentary life. The settlement of tribes has been a policy of the Iraqi as it was of the later Ottoman Government, serving to break their armed threat to the authority of the State but also to develop the national economy. Between unmixed nomadic herdsmanship and unmixed agriculture lies a whole spectrum of combination which makes Iraq a living museum of nomad settlement.

Pure camel-raising nomadism, confined to the Arabs of Iraq's western deserts and the Jazira, is comparatively rare and becoming rarer. Modern means of communication have diminished the trade in camels on which the major tribes depended, and the enforcement of governmental authority has deprived them of protection money and more violent sources of income. There is every inducement for the camel-herdsman to accept the humiliation of farming grain, then vegetables and finally the despised tomato.

The nomadic tribes that survive as such live much as did their ancestors. They move with the season between grazing grounds and water holes, to whose use they have a traditional right. From their animals they derive many of the necessities of life and obtain the rest from the settled areas in exchange for the animals and their products. The largest unit of instinctive loyalty is the tribe, which is regarded as having a basis of blood relationship. The shaikh of the tribe, drawn from one of its aristocratic houses, is its representative with other tribes and the government, orders its internal and external relations in consultation with the other tribal notables, and, to subsidise the guest tent he maintains on behalf of the whole tribe, draws certain dues from its members, all of whom have free access to him. The position tends to pass from father to son, but is held, as it must be if the tribe is to prosper, in consequence of personal qualities, and if these are lacking tribal opinion will force the succession along other lines.

The semi-nomadic tribe-groups combine agriculture with sheep and goat breeding. Most of their component sections are settled, but some move their flocks to pasturage in the spring and early summer and later return to their settlements.

Other Arab tribes are completely sedentary. By far the greater part of Iraq's tribal population is in fact settled in villages. Its tribal coherence is less marked than in the nomadic tribes; and although the shaikh exercises tribal authority and tends among his tenants to be lawgiver, arbitrator, magistrate and tax-collector, he is also an independent and sometimes absentee capitalist, being, as we have seen (p. 120), not only the landlord but also the market and the supplier of capital. The peasant is not necessarily a resentful victim of oppression; he usually feels a certain tribal loyalty to the shaikh, regarding him rather as a patron and protector—not least against the government—than as a tyrant, and accepting the onerous terms of tenancy as part of the natural order of things. The system contains, indeed, an element of social security; miserable though the peasant's lot may be, neither his fellow-cultivators nor the shaikh himself will let him and his family starve.

This relationship is still valid over the greater part of rural society, though a great many holdings are cultivated by independent farmers and their number is increasing steadily with the distribution of State land; there are suggestions, however, that it may gradually be modified. On the landlord's side we have noticed a move towards more efficient farming and perhaps a more enlightened outlook. He is in any case confronted with a rising tide of reformist opinion, from which, if of a younger, educated generation, he may not himself be immune. The peasant, for his part, is no longer isolated in rustic ignorance. Communications are improving. He can be informed and influenced by the radio, to some extent by political activists and most of all by his own relatives who have migrated to the towns and open his eyes to the advantages of another life. There are increasing signs of restlessness in the country-side, in some small degree political but mainly social and economic. It takes the form of general dissatisfaction with the peasant life when money can be made more easily in the towns, and of resentment against the social and economic domination of the landlord. Its intensity and manifestations vary from district to district; in some cases there is a spontaneous reference to the local administration of matters which would previously have been referred to the shaikh. With doubts of the traditional system implanted in his mind and work in the towns or on development projects exercising their appeal, the cultivator will no longer defer unquestioningly to the shaikh's authority; and the systematic expansion of rural education that the government is planning will help to disrupt a social order that is outgrowing its utility.

Much of what has been said of the Arab rural region applies in general to the Kurds of the north-east and extreme north but would require modification in detail to conform with their different tribal structure, historical background and geographical environment. Holdings are smaller than in the south and a high proportion of them are cultivated by independent farmers. The landlords (*aghas*) who nevertheless control much of the cultivated area are themselves largely tribal in organisation but have in some cases no tribal connexion with their cultivators, having imposed themselves as a military caste on a non-tribal agricultural population. Terms of tenancy are hard, but on the whole, perhaps, rather easier than in the south; and, divided and isolated as some of the population is in remote mountain valleys, it is unlikely that ideas of social change will influence it as rapidly. The Kurds also have their semi-nomads, whole tribes which, according to the season, move their flocks from the foothills of Iraq to fixed mountain pastures in Persia, leaving a few representatives on their Iraqi cultivation.

Urban and tribal society are by tradition mutually exclusive, hostile and contemptuous, the townsman's contempt mixed liberally with fear. There has nevertheless been continuous economic contact between the two; some of the towns, indeed, contain what clearly were once tribal quarters. With the steady extension of governmental control and establishment of rural security since the First War there has been increased intermingling. Once the administration had established itself in tribal eyes as a thing to be placated and cajoled the chiefs began to frequent the centres of administration and government. Sessions of Parliament kept tribal deputies for long periods in the capital and led some of them to buy houses there. The growing amenities of the town and a lessening devotion to tribal life combined to the same effect. The development of agriculture not only helped diminish tribal and urban prejudices but created common interests between tribal landlords and city merchants, carrying the former beyond mere sale and purchase to the acceptance of urban capital and urban partners. In the south the vicissitudes of sharecropping have driven sharecroppers in a steady flow to the towns, where they may constitute a large and undigested portion of the population. On the periphery of Baghdad's urban population, for example, is a tribal settlement of perhaps two hundred thousand immigrants, maintaining in social isolation its own village life and mores.

In the cities the Iraqi Kingdom inherited a society which had changed little in centuries. There was an upper class of leading administrative and religious families, rarely of great antiquity though in some cases manifestly aristocratic; such, for example, were the families of the *naqibs*, particularly the ancient Gailanis of Baghdad, and of princes of the past, like the Jalilis of Mosul and the Kurdish Babans. Below them were the less distinguished men of religion in their grades, then the tradesmen of the bazaar, no longer organised in guilds, and the police and petty government employees. The upper class enjoyed inherited fortune, held land or engaged in commerce; Shi'is and members of the religious minorities were at various levels particularly active as business men.

Beside these traditional social groups, imbued with the principles of their religion and with varying degrees of traditional learning, a new society began to develop in the second half of the nineteenth century, whose frontiers were to cross and confuse some of the existing divisions. Its distinguishing mark was a secular education imitated from the west, and it arose to meet the demands of a reformed administration and system of law and a western type of medicine and engineering. To meet similar demands and for other reasons (p. 172), the Iraqi successor government adopted and extended a western type of education, with a corresponding enlargement of the new society. Membership of this society might be considered to depend on secondary education, which has become a watershed, determining culture, social habit, political attitude and economic function, though not necessarily wealth.

On one side of the watershed lie the practical men, mostly illiterate but often well informed by radio news and newspaper recital, immersed in their work, conscious of their skill and imbued with shrewd common sense. In social loyalty they are hardly less compartmented than their fathers, owing it to family, town and town quarter, and religious sect. Beside the great mass of urban labour, divided among thousands of small and varied enterprises, the modern industrial establishments, and in particular the oil companies, the railways and the Port, have begun to create a new working class, derived partly from existing urban occupations and partly from the rural population. Concentrated employment in modern industries tends to blur social divisions and encourage a consciousness of wider identity. The numbers affected are still, however, small, and labour organisations have had to face the existing social divisions, a marked individualism, and at times governmental repression. Especially where large companies provide housing estates for their employees the effect is sometimes to establish an independent new community, a new piece in the mosaic, rather than to promote the general solidarity of labour. Modern training and working environment also affect the workman's outlook in other ways. He is likely to have a sharpened awareness, to be more adaptable and progressive. On the other hand service in a large, impersonal organisation may disturb that harmony of life and emotion which is characteristic of traditional society. Religious belief may perhaps be unaffected; but the substitution of printed regulations for the personal relationship with a small employer or master craftsman may sometimes, in spite of good pay and conditions, cause an underlying dissatisfaction.

On the other side of the educational watershed lie officialdom, the professions, politics and the office. This is a self-consciously white-collar world with some rudimentary tendency to a social cohesion bridging differences of religion, family, wealth and function. Birth in itself is no longer very significant except to those who boast it; wealth is of much greater importance, official position and connexion with the régime more important still. Economically this educated society is roughly divisible into three. There is a small upper class consisting of the distinct ministerial group we shall discuss in a political connexion, of the most senior civil servants and service officers and those with sources of income apart from their salaries, of rich business men and urban landholders, and of the most successful members of the professions. There is a middle class, also small, which lives more or less adequately if not comfortably by its own standards; it is composed of senior civil servants and service officers, higher teachers and ordinarily successful business and professional men. Below them lies the great mass of the educated public, the lower and lower-middle grades of the administration and services, the junior teachers, the part-time lawyers and newspaper editors and all the under-employed whom the educational system has created. These have been among the principle victims of rising prices during and after the Second War; a major factor of instability in the country has in fact been the divorce of intellectual dynamism and material well-being. Their penury has been emphasised by what they consider the growing ostentation of the upper class, to most of which they believe themselves intellectually superior. The example of luxury in the country itself, or in books and films, has created appetites which they have no hope of satisfying; they have similarly formed ideas of romantic relationships for which their society has so far made no provision. In their careers they have suffered from those traditional principles of loyalty which have not infrequently influenced professional advancement, not least in the administration. Psychologically and spiritually they, most of all, have been stricken with the malaise born part of vacuum, part of discord, which besets the modern Islamic world. Politically, as we shall see, these 'angry young men', considering themselves deprived of their due influence, have formed the great body of the opposition, the violence of their convictions perhaps sharpened by these many frustrations and by the nature of their education.

The progress of national development is beginning to affect urban as well as rural society. Its direct benefit has so far gone mainly to engineering contractors, industrial capitalists and business men and to skilled and certain categories of unskilled labour. The bulk of educated society may not yet have derived much profit from it and may on the contrary have suffered from the effect on prices; but salary increases and housing schemes have alleviated its present condition and given it some assurance for the future, and development will in time create remunerative positions which it can hope and is indeed being trained to fill. And it enjoys no less than other classes the new urban amenities, better transport facilities and expanded social services.

Movement between the various groups of society has so far been considerable, without, however, constituting a flux. Any reasonably intelligent boy can obtain a higher education at State expense and a clever boy is likely to secure a State or foreign scholarship to study abroad. In that case, given good fortune and possibly a certain influence he may rise to some of the highest positions of State. On the other hand his family may have neither the tradition of education nor the financial means of dispensing with his labour; and if he receives his education in the country itself and has no outstanding advantages he will quite likely have exchanged reasonable prosperity as an artisan for white-collar under-employment. On the whole peasant families have tended to produce peasants, artisan families artisans, official and academic families officials and teachers, the most considerable change in occupation arising from the migration of peasants to the towns. As technical education is extended to meet the needs of development, it will possibly tend to confirm this continuity of occupation, but will offer improved skill, status and income within the occupation itself.

An important social consequence of technical education is the creation of a new class of technologists and managers, who are enlarging the middle at the expense of the lower-middle class. Unlike the latter, they are not a class of frustration; they are moderately satisfied with their work, their status and their economy, and for this reason, and because of their different training and greater practical experience, have a different view of affairs. They are less interested in politics than the lawyers, and particularly in foreign politics; they would like to see Iraq internally strong before they plan her role on the international stage. Their criticism of government is on grounds less of politics than of technical and administrative efficiency. In the sphere of administration and economics, indeed, they will supply one of the country's most pressing needs; politically they may well come to constitute a new element of stability.

THE FAMILY AND THE SEXES

THE IRREDUCIBLE atom of traditional society was the family and for much of the population it retains its authority. For others modern education and foreign influences have weakened its ties; but although it may no longer be the prime focus of their loyalty it still commands their devotion and respect, serves as an instrument of mutual aid and, like friendship, imposes obligations which may outweigh those of profession or the State. Change, where it has occurred, has consisted in the departure of married children to homes of their own and in a lessening of parental authority, particularly in the choice of a wife or husband. The same factors of change are profoundly affecting the position of women.

The Iraqi woman, like those of other Muslim societies, has exercised considerable influence, but largely from a position of seclusion. In rural society, indeed, polygamy, laborious work and some degree of segregation go with unveiling and a certain physical freedom, in which sexual freedom is not included; unchastity is apt to be requited with death. Among the Kurdish tribes women have from time to time risen to pre-eminent position, even to military command. In the towns, and especially among the upper and middle classes, where polygamy is now almost extinct, seclusion and veiling have been the custom, sanctified by a millenium of social habit. They are still observed in provincial towns, but in the major cities are beginning to pass away.

The movement for emancipation started at the top of society, where there was more opportunity for foreign travel and for contact with resident foreigners. It has progressed farthest in Baghdad, where, in the households of a few of the younger Muslim

Ministers, administrators and business men the position of the wife differs little from that of her English counterpart. She holds and attends mixed parties with her husband, joins social clubs, dances at club and charity balls, does her shopping bareheaded and in European dress and drives her own car. Between this small emancipated group and the still secluded women of conservative families there are many gradations. Outside the family circle some women attend only the most intimate of mixed parties, some only in the presence of foreigners; and although the face veil has practically disappeared comparatively few women will appear in public without the voluminous black silk 'abba that has survived it. The middle class is less enterprising, the lower educated classes almost as conservative as the working people. Although they profess the social and political theories of the west and deplore the existing social conventions, they are rarely prepared to disregard them and criticise any colleague who does. Emancipation has demanded courage from wife and husband alike; public censure apart, ingrained feeling is so strong that even those enamoured of its theory may be acutely embarrassed by its practice.

Education, foreign example and the substitution of the individual household for the family are changing the approach to marriage itself. It was traditionally a physical and economic relationship; parity of education is now making companionship possible, mainly in the upper and middle classes, where female education is most common. Where companionship exists the time devoted to it may nevertheless be small, the residue—as anywhere else—when the claims of business and society have been met. Even the most progressive and devoted couples spend much of their leisure in the company of their own sex, others virtually the whole of it. Except on the higher social levels the house is the women's place of meeting; many men return there only to eat and sleep, sometimes only to sleep. This does not prevent good relations between husband and wife, mutual respect and even considerable affection; but it does tend to deny a home.

The choice of a wife is increasingly a matter for the individual. In the urban society of the past nothing was more subject to the authority of parents; husband and wife, often very young, were not permitted to see one another before marriage, though curiosity sometimes went to ingenious lengths of circumvention. Now the educated young man, given that he observes rules of social compatibility which would apply in many countries, has often almost complete freedom of choice and even of initiative, though he may still have to base the choice on hearsay rather than personal knowledge. Young Muslim men and women, except in very few families and in small, carefully chaperoned groups, may still not join in social activity together; but academic association in the mixed colleges is permitted and it is becoming more common for a young man to see and even speak to his wife before marriage, though rarely to know her very closely. It is nevertheless possible to form close attachments and maintain them surreptitiously by telephone, post and planned coincidental meeting; here and there young people are for the first time falling in love. The immediate result may be to sharpen their emotional problems, for marriage may be prevented by unequal social status or by other arrangements which the girl's parents may have made. The educated girl is less free than the boy. Her family are more likely than his to exercise the right of veto and compulsion. Usually she is accorded the privilege of a rather passive choice; her parents make suggestions which she is free to reject, and it is only after persistent rejection that pressure is applied. To girls influenced by films and novels this may be a frustrating procedure; most of them are, however, realistic about marriage. They appreciate that, until association is freer, happiness may lie rather in a list of candidates prepared by conscientious and indulgent parents than in personal choice based on the impressions and emotions of a few meetings.

Among the uneducated and humbler educated classes of the town the girl is completely under parental control until she is married and the man, through intermediaries, chooses a wife on almost entirely practical grounds. Marriage between relatives is common; it is even commoner in the tribes, where a girl's first cousin traditionally has the right to marry her. In tribal custom runaway marriages may lead, as much as unchastity, to murder, although peace may be negotiated against an indemnity. With the acquisition of a new economic outlook shaikhs have tended to deny the claims of nomadic custom and to marry their daughters as peremptorily and prudently as a city grandee.

Arbitrary divorce of a wife without reciprocal right is, like polygamy, now eschewed by educated society but still facilitated by the Islamic law of the land. The legal and political disabilities of women—the latter are shortly to be alleviated by the grant of the vote to educated women and perhaps their eligibility for parliamentary election—are a prime concern of the five federated women's organisations of Iraq. Led by women of character, culture and social standing they have fought for female rights with persistence, skill and the courage of personal example.

Women of this quality are increasing in number. The Iraqi woman is by nature strong in character, intelligence and ability. Given education and responsibility she displays emotional balance, a keen intellect, a power of organisation and command and a capacity for social service. In society she can be smart, sophisticated and amusing, at home she is a devoted mother and a good housewife, in politics often forthright to the point of aggressiveness. Behind the scenes until yesterday, to-day in public with an assurance as though of ages' experience, she is a powerful and indeed formidable force. She emerges from confinement under pressure, maintained by the restrictions that still exist. She is apt to approach any activity open to her with the intensity of a *jihad*. The Muslim girl is still, by public and family feeling, restricted in her occupation. She may teach or be a women's and children's doctor and now a social worker; but by exceptional power of will, which some have had, she can engage in almost any activity she wishes. One or two have been diplomats, one the head of a government office. Some have graduated highly from the Engineering College. Christians, less limited by the opinion of their communities, also become nurses, typists and clerks. In all these activities women are in energy, efficiency and undemanding adaptability redoubtable rivals to men.

Iraqis are extremely fond of children, and educated parents are beginning to devote much time and thought to their upbringing. Childhood is not usually regarded as having significance in itself, but rather as a simple absence of adulthood. For a few years poor children play together in the streets, others in the household with whatever playthings come to hand—toys are becoming increasingly abundant—and then, almost without transition, they become socially adult, the poor when they start at an early age to work, the richer when they begin their secondary education. Until then they have been subject to no very rigid discipline; but when the brief period of childhood is past a discipline is indeed imposed, that of adult society, exercised through family, social convention and, for the student, not so much the school organisation as the student body itself, with its con-

G

sciousness of status and its claim to a political and social role. The result is an early gravity and in some respects maturity, not less marked in the country-side than the town. The sons of many tribal landlords, indeed, Arab or Kurd, receive an excellent training in character, illiterate though some of them are; for in silent attendance at their fathers' audience chamber and later as their active deputies they learn to pass responsible judgment and exercise confident command.

The absence, however, of a period of adjustment, in which child and adult can alternate, may have attendant disadvantages. The problems of adolescence are resolved rather by ignoring their existence, and adolescents who are incorporated in adult society are not unlikely to rebel against it. There is similarly no period of inutile discovery and experiment; in life as in the school library young Iraqis have little time to browse, little chance to enrich their experience before it is frozen by the responsibilities of early adulthood.

DAILY LIFE

OUTSIDE THE towns daily life has hardly felt the impact of the west. The tribal nomad or villager lives in the immemorial black tent or a simple dwelling of what material is available, mud or reeds or stones. His furniture may not exceed a mat, bedding, cooking and eating utensils and a wooden chest. He wears the traditional dress of his people. For the Arabs it is basically a long shirt, in which alone they tend their crops; it is supplemented with head cloth and encircling cord and, by those who can afford it, a woollen or camel hair cloak. Kurds wear a turban, short, tight jacket, waist sash and baggy or straight, wide trousers according to district, sometimes assuming features of Arab dress where Arabs are neighbours. The women of both races wear brightly coloured dresses; the Arabs cover dress and head with a black 'abba, the Kurds wear a skull cap or turban. Female dress accounts for most of Iraq's considerable importations of printed cotton and artificial silk. Fabrics are also imported for the men, in particular plain white cotton material. The cloak and rustic 'abba are still woven locally and for their distinctive costume the Kurds manufacture cloth of wool or goat hair, some of it richly dyed and delicately decorated. The shaikhs and aghas may have their cars, and town houses furnished in western style, and may even, while occupying them, wear western clothes; but on their estates or in the tents of their tribe most of them live simply, with only the fewest and most portable of foreign innovations. The mark of their position is the audience tent or chamber, where they spend their rural existence in tribal government and reception.

In the cities material life tends to follow the educational watershed and the functional division that accompanies it. On the educated, white-collar side there are more, on the uneducated, manual side less western externals; there is, however, a neutral zone where clerical and artisan incomes overlap. Members of the first group tend to live in the newer houses of the suburbs, to have furniture of a western type and to wear completely western dress. The poorer working families are usually concentrated in the older houses of the city centres and furnish them hardly more elaborately than the villager. Many of the older artisans and tradesmen wear the traditional tight turban and coat-like gown of the townsman, but western working clothes are quickly replacing them. Western hats, on the other hand, have never become popular among Muslims of either sex and the *sidara*, a usually black version of the army side cap which the first King Faisal introduced as the national male headdress, has practically disappeared in educated society except on ceremonial occasions and among elderly government officials.

Of western innovations the cinema has to some extent altered the pattern of urban life; others have not, except in the richer families, changed more than its details, fitting neatly into the place of the old and more modified themselves than modifying. The radio is universal, but in the tea shops it has merely replaced the traditional reciter of epic. The country bus has nothing western European in its character, but is the traditional caravan compressed or the traditional caravanserai made mobile.

Iraqi life is still marked at nearly all levels by a simplicity that approaches austerity. Among the rich western importations have, it is true, encouraged a more conspicuous luxury, but luxurious only in contrast with the general environment and even so in their entertainment rather than their domestic life. In their houses and their appointments it is by western standards a rather modest middle class state that most of them maintain. In hospitality Iraqis are the most generous of people; the peasant will kill his last lamb or chicken for the traveller, the townsman entertain his friends beyond his means. Hospitality is nevertheless offered without formality or ostentation, a pleasant characteristic of Iraqi life in general.

Simplicity is nowhere more apparent than in the townsman's daily diet. The educated have adopted western utensils and table habits but are otherwise uninfluenced from abroad. Of the three daily meals the first commonly consists of tea, bread and cheese or cream, the others of the national dish of rice and vegetable stew—with or without meat—and bread, fruit and tea, or a snack of bread, cheese and cucumber, *kebabs*, or various preparations of crushed wheat. Such a diet is considered adequate at most levels of society, but since the Second War was beyond the reach of the poorer working families and is only now being restored as wages rise. For the very poor the staples have been bread, tea and dates. The bread, of wheat or barley, is unleavened and made in large, thin, pliable discs which can be eaten pleasantly unaccompanied; it also serves conveniently as a spoon, to be consumed with each mouthful. It is at receptions and parties that the full resources of the country's cuisine appear: lamb roasted and stuffed with rice in the tribal manner, Tigris fish roasted before a wood fire and flavoured with savoury sauce, and numerous Turkish dishes whose delicate perfection may require hours of preparation. The traditional drinks, apart from tea and coffee, are sour milk, cinnamon and lime tea, fruit juice, and date *'araq*, which is responsible for what little drunkenness exists. Wine is made by Christians of the north but is not widely consumed. Some of it is very palatable—not, however, the wine that is marketed. Of foreign drinks the American 'colas' have taken pride of place in summer; their advertisements have become part of the urban scene, their bottling a national industry and their relationship an inspiration for political cartoonists. Beer of excellent quality is made in the country and has established itself mainly among the educated classes. Whisky is the social drink of the rich and is taken by the political opposition as a symbol of its anathemas, just as it takes the cocktail (which usually means whisky or lemon squash) to symbolise wealthy mixed society.

Urban leisure is still spent on the principle that men and women, even if married, are socially divided, mixed society and companionship in marriage, where they exist, providing an addition rather than an alternative to the traditional pattern. The house serves, as we have seen, mainly for feminine association. Among wealthier women this may be frequent and well organised.

There are card parties and parties where singers entertain the guests, and some women hold an open reception on a fixed day of the month. A few distinguished men hold a similar weekly reception and others keep open court or receive by appointment; and men of the middle classes also use their houses for occasional entertainment, while passing most of their leisure in other places.

The places at which men gather vary with the social group. The leisure life of the working and lower clerical classes is based on the *mahalla*, the town quarter, and is determined by the nature of their work. Shopkeepers and craftsmen work late and receive their friends on their business premises, which are usually separate from their dwellings. Others frequent their *mahalla* tea house. This is not only their club but their home, which they visit informally and often in domestic undress, leaving their own cramped houses to squalling children and their wives' female relations. It offers refreshment and the *nargila*, company, radio and newspapers; and vendors are ready with food. The radio is replacing some of the traditional pastimes, but they are not altogether dead. Dominoes and backgammon are universal, and during the festive nights of Ramadhan, when tea houses stay open until two or three in the morning, their patrons play traditional games of the type of hunt-the-ring. Cards are forbidden, but there is mild betting on other games. Cock-fighting is occasionally revived, but ram-fighting, once common, and combats of sword and singlestick have passed away, and the epic recitals of 'Antar and the Bani Hilal are passing too. Some tea shops are the meeting places of nightingale fanciers, who debate the training, performance and market price of their birds. Friends may also meet at the *mahalla* barber's, and in Baghdad groups of artisans walk outside the city to discuss and to sing the traditional and intricate Iraqi *maqam* under expert guidance. Members of the same trade, especially among the Shi'is, at times join in an excursion to some holy place, thus preserving memories of the former guilds.

At the other social extreme are the better hotels and in Baghdad and Basra the western cabarets, where the rich meet habitually and others when they can afford it. The upper class spends its evenings alternatively in the expensive social clubs, male or mixed according to the society, the middle class in the increasing number of professional clubs. Business men and lawyers regularly receive social calls in their offices not only in the evening but throughout the working day; and daytime visiting is a familiar embarrassment to the conscientious civil servant. Students and lecturers meet separately in their colleges after hours. Between these private and more expensive public meeting places on the one hand and the life of the *mahalla* on the other there is a range of minor hotels, restaurants, central and suburban tea and coffee shops and oriental cabarets which the educated and other classes frequent according to income, taste and social preference. For some group or other all these are clubs. Iraqis like to have a circle of friends whom they can meet without formality or prearrangement.

A popular pastime in clubs and private houses, particularly among the upper classes, is card-playing; Iraqis engage with equal zest in games of skill, in which they excel, and those of chance. The element of chance exerts a particular attraction for them, a characteristic demonstrated by the sale of lottery tickets in the streets and by the large crowds which attend the Baghdad races. In the latter case public interest may owe something to the important role which the horse has played in Arab history and social life. With the advent of the motor car and the disappearance of the foray, the Arab horse has lost most of its traditional importance for the tribes (some of whom, however, still guard jealously their own pure strain of mare), and it now owes its preservation in Iraq mainly to horse racing, which is highly organised and of some economic importance. There are two Racing Companies in Baghdad and meetings, held twice a week, draw an attendance, according to the day, of some nine or fifteen thousand. The turnover at the totalisators of the two companies averages two million dinars a year. Racing is regulated by law and supervised by the Iraqi Turf Club, with which some 4,000 pure Arab horses are registered.

CULTURE

IN MODERN times it is the life of the educated classes of Iraq which has perhaps been poorest in variety. Tribal society, with its economic self-sufficiency and social complication, has possessed a large body of diverse technical skill and natural and tribal lore. The urban craftsman has had his trade, the education of the bazaar, his hobbies, pastimes and favourite stories and his recurring family and religious ceremonies. Many of the educated have by contrast lacked a dimension. A very few young men who could afford it have collected stamps, taken photographs or driven sports cars. More, not usually the best educated, have taken an interest in football, wrestling or other sport, and card-playing and the races have also had their devotees. But the leisure occupation of the overwhelming majority, and particularly of the students, has been the discussion of politics, conducted in teashop, hotel and club, and varied on the rather lower levels by attendance at the cinema or oriental cabaret.

Among these classes there has always been a true intelligentsia which has pursued political and other speculation on a high intellectual level, and a body of scholars, professional or amateur, who wrote on the geography, customs and antiquities of the country and, in certain aristocratic cases, on family history. More, indeed, was written than published. There has been no private and until recently no governmental patronage; the printing and sale of books has consequently been the responsibility of the author, with distribution by no means so organised or demand so great that he could usually recover his expenses. The domestic market has been small, smaller still since the Jewish emigration of the early 1950's; and foreign markets, even had the means of reaching them existed, have been dominated by the better printed books of Egypt and the Lebanon. Topical expositions of political or social problems have been in greater demand and more often published than academic works, sometimes only to meet the censor's ban.

The Press has suffered from similar and additional disabilities. Small circulation in a country of limited literacy has been reduced still further by the reading habits of the public; a newspaper is regularly passed between friends, read at a tea shop or hired out to its patrons by an enterprising vendor. Even with advertisements few papers can support themselves, let alone their owners; the rest are run as a sideline by a lawyer-politician or business man, or depend on a subsidy from the government, a political party or private individuals, who sometimes subscribe for a single panegyric issue. Subsidies make it possible to earn a living by journalism, even if publication is intermittent; but many newspapers are published rather for the political and social contacts they promote or out of political conviction. In spite of these discouragements the country has sometimes had as many as forty or fifty newspapers, most of which have succumbed, within a few weeks of appearance, to lack of capital or to official censorship; two or three, however, have survived for decades. Few of them

are newspapers in the literal sense or even the entertainment
sheets which sometimes pass as such elsewhere. Their existence
is too precarious for most of them to employ a staff of reporters
within the country or to subscribe to a foreign news service, the
items of news they publish being gathered perforce from radio,
foreign newspapers or the governmental Department of Guidance.
(There are, however, notable exceptions; one newspaper even
maintains correspondents in European capitals.) It is indeed to
the radio or foreign Press that the public tends to turn for its
factual information, reading the newspapers rather for their
political comment, which is esteemed in proportion to its
eloquence, wit, and audacity in attack. Distinguished names in
current Iraqi journalism include Yahya Qasim of *Al-Sha'b*, Salman
al-Safwani of *Al-Yaqdha*, 'Adil 'Auni of *Al-Hawadith*, Jibran
Melkun and his sons of *Al-Akhbar*, Taufiq al-Sim'ani of *Al-Zaman*
and the author-editor Ja'far al-Khalili. The celebrated Rufa'il
Butti of *Al-Bilad* died in 1957. Many of the political leaders have
also earned a reputation as able journalists. A number of newspapers express in their writing and their cartoons the dry humour
for which Baghdad is famous; the newspaper of the writer Khalid
al-Durra was long applauded for its pithy cartoons, and the
weeklies *Habazbuz* of Hajj 'Abud al-Kirkhi and *Qarandal* of
Sadiq al-Uzdi have been notable for their political and social
wit. In addition to the Arabic Press there is a long-established
daily newspaper in English, *The Iraq Times*.

Aesthetic activity was long confined to poetry and the traditional
forms of music. Between the two wars Iraq produced two of the
greatest contemporary Arab poets, Ma'ruf al-Rasafi and
Muhammad Mahdi al-Jawahiri, but apart from poetry the
significant literary output was limited; it included the novels of
Ja'far al-Khalili and Anwar Sha'ul and the earlier work of Dhu'l-
Nun al-Ayyub.

The Second War was followed by a perceptible intellectual and
artistic awakening. Intellectually Iraq can now claim a growing
élite, educated first in foreign universities and now increasingly
at home. Academic theses have been published in some quantity
with governmental support, and as research establishes itself in
the colleges they will clearly multiply; there are also articles of
quality in various professional and technical periodicals. The
same élite is beginning to provide an appreciative and critical
public, which never before existed, not only for foreign literature

and art but also for the growing body of young Iraqi writers and artists. To its aesthetic education the British and other cultural institutes have made a devoted contribution; and more serious art teaching in the schools is no doubt having its effect.

It was with the Second War, indeed, that Iraqi prose literature began on any scale. Its form and style have been moulded by western influences, absorbed directly or through the writers of other Arab countries. Much of the initial inspiration was also from the west, consisting in that newly awakened social sense and eagerness for reform which were no less fundamentally to affect the political scene. The result has been the short stories of several young writers—among whom are 'Abdul-Malik Nuri, Fu'ad Takarli, Murtadha Shaikh Qadum, 'Abdul-Wahhab Amin, Shakir Khasbak and Jabra Jabra, who is also poet and artist—and a new impulse in the case of certain of the older ones. Most of the writing is realistic and imbued with political and social purpose; this has gained it a certain popularity outside the intellectual élite. A modern school of poetry has arisen beside it to comple- ment, though not replace, the traditional models; it is marked not only by greater freedom of form but also by the current realism and social awareness. Plays are also being written and occasionally produced; though there is no modern professional theatre there are a number of private dramatic societies, schools and colleges which regularly produce plays, and dramatic art is taught in the Baghdad Institute of Fine Arts. In literature, as also in the visual arts, young women are as interested and talented as the men, and have won wide Arab recognition with a poetess, Nazik Mala'ika, and a writer of short stories, Safira Jamil Hafidh. As social outlook changes they will no doubt turn to the theatre; at present few families will permit their daughters to act in public.

Of the non-Arab communities only the Kurds have produced a significant—if limited—literature in their own language. They have a long oral tradition of epic and lyric poetry and since the First War have developed the Kurdish dialects of Iraq and particularly that of Sulaimaniya into a flexible instrument for modern writing. There have been collections of modern verse, academic and literary prose in some quantity and a small Kurdish Press. Kurdish broadcasts and magazines which were sponsored by the Allies during the Second War and prepared with loving care by Kurdish scholars such as Taufiq Wahbi, not only endowed

G*

the written language with a new richness and subtlety but also
secured for the same favoured dialect a wider literary currency.
Education in the Kurdish areas has had a varying effect. On its
higher levels it has familiarised many Kurds with Arabic and has
brought some of them into the main, Arabic-speaking stream of
national life; but, being on its lower levels exclusively in Kurdish,
it has given much larger numbers a greater command over their
own language and a pride in it which both nourishes and is
nourished by Kurdish nationalist feeling. While these sentiments
remain so will a Kurdish literature.

Painting and sculpture were similarly a direct product of the
Second War, when a group of young Iraqis fell under the influence
of Allied artists in the country, some of them later to study art in
Europe. Others were moved by the growing interest to enter the
Institute of Fine Arts, and in time groups of artists began to hold
exhibitions. They have created a serious public, whose wealthier
members have become ready patrons of their work. Among those
to win—in some cases international—recognition are Jawad,
Lorna and Naziya Salim, of whom Jawad is also a sculptor,
'Ata Sabri, Jabra Jabra, Mahmud Sabri, Isma'il Shaikhli, Fadhil
'Abbas and Faraj Abbo. Their work cannot yet be said to constitute
a peculiarly Iraqi art. Art, unlike Arabic literature, has had no
continuous tradition in the country. A tradition will no doubt
evolve naturally, as foreign models are subjected to internal
influences; it might also be created artificially through psychological identification with the past, though that cannot be achieved
by mere act of will.

The problem of the Iraqi architect is different. There is a
continuous tradition of Muslim public and domestic architecture,
but it does not conform to the material requirements and the
spirit of the new age. Here it is also premature to speak of a modern
Iraqi style, though peculiarities of climate and material have
from the first imposed their demands on design and construction.
Within the house, furniture is for the first time being designed by
artists with the same reference to climate and material, and upper
and middle class homes are beginning to display a conspicuously
modern taste. Artists and architects are already influencing the
design of schools; perhaps they will also turn their attention to the
tea houses, so that the young may not only have their minds
moulded in tasteful surroundings but also pass their leisure in them
as they grow up.

The music of the country has a vigorous tradition. Although tea shop concerts are no longer fashionable, it is kept alive in its various forms on religious occasions, at weddings and other celebrations, in the oriental cabarets and now also by radio and television. Its appeal is universal and certain types of western music are almost equally popular, particularly that of South America, which has certain similar characteristics. Western orchestral music is gaining a wide circle of educated adherents. Concerts of visiting musicians are well attended and there are a number of private orchestras, mainly Armenian, as well as a national orchestra, whose conductor has performed with acclaim in the Albert Hall. Outside the circle of musicians and a small section of the intellectual élite detailed knowledge of western music hardly exists. Technical appreciation of traditional Iraqi forms is found mainly among working men, though a few intellectuals have studied them seriously.

It is as a purveyor of music that the radio earns its greatest popularity. In this the national studios, owned and controlled by the State, serve the masses well enough; but they have yet to plan programmes which can satisfy the educated public or compete with Egyptian broadcasts. In the mechanically competent television station which has recently been installed the problem of programmes is still more difficult and has so far been solved by copious use of films; the most useful transmissions have perhaps been those to schools.

Of all Iraq's aesthetic accomplishments since the Second War the most spectacular has been the most recent: the production of excellent films. First came a documentary series about the country, made by the Iraq Petroleum Company, whose systematic training of Iraqi technicians may have helped create a national film industry. At the same time other Iraqis were trained abroad; of these some are now staffing the audio-visual services of the State education department while others have made two admirable feature films. These won an immediate success, with the ordinary public for their realistic treatment of social problems, and with the connoisseurs for their high artistic merit. It would be gratifying if the government were moved by such private achievement to give still more encouragement to scholarship and the arts, for it is through these, as much as by material triumphs, that it will establish Iraq's position among Arab nations.

RELIGION

SOME OF the remarks offered in this chapter have been of universal
application; others refer rather to the Muslim majority and adjustment must be made for the other religious communities, which
have been described earlier in the book.

By the terms of the constitution all Iraqis are equal before the
law, whatever their religion; constitutional equality has not, however, been followed by complete social integration, the extent of
the divergence varying with the social group. Among the working
classes there is often a physical division, for cultivators of different
faiths usually concentrate in separate villages and town labour
in separate *mahallas*. Separation has been confirmed by a certain
prejudice or antipathy. Of the Muslim sects the Shi'i could look
back on centuries of underprivilege at the hands of the Sunni
Turks, and both sects tend to regard the other as heterodox, while
sharing a consciousness of superiority over other religions.
Christians and Jews, on their side, have tended to combine a
wariness of Islam in its less tolerant moments with a pride at
their own greater literacy and an equal conviction of religious
worth. Among the educated public contact between the communities ranges from self-conscious association at work and
complete isolation after it to the professional and social unity of
the richer, more progressive business and professional groups;
a typical attitude is one of conscious denial of difference and sub-
conscious acceptance of it. It is still almost impossible for a Muslim
girl to marry a Christian who refuses to change his creed; and
between an educated Sunni and Shi'i, neither of them a practising
Muslim and each a fervent Arab nationalist, the religious prejudice
of a previous age may be replaced by a hint of political suspicion.
The instinct of communal cleavage has been confirmed by centuries of administrative practice; for in the Ottoman Empire
the religious communities constituted small vassal nations, responsible to the government through their own religious heads.

Between communities with so individual a history there is, not
surprisingly, a difference of general attitude and social habit. This
is a further impediment to communication, which is being
gradually overcome by education, economic interest and social
change. Christian and Jewish society permit a mixing of the
sexes, at any rate within the circle of personal acquaintance, and
are based on a home life which does not differ radically from our

own. Their tastes, interests and outlook have tended, income for
income, to be more western than among Muslims. There has
been longer association with the west, on the Christian side
religious, on the Jewish commercial, and both have a longer
tradition of education abroad. For a time, moreover, their
communities were provided with more modern and relatively
more abundant educational facilities than the Muslims; and in
the towns they have tended not only to practise the professions
but also to have a large proportion of business in their hands and
to form a significant section of what could be called the middle
class. Much of what has been said about Iraqi upbringing,
education and jejuneness of life does not apply to them; in
different degrees they have long had literary and aesthetic
interests, mostly derived from the west, and the Jews in particular
have maintained a varied intellectual life. The expansion of a
Muslim élite will lead to greater intellectual and aesthetic uniformity; and on the level of the State colleges there has already
been a large measure of intellectual integration, for the religious
communities have not provided their own facilities for higher
education. The gradual thaw in Muslim social life will also draw
the communities closer.

Another factor of integration is the lessening spiritual and
doctrinal hold of religion on the educated public. The breakdown
of the Ottoman Sunni caliphate has been reflected in the smaller
sphere of every other community. Many intellectuals now tend to
profess agnosticism and to view religion rather in its historical
perspective, as the expression of material forces. In the present
age they are apt to regard it as obscurantist and, if they are
politically inclined, even as an instrument of reaction or of
imperialist 'divide and rule'; Iraqis of any sect should, they
believe, put the cause of progress, independence and democracy
above mere religious creed. Muslims have probably gone farther
in admitting doubt than the other communities, to whom religious
cohesion may seem to guarantee their continued identity. A
minority of educated Muslims still perform the ritual practices
their religion enjoins, and it is almost inconceivable that any
political movement should attract them by sole appeal to religious
feeling. The Muslim Brotherhood has notably failed to win
adherents. But a religion like Islam cannot be jettisoned as easily
as a dogma or ritual; its moral and social instincts adhere more
closely and influence even its deniers in ways of which they are

unconscious. Nor are denials very loudly voiced. It would take courage to publish a criticism of Islam or even, in the course of scholarship, an unorthodox interpretation of Islamic history. The men of religion, though they have lost their positive hold over the educated population, still command some power of veto. Despite the growing force of modern education they are still trained in the traditional Islamic sciences at the Sunni and Shi'i religious schools; in Najaf, indeed, Shi'ism still maintains its medieval university. They still publish their works of religious exegesis, faithful to the canons of a scholarship that is sundered by centuries and a whole mode of thought from the new generation. There are still Muslim charitable societies which support orphanages and other good works. And Iraq still preserves her religious (Shari'a) law, however limited in scope, retains a governmental department to administer mosques and religious endowments, and continues by her constitution to be a Muslim State.

For the uneducated majority, and for many women of all classes, religion is still a reality and a necessity. The mystical brotherhoods of Islam still attract a small number of novices and the Shi'i masses are still moved to exaltation at the more vehement of their annual ceremonies. But for most of the ordinary people religion has usually a quieter significance; they seek in it something to sustain them and give colour, meaning and coherence to the life they live. Nothing in life escapes it; but it is not so much a code of prohibitions as a habit of action, speech and thought, a rich body of familiar duties, observances and enjoyments that is conterminous with life itself. Educated society, which accepts so much of it because it is unaware of the acceptance, has still to provide a substitute.

Chapter 9

Politics

IF THE Ottoman legacy to Iraq was an impediment to the economy and administration of a modern State, the political foundation of her Statehood was hardly less precarious. From the Ottomans themselves she inherited a fragmented society which not only lacked any single focus of loyalty but contained mutually hostile or suspicious elements. By the disposition of the Allied Powers, and greatly to her own satisfaction, areas were allotted to her which contained desirable quantities of oil but also a large population of Kurds, Turkomans, Yazidis, Christian Arabs and Assyrian newcomers, none of whom were anxious to be incorporated in a predominantly Muslim-Arab State. What political thought existed favoured constitutional democracy, a preference shared by the Powers and the Mandatory herself; but this form of government had no basis in urban tradition or in the temperament or intellectual development of the vast majority of the population. During the mandatory period, as we have seen, these problems were recognised; and in addressing herself to their solution Iraq began her evolution as a modern State. But at the same time other problems were added. Of these the most distracting was the relationship with Great Britain, not least for the divisions it created among Iraqis themselves and the complications it was later to cause in their delicate contact with other Arab countries. Each of these problems could arouse destructive passions in a State which had still to strengthen its fabric against disruption. The extent to which Iraq has nevertheless consolidated her statehood, maintained her machinery of government, improved her material existence and balanced what problems she could not completely solve is an achievement for which some of her own citizens have allowed her too little credit.

THE NATION

ON THE disparate groups which compose the Iraqi State economic
evolution and administrative routine have in time imposed a
large measure of unity. A coherent economic system has grown up
within its frontiers, controlled from the national capital, depending on the national network of communications and looking
increasingly to the national government for guidance and support.
In every area families depend for their living on the large State
organisation. In every area police and the public courts enforce,
if not yet one law, at least a choice of State and tribal law, and the
State has established relations with an increasing number of
citizens directly, instead of through tribal or communal heads
as before. The mere existence of a distinctive government and
State machine, military organisation, official uniform, passport
and flag help to create a feeling of common and distinct citizenship, particularly among the growing number of Iraqis who are
in touch with other States or their citizens. For them the
inheritance common to all social and communal groups in Iraq—
distinctive environment, way of life, linguistic and cultural
tradition and even temperament—are likely increasingly to outweigh the differences.

The Iraqi State has not in itself, however, been the focus of
intense or exclusive political loyalty. Intense loyalty has been
rather of two kinds. The first has been the still surviving devotion
to the tribe or in some cases to the religious community, the latter
still conceived, in the Ottoman tradition, as a political unit or tiny
nation. Uneducated Shi'is can still be moved to emotional vindica-
tion of their community, and some even of the educated see the
good of the State in terms of that community's advantage. Many of
Iraq's 150–200,000 Christians of all classes, impeccable citizens of
the Iraqi State, have retained an instinctive attachment to their
various *millet* communities, which are constitutionally recognised
in the right to their own schools, personal law and courts, and
parliamentary representation. The position of the Jews was similar,
but their community, which with its 150,000 members originally
approached the Christian in size, was reduced to a mere 10,000
by the exodus which followed the Palestine war and is considered
no longer to justify special deputies and courts, though its law of
personal status is still applied. Relations between the minorities
and the Muslim communities have been good, on higher social

levels excellent, with nevertheless a certain political circumspec-
tion on both sides. The majority of Iraqi Jews were never Zionists,
but after the Second War the activities of a small section drew upon
them the suspicion of the nationalist public, passionately concerned
with events in Palestine; while distrust of Great Britain and France
has tended to reflect upon the Iraqi Christians. Incidents between
the communities have been few, but the minorities have been
apprehensive at signs of religious discrimination which Arab
nationalism has sometimes displayed in moments of emotion, and
Christians long remembered the bloodshed of the Assyrian crisis.

The second form of intense loyalty, and the one more capable
of political expression, is embodied in two separate nationalisms,
Arab and Kurdish, neither directed to the existing Iraqi State
or to any nation yet realised within political boundaries. Kurdish
nationalism seeks to divide the existing State, Arab nationalism
(or pan-Arabism) to incorporate it in a larger unity.

The Kurdish movement for autonomy or independence has
been vigorous. Its militant expression has lain in the rebellion of
tribal chiefs; its ideology has been the product rather of educated
townsmen. Tribal leaders have at times employed the language of
nationalism; but, if this was partly from a genuine consciousness
of Kurdish identity, it was more often, perhaps, in the interests of
their own lawless independence. Warlike and predatory, they had
in the past exercised feudal sway with at the most nominal acknow-
ledgment of Ottoman or Persian suzerainty, and had maintained
their economic life, their dynastic groupings and their bloody
feuds without regard for political frontiers. They were as fiercely
proud of their ancestry and tradition as the desert Arab, and little
disposed to submit to Arab rule; and the initial British dispositions
after the First War had indeed led them to expect some measure
of autonomy. There has never been a concerted Kurdish rising,
for the Kurdish tribes have been as divided as the Arab. Resistance
to the government has had two main sources, Shaikh Mahmud
Barzinji at Sulaimaniya and the Shaikhs of Barzan, all of whom
could appeal to religious sentiment as well as to racial pride and
material interest, the title 'shaikh' among the Kurds denoting
pre-eminence in a mystical brotherhood. Shaikh Mahmud, who
proclaimed himself King of Kurdistan, took the field against
British forces in 1919 and Anglo-Iraqi forces during the Mandate.
Shaikh Ahmad of Barzan caused disturbances in 1919, 1927,
1931–2, 1933, when he was defeated by joint Turco-Iraqi action,

and in 1935. In 1943–45 his brother, Mulla Mustafa, led a rebellion which proved beyond the power of the State to crush by force and was eventually disrupted by political and financial persuasion exerted upon his Kurdish allies. He withdrew first to Persia, where he assisted in the establishment of the Russian-sponsored Kurdish People's Republic of Mahabad in December 1945, and, after its collapse late in 1946, to Russia, with the rank of Marshal of the Soviet Union. Since then there has been no organised Kurdish resistance to government.

The rebellion of Mulla Mustafa combined to some extent the force of Kurdish tribalism with an ideology which had developed mainly in the towns. This had appeared towards the end of the nineteenth century in Turkey, but it was not until the initial liberalism of the Young Turk revolution in 1908 that Kurdish political clubs were established in Iraq. Their aspirations were encouraged by President Wilson's Fourteen Points and other Allied promises of autonomy to ex-Ottoman subjects and were formally confirmed in 1920 by the Treaty of Sèvres, which provided conditionally for an autonomous and eventually independent Kurdish State; but the proposal did not survive the Treaty, which was never ratified. The Kurdish areas of Iraq, which the British authorities had administered as a partially separate zone, were included in the Iraqi State, against the will of urban nationalist and tribal baron alike; the Kurds, indeed, like the Arabs, were bitterly disappointed at the peace treaties. They were, however, accorded special safeguards: the Iraqi Constitution ensured them the right to have Kurdish taught in their schools, and when the League of Nations assigned the Mosul vilayet to Iraq in 1925 it provided that Kurdish officials and teachers should be appointed to the Kurdish areas and Kurdish be an official language in them. These undertakings were honoured by the government, which has given its Kurdish subjects parity of treatment with the Arabs; but only markedly superior treatment, if that, could have reconciled the more fervent Kurdish nationalists. Some Iraqi statesmen, and particularly Nuri al-Sa'id, have been prepared to grant a limited Kurdish autonomy; others have firmly resisted such concessions—partly from fear of similar Shi'i demands.

Nationalism among Kurds as among Arabs is on the whole most ardently professed by publicists, students and young men of the less prosperous educated classes; the older and wealthier recognise the economic problems which would beset a Kurdish State. As for the agha on his land, economic interests, especially in an age of development, have helped reconcile him to inclusion in Iraq.

During the Second War Kurdish nationalism began to look to Russia as the vindicator of its claims. While the Russians controlled northern Persia they made contact with Kurdish intellectuals and aghas. The Republic of Mahabad was a premature first-fruit of the new alliance, and Mulla Mustafa soon afterwards received his Soviet honours. Soviet contacts have since been intensified and in the early 1950's Sulaimaniya, the intellectual headquarters of the Iraqi Kurds, was considered a major centre of communism in the country. The greater part of Kurdish as of other Iraqi 'communism' has consisted of a desire for Soviet support against, in the one case the Arabs, in the other the Western Powers, combined with a desire for social reform which is rather socialist than communist. It could, no less than genuine communism, provide a channel for Russian intervention in Iraqi affairs, the more dangerous because the Kurdish area adjoins the country's most productive oil-field and contains its north-eastern gateways.

Arab nationalism in Iraq, like its Kurdish counterpart, was born at the beginning of the century. Previously Iraqi Arabs, with no more political attachment to Arabism than to the territory which was later to become Iraq, were loyal rather to tribe, town and religious community, and Sunni Muslims to the Ottoman caliphate. There had not yet occurred in Iraq either the spread of western political concepts or the Arabic cultural renaissance amid which the nationalist movement had appeared in the nineteenth century in Syria and the Lebanon, and it was not until the revolution of 1908 that Arab nationalist ideas aroused any considerable interest there or close contact was established with the nationalists of the Mediterranean coast. Iraqi officers in the Ottoman army were particularly associated with the pan-Arab movement; of the other Iraqi nationalist groups—for the movement was by no means united—some would have been content with a measure of local autonomy within the Ottoman framework. Loyalty to the Ottoman State continued indeed as a political current in Iraq as long as that State existed and as a nostalgic memory after its disappearance, to be replaced in some cases by admiration for Kemalist Turkey. A younger generation of nationalist Sunnis has come however to hold anti-Turkish feelings

as strong as those which, for different reasons, the Shi'is have
inherited. To many Turcophiles the installation of King Faisal
in 1921 was unwelcome; but, once installed, he and his entourage
of Iraqi officers set the tone of political feeling. Arab unity was
thereafter the creed of every Iraqi Government, and any want
of fervour in its profession was immediately castigated by the
political public. The rural masses have remained comparatively
unaffected by it, though radio and increasing contact with the
towns have had some influence; but the educated urban population, in which political consciousness and energy reside, has been
deeply indoctrinated, and as its numbers and moral influence
have increased so has the force of pan-Arabism.

What emotional political loyalties the Iraqi State has inspired
were part of this wider Arab nationalism, whose feelings both
attached themselves to it and derived new intensity from its
existence. For a time the Iraqi pan-Arabist was inevitably preoccupied with his own country; during the Mandate his first
thought was for its independence, and once this was achieved
his attention was distracted by the turbulent course of domestic
politics. Until the end of the Second War, indeed, no larger
political entity was apparent to which Iraqi pan-Arabism could
direct its loyalty. Egypt was neither by herself nor by the Arabs
considered politically part of the Arab world, with Ibn Sa'ud
there was no desire on either side for closer relations than those
established by the treaty of 1936, 'Abdullah of Transjordan was
content with his dependence on Great Britain, and Palestine,
Syria and Lebanon were still under mandatory authority. It was
only with Egypt's self-discovery as an Arab State in the early
1940's, the formation of the Arab League in 1945, and the effective
independence of Syria and Lebanon in that year that loyalty to
a larger Arab State became feasible. Iraqi nationalists at once
extended their horizons; meanwhile the strong emotions displayed
over Palestine and the Franco-Syrian crises had demonstrated
the strength of their pan-Arab feeling. It has been reinforced by
Arab vicissitudes since the foundation of the League: the attempts
to create a Greater Syria, the Palestine War and its aftermath,
the hostilities of 1951–52 in the Suez Canal Zone, domestic events
in Syria and Egypt, the Baghdad Pact, the appearance of Russia
as the self-appointed champion of the Arabs, the Suez crisis
of 1956 and above all the creation of the United Arab Republic.
Many Iraqi nationalists now express unequivocal and passionate

loyalty to an Arab political unit larger than their own country and, in the belief that the governments of Egypt and Syria upheld their political doctrines more than did their own government, have looked increasingly to those States for leadership and to Gamal 'Abdul-Nasir as the symbol of their aspirations.

Those responsible for the conduct of Iraq's affairs have usually been too influenced by the regionalism in her tradition and too conscious of special interests, arising particularly from her production of oil and her proximity to the Soviet Union, to favour incorporation in a unitary Arab State. Many Christian Arabs also feel an interest in an Iraq that retains her separate identity rather than merges in a larger Muslim unity, though some of the most fervent Arab nationalists have been Christians. Similarly many Shi'is, although pan-Arabist in sentiment, do not favour so close a union with other Arab States that, as against Sunnis, they would become a small minority. Kurdish nationalists are naturally opposed to complete absorption in a larger State based on simple Arabism, and some of the pan-Arabists, indeed, not yet burdened with political responsibility, have declared themselves ready to accept an autonomous Kurdish province within an Arab federation or unitary State.

In proportion to the strength of their pan-Arab convictions, the various elements of the public continue to look on the destiny of other Arab countries as their own, particularly when Arabs are in conflict with foreign powers. Since the Second War there has been considerable public sympathy with Egypt in her relations with Great Britain, with the Algerian insurgents, with Bahrain in the face of Persian claims and with the Imams of Yemen and Oman when engaged with British troops. Above all, the threat of hostilities between Israel and any of her Arab neighbours has immediately provoked declarations of support for the Arab State concerned.

IRAQ AND THE ARAB COUNTRIES

IT WAS only after the Second War that the pan-Arab sentiment of the educated public diverged from official policy. The first King Faisal led a revolt in the hope of creating an inclusive Arab State and he pursued it to the end of his life. In the 1930's, Iraq, as the first Arab mandatory State to gain her independence, became the centre of pan-Arabism and a refuge for Palestinian and Syrian nationalists, to whose cause successive governments gave support. The Palestine problem was of particular concern to them; in 1936 Nuri al-Sa'id, and then King Ghazi himself, mediated informally to end the Arab strike there, and in 1940 the Iraqi Government was prepared to offer full belligerency on the Allied side in exchange for a solution acceptable to the Palestine Arabs. With Sa'udi Arabia and with Egypt, which in a political sense was hardly yet considered an Arab State, Iraq maintained amicable relations. In 1936 she signed a treaty of brotherhood and alliance with Sa'udi Arabia, which was joined by Yemen the following year.

When in 1941 the British Government promised to support any generally approved scheme for strengthening the political ties between Arab countries, it was Nuri al-Sa'id who took the initiative; he had been tireless in attempting to gain concessions for the Palestine Arabs and had in 1940 tried to establish a common policy with Turkey in case Syria and Lebanon gained independence. In 1943 he circulated a proposal for a league of Arab States to comprise, in the first instance, Iraq and a Greater Syrian State consisting of Syria, Lebanon, Transjordan and Palestine. The scheme gained little Arab favour and the Egyptian Government, apparently with Iraqi and other encouragement, initiated the negotiations which resulted, in 1945, in the foundation of the broader and looser Arab League.

The creation of the League marked a transfer of Arab leadership from Iraq to Egypt. This was inevitable as soon as Egypt interested herself in Arab unity, for her ambitions were supported by political sophistication and a long history of nationhood, apparent prosperity, industrial development, manpower, metropolitan grandeur, a central geographical position and undisputed cultural supremacy in the Arab world. The years that followed have been marked by a conflict between the Hashimite States—Iraq and Jordan—and Egypt, each side with its own interpretation of Arab unity: on the one hand a close unity of the Fertile Crescent as envisaged in Nuri al-Sa'id's proposals of 1943, and on the other some broader association with Egypt as its centre. To this a unity of the Fertile Crescent would be an obstacle; Egypt accordingly opposed it with the assistance of political allies in Syria and her influence over the Arab League, which became increasingly an instrument of her policy. Sa'udi Arabia was in this her active ally, for, however formally good her relations with the Hashimite countries, she had no wish to see their power consolidated and extended.

The struggle was essentially for Syria, and of the two Hashimite States it was Jordan, under King 'Abdullah, who first sought union with her. His persistent efforts to effect it with himself as head aligned Syria with Egypt against the Hashimite States; the division was confirmed by the treaties with Turkey which Iraq and Jordan ratified in 1947. As the Palestine situation deteriorated King 'Abdullah transferred his attention there, with the idea of incorporating as much of it as possible in his own State; Egypt responded by supporting the Mufti of Jerusalem against him. The mutual suspicion with which the Arabs fought the Palestine War in 1948 was largely responsible for their failure. When Jordan formally incorporated Eastern Palestine in 1950 Egypt and Syria attempted to expel her from the Arab League, but were prevented by the opposition of Iraq and Yemen.

Even before the assassination of King 'Abdullah in 1951 Iraq had replaced Jordan as a potential partner of Syria, but with considerable caution. 'Abdullah's ambitions had been approved neither by part of her ministerial group nor by much of her public; and Iraqi advocates of union realised that differences of government and foreign policy could be reconciled only by patient negotiation. Within Syria herself there was a considerable body of support for union, and when Colonel Husni Za'im assumed power by military *coup d'état* in March 1949 he was initially in favour of association with Iraq; but while the Iraqi Government was considering his limited advances, Egypt and Sa'udi Arabia intervened swiftly to win him to their side. Colonel Sami Hinnawi, who displaced him in a second *coup d'état* in August 1949, represented the supporters of union, which seemed likely to be approved by the Syrian Constituent Assembly; this prospect probably provoked the third military *coup d'état*, of Adib Shishakli, in September 1949, after which union with Iraq was put aside and close political, economic and military relations were established instead with Egypt and Sa'udi Arabia. Relations with Iraq were strained, particularly in February 1954, immediately before the fall of the Shishakli régime, when Iraq was accused of intervening in Syrian internal affairs. In the course of their rivalry over Syria, Iraq's relations with Egypt had also worsened, the continuous vituperation of the Egyptian radio playing no small part. One group of Iraqi statesmen was particularly anxious to

restore amity, and in 1950 Muzahim al-Pachachi, Foreign
Minister in the cabinet of 'Ali Jaudat al-Ayyubi, visited Cairo
and agreed that Iraq should defer any plans for union with
Syria; the cabinet was forced to resign in consequence. Shortly
afterwards Egypt proposed an Arab collective security pact,
which was clearly designed to discourage such union; Iraq joined
it only in a modified form, Jordan not until King 'Abdullah's
assassination. In 1954, after the fall of Shishakli, the Iraqi Prime
Minister, Dr Fadhil al-Jamali, submitted to the Arab League a
proposal for its transformation into a federal State, which failed
for want of support.

From 1952 onwards the rivalry between Egypt and the Hashimite kingdoms assumed a new form, to which the growing wealth
of Iraq and her economic development, in contrast with the
precarious economy of Egypt, added bitterness. Against the
material power of Iraq the Egyptian military régime was able to
pit the force of the new nationalism, of which it had appointed
itself the standard-bearer, and to convert a competition between
governments into one also of ideologies. It thereby won the
support of much of the politically dynamic public in other Arab
countries, including the Hashimite States themselves, and was
strengthened by the triumph of a similar ideology in Syria. The
new nationalists, in Iraq as elsewhere, pointed a contrast between
the spectacular agrarian measures in Egypt and the slow progress
of land reform in Iraq, and between the evacuation of the Suez
base, the Soviet arms and economic agreements, and the nationalisation of the Canal of the one hand and, on the other, the alliance
with Great Britain and Turkey in the Baghdad Pact.

The challenge to Egyptian leadership implied in the Pact and
its possible extension to other Arab States caused mounting tension
between the countries in recent years. At the end of 1953 members
of the Egyptian Government had accused Iraq of planning to
join an enlarged Sa'dabad Pact, and, after the Iraqi premier
had announced his intention of seeking arms from the west
and King Faisal had paid his State visit to Pakistan early in
1954 (p. 107), Egypt countered by unifying her military command
with the Sa'udi, the two States declaring their opposition to any
western-sponsored defence organisation pending the settlement
of the Palestine and Suez Canal questions, and to any association
of Arab States with the recently concluded Turkish-Pakistani
alliance. After the Anglo-Egyptian agreement of June 1954 it

seemed that relations might improve; Salah Salim paid a successful goodwill visit to Iraq and late in the year Iraq was apparently considering, in agreement with Egypt and the other Arab States, a treaty with Great Britain on similar lines to the Anglo-Egyptian. With the Turco-Iraqi agreement of February 1955, however, the division became final. Over the next two years Egypt promoted a network of joint military commands which covered herself, Sa'udi Arabia, Syria and Jordan and explicitly excluded Iraq, against whom she intensified her radio campaign.

Relations with Syria improved after the fall of the Shishakli régime and in 1955 Syria tried to mediate between Iraq and Egypt. From the middle of 1956, however, the Iraqi Government watched with apprehension the connexions which the coalition of Syrian officers and Ba'thists was establishing with the Soviet bloc; it suffered moreover from Syrian radio propaganda and deeply resented the sabotage of oil pumping stations in Syria during the Suez crisis. This caused Iraq heavy loss and threatened her development programme, her standard of living and her political stability; the Government of Damascus retorted with charges of an Iraqi plot against Syria. Once the flow of oil was resumed, in March 1957, Iraq tried to secure guarantees against future mishap; but formal talks held in the autumn reached no conclusion, and in April 1958 the Iraqi Government, on the grounds of its loss of revenue, declined to pay its share towards the budget of the Arab League. Members of the Iraqi Government nevertheless expressed their opposition to any oil pipeline which might by-pass other Arab countries in carrying Iraqi oil to the Mediterranean. Where their relations with foreign States were concerned Iraq in general maintained a correctly Arab attitude towards Egypt and Syria. She supported Egypt in her treaty negotiations with Great Britain, during the Anglo-Egyptian hostilities in 1951-52, in her nationalisation of the Suez Canal, and at the time of the Anglo-French intervention in 1956, and she was quick to offer assistance when either State considered itself threatened by Israel.

On the subject of Israel the attitude of both government and opposition was equally uncompromising. Iraq prides herself on being the only Arab combatant in the Palestine War not to have concluded an armistice with Israel, with whom she is still in a formal state of war, and on the considerable losses she has sustained from refusing to re-open her southern pipeline to the Mediterranean through Israeli territory; and in the face of

criticism of its home and foreign policies the government tended
increasingly to point to Israel as the root of evil in the Middle
East. Nor, in the present state of public opinion, could any
government, even supposing that it wished to establish relations
with Israel, attempt with impunity to do so. In the eyes of nationalists although, as we shall see, the ultimate menace is from the
west, it is Israel who is the immediate enemy, and any attempt
to convince them of danger from Russia founders on this fundamental principle. As a condition of friendship with the west they
demand not only the surrender of remaining privileges in the Arab
world, but also a change of attitude towards Israel. What inflamed
nationalist emotion at the time of the Suez crisis was not even so
much the fact that the government was in alliance with the
assailant of an Arab country as the belief that the assault was
co-ordinated with the Israeli invasion.

With her ally Jordan, also a Hashimite monarchy and in treaty
relationship with Great Britain and Turkey, Iraq was in close
contact. The two governments commonly consulted each other
on foreign policy before the death of King 'Abdullah; their
specific union would be an obvious nucleus for the unity of the
Fertile Crescent which they both advocated. This was discussed
before the end of the Second War, but, faced with criticism in
Iraq and elsewhere, the plan was in 1947 diluted into a treaty of
brotherhood, which however permitted military assistance by
one State to suppress internal disorder in the other. Further
suggestions for union, made shortly before and immediately after
the assassination of King 'Abdullah, during the illness of his
successor King Talal, and again in 1954, after the accession of
King Husain, also came to nothing. King Husain and his second
cousin King Faisal assumed their constitutional powers on the
same day in 1953 and maintained close personal relations. For a
year and a half, indeed, from the end of 1955, when Jordan
rejected the Baghdad Pact, their governments pursued divergent
policies, that of Jordan leading her into closer relationship with
Egypt, Syria and Sa'udi Arabia and to the abrogation of her
treaty with Great Britain. Under the neutralist, pro-Egyptian
chamber and cabinet which were established in 'Amman in
October 1956 relations with the Iraqi government were strained,
to be restored during the Jordanian crisis of April–May 1957,
when King Husain successfully asserted his authority against an
opposition movement of politicians and officers who had Egyptian

and Syrian support. These two countries, which had already shown their influence on nationalism in his kingdom, now unleashed against him a violent propaganda campaign, inciting his subjects to revolt and assassinate him. Their formal combination on 1 February 1958 in the United Arab Republic appeared to threaten the integrity of his kingdom, and the federation of Iraq and Jordan, so long proposed, was now effected to counter it; federation might also help solve the financial difficulties which had beset Jordan since abandoning her British subsidy. On 14 February the two kings signed an agreement uniting their countries in an Arab Federation, which by 18 February had been ratified by their respective parliaments.

By the terms of its constitution, which was immediately drafted, membership of the Federation was open to any Arab country. Each member State retained its independence and existing system of government; there was to be joint conduct of foreign affairs and diplomatic representation, unification of armed forces and education, and co-ordination of financial and economic policy and communications. Existing international agreements would be binding only on the States which had already contracted them; this represented a compromise over Iraqi membership of the Baghdad Pact. There was to be a federal government consisting of a head and of legislative, executive and judicial authorities; its seat was to be alternately in Baghdad and 'Amman or might be made permanent. The head of the Federation was to be the king of Iraq and in his absence the king of Jordan; when another State adhered the position would be reconsidered. The head was the supreme commander of the joint army, with the king of Jordan supreme commander of forces stationed in his country. Legislative authority was vested in a Chamber (consisting equally of Iraqis and Jordanians) and the head of the Federation; executive authority was vested in the head, who exercised it through a Council of Ministers. The federal government was to command a permanent source of revenue; for the first year Iraq was to pay 80 per cent of its revenues and Jordan 20 per cent.

The amendments required in the individual constitutions of the two countries were ratified by the Jordanian parliament on 26 March and doubly by the Iraqi, on 26 March and 12 May, a new parliament, in accordance with the existing Iraqi constitution, having been elected in the meantime. On 19 May the first federal cabinet was appointed, with Nuri al-Sa'id as Premier and

the Jordanian Ibrahim Hashim as Deputy Premier and containing
Ministers for the Treasury (Iraqi), Defence (Jordanian) and
Foreign Affairs (Iraqi), and Ministers of State for Defence (Iraqi)
and Foreign Affairs (Jordanian). On 27 May King Faisal opened
the first session of the federal parliament (composed of 20 repre-
sentatives of each country) and took the oath as head of the
Federation; his Speech from the Throne referred to settlement of
the Palestine and Algerian situations. On 3 June the Iraqi Chief of
Staff, General Muhammad Rafiq 'Arif, was appointed Chief of
Staff of the combined armies and the Iraqi Air Force commander,
Commodore Kadhim 'Abadi, commander of the combined air
forces.

It was believed initially that Sa'udi Arabia might join the
Federation. In the latter part of 1956 her relations with Iraq had
greatly improved. Hitherto she had played her part in discouraging
Fertile Crescent unity and had placed her resources behind the
bloc that crystallised, under Egyptian leadership, against the
Baghdad Pact. The increasing connexions between Egypt and
Syria and the Soviet countries, together with the threat to oil-
transit contained in the sabotage of November 1956, revealed
common interests with the Iraqi Government. State visits were
exchanged between the two countries, cultural, economic and
trade agreements were concluded, and Iraq was invited to send a
military mission. The federal constitution was so drafted as to
permit King Sa'ud's becoming its Head in the event of his
adherence. While he was considering his position it was affected by
three moves on the part of the United Arab Republic: the latter
secured the adherence of the Yemen, the Egyptians laid claim to
Sudanese territory opposite his coast, and he himself was accused
of plotting to assassinate President Nasir. In the wake of these
events and of a financial crisis at home, on 24 March he committed the country's financial, internal, external and military
affairs to his brother, Crown Prince Faisal, who was believed to an
uncertain degree to have Egyptian sympathies. There was no
apparent decrease in cordiality, however, between the Sa'udi
Government and Iraq.

Similar hopes were entertained for Kuwait. Iraq, whose
economy was already committed, if not over-committed, to the
development programme, was embarrassed by her new federal
undertakings, and the government made no secret of seeing
Kuwaiti oil revenues as the solution; the Ruler of Kuwait, it was

affirmed, would retain his full powers if he joined the Federation. The Ruler, however, evinced no matching enthusiasm. Apart from his interest in controlling his own revenues and in conciliating pro-Egyptian elements in his State, there was a history of uneasy relations between the two governments, founded on a dispute over frontier territory which was not completely resolved by an attempt at delimitation in 1932. Iraqi resentment was aggravated by extensive smuggling from Kuwait into Iraq, while the Kuwaitis were little conciliated by Iraqi claims to Kuwait itself, formulated before the Second War and since raised periodically in the Press, with no less emphasis in consequence of Kuwait's new oil wealth. Proposals in recent years for piping Shatt al-'Arab water and Basra oil from Iraq to Kuwait came to nothing; the water pipeline would have augmented the Kuwaiti water supply and the oil pipeline have permitted the use of larger tankers for exporting Iraqi oil than can use the oil port at Fao.

The Lebanese Government expressed its intention to co-operate with both the Arab Federation and the United Arab Republic, but to join neither. Under Camille Chamoun's pro-western presidency Lebanon maintained good relations with Iraq, who on her side had acknowledged the special position of Lebanon in the Arab world. To a country so placed Arab divisions have been an embarrassment, particularly when reflected increasingly in her domestic politics. In 1956 a pro-Egyptian cabinet assumed office in Beirut and declared its hostility to the Baghdad Pact; but at the time of the Suez crisis the President joined King Faisal and King Sa'ud in resisting the uncompromising attitude of Egypt and Syria towards Great Britain and France, and the cabinet which succeeded accepted, as did Iraq, the Eisenhower Doctrine.

The Lebanese crisis, which assumed its more acute form in May 1958, was a source of concern to the Iraqi and Jordanian Governments. The federal Foreign Minister assured the Lebanese Government of support for its complaint against the United Arab Republic at the Security Council; and Nuri al-Sa'id, who considered that Lebanon's inclusion in that Republic would complicate the position of the whole Baghdad Pact area, expressed his willingness for intervention, if requested by the Lebanese Government and recommended by the United Nations, and believed that Iraq, after consultation with Jordan, would be prepared to take part in it. It was reported that the Muslim

members of the Baghdad Pact would discuss possible assistance
to the Lebanese Government when they met in Istanbul on 14
July prior to the full Council meeting in London.

The official attitude of the United Arab Republic towards the
Federation was at first one of cautious politeness; but after his
own Union had been criticised by members of the Iraqi Government President Nasir himself attacked it in the strongest terms
as an imperialist fabrication which would be dispersed like dried
leaves in the wind. Cairo radio urged the Iraqi and Jordanian
people to overthrow the Hashimite dynasty and began inciting
the Kurdish populations of the Baghdad Pact countries against
their governments.

Egyptian disapproval was shared by the Iraqi opposition, which
considered the Federation a reinforcement of reaction and a
check to the type of Arab unity to which they aspired, that
represented by the United Arab Republic. There were also, as
we have seen, very general misgivings about the economic aid
to Jordan involved, which on the Jordanian side had been a
principal incentive towards federation and on which, indeed, the
acquiescence of part of the Jordanian public was conditional.
Iraq's 80 per cent share of the federal (mainly military) budget
was likely to amount to some ID 32–36 million, representing an
increase of some ID 5–9 million over her present military outlay.
Her Government was quick to point out that federation was not
meant to solve the problem of the half million Palestinian refugees
in Jordan.

IRAQ AND FOREIGN POWERS

IRAQ'S PRIMARY foreign relationship has been with Great Britain,
who, even with the growth of American influences in the area,
remained her chief customer and supplier and her sole western ally.
Under the treaty of 1930, which continued to regulate their relations until March 1955, the two countries were to consult on all
matters on foreign policy affecting their common interests and
avoid foreign policies embarrassing to the other. They were to
assist one another if either were involved in war, Iraq's responsibility being to furnish communications and other facilities and
particularly to assist the passage of British forces across her
territory. She was to grant Great Britain sites for air bases, at
which forces might be maintained with immunity from Iraqi

jurisdiction; bases were in fact established at Shu'aiba near Basra and at Habbaniya west of the Euphrates. Great Britain was to have precedence for her ambassador, to provide what foreign officials and military instructors Iraq might require as well as receiving her officers for training, and to supply her forces with arms and equipment.

The treaty marked a further stage in the policy of material disengagement by which Great Britain was to protect her oil supply and imperial communications with minimum expenditure, forces and, it was hoped, offence to nationalist feeling. To one body of Iraqi opinion it seemed a reasonable compromise; while immature Iraq would require assistance in her development and protection in the political jungle, and they believed that she was better served by association with a Power of known and limited interests than with others of possibly wider ambitions.

Other Iraqis, however, were prepared to grant Great Britain her facilities, if at all, only by agreement between willing equals and asserted that the majority of Iraqi political opinion rejected the treaty. The presence of British forces, which by its terms was not to constitute an occupation or prejudice the sovereign rights of Iraq, they considered to do precisely that and firmly believed the British Embassy, advisers and military mission to form the real government of the country. Resentment was inflamed by the situation in Palestine, by the bitterness of its political refugees and by sedulous Axis propaganda. Between the two European blocs of that period many nationalists favoured what was later to be called positive neutralism; they were hostile to Great Britain, looked on the Axis as a possible counterpoise or active ally, wished to avoid involvement in a war between the two, especially on the British side, and if war came might expect and even prefer an Axis victory. It was this feeling which Rashid 'Ali, partly from predisposition, partly from pressure of circumstances, came to represent in 1940 and 1941. His unwillingness to implement the terms of the 1930 treaty led, as we have seen, to brief hostilities between the two countries in May 1941; after his defeat and flight and the restoration of the Regent the government co-operated fully with its British ally.

After the Second War the independence of India did not lessen Great Britain's interest in Iraq. Communications had still to be maintained, Middle Eastern oil was every year of greater importance, and Russia, the traditional bogy of her Middle East policy, had reappeared with grimmer menace. Britain must block any Soviet advance into the area, which would threaten her position not only regionally but in Africa beyond; she would hesitate to surrender her special relationship with Iraq, unless against some adequate guarantee. The Iraqi government was similarly conscious of a Soviet danger from without and its fifth column within, and, while unprepared to renew the existing treaty on its expiry in 1957, was not indisposed to offer some form of guarantee. A new formula was eventually devised: while the general relationship was to continue as before, the British bases were to revert to Iraq and a joint board was to co-ordinate the strategy of the two countries. A treaty embodying these terms was signed at Portsmouth in January 1948.

The new nationalism of the post-war years was, however, even more determined than the old to deny Great Britain a special position and, quite apart from the ideological sympathies of its left wing, was inclined to see Russia in the role for which the previous generation had cast Germany. With the city populace as its instrument it effected the repudiation of the Portsmouth Treaty in an outburst which has taken its place in nationalist legend beside the uprising of 1920; and until 1952 the political parties which represented such opinion were conducting a campaign against the international oil companies operating in Iraq. They were quick to adopt the idea of nationalisation from the Persian Government, some of them demanding it immediately, others when Iraq should have trained men competent to run the industry. The negotiations for the new oil agreement of 1952 were a particular target of attack; once it was concluded the violence of criticism subsided. Even so companies registered in a country which nationalism distrusted and employing numbers of its nationals, equipped with an organisation and installations enormous by comparison with other industry in Iraq, and topographically remote from the centre of political feeling were apt to appear alien and disquieting to a section of the public. Their increasing integration with the life of the country and above all the training of Iraqis to occupy positions at all levels of the industry might be expected to diminish this impression; and meanwhile the government, while seeking to maintain its oil revenues at a maximum, has considered that this can be most effectively achieved by organisations with long experience, a record of technical success and full access to markets.

With the failure of the Portsmouth Treaty in 1948 the two

governments sought a formula more acceptable to political opinion. This seemed to be offered within the comprehensive arrangements for Middle East defence against Russia which the western powers had begun to contemplate; for it was clear that British dispositions in Egypt and Iraq, even if maintained, were inadequate to meet a Soviet threat. The Iraqi Government was equally sensitive to the possible danger and had little confidence in the Arab Defence Pact which was declared by Egypt to be sufficient. It consequently showed some interest in the abortive proposal in 1951 for a joint Middle East Command, made by the United States, Great Britain, France and Turkey, and from 1953 onwards advocated co-operation between those 'Northern Tier' governments which were most immediately exposed to Soviet aggression and most apprehensive of it. In February 1955 Iraq signed a defence treaty with Turkey and later in the same year made similar agreements with Pakistan and Persia.

As the new association, known as the Baghdad Pact, began to crystallise, it seemed to offer Great Britain, if she participated, an adequate substitute for the guarantees of the existing 1930 treaty; and its Muslim sponsors were anxious to reinforce it by western adherence. Britain accordingly acceded in April 1955 and simultaneously concluded a new defence agreement with Iraq, which replaced the existing treaty. It involved Iraq in no obligations beyond her own frontiers; in the event of an armed attack against her, or the threat of it, the British Government undertook at her request to assist in her defence, if necessary with armed forces. There was to be co-operation in planning, training and equipment and Great Britain was to assist Iraq particularly in maintaining her air force and airfields and developing her defences against air attack. British bases were to pass to Iraqi command in May 1955 and British forces to be withdrawn.

It was affirmed at the first meeting of the Baghdad Pact Council in November 1955 that the Pact was consistent with both the United Nations Charter and the Arab League treaty of joint defence and economic co-operation. Its aim, it was stated, was to work for peace and security in the Middle East, to defend its members' territories against aggression and subversion and promote the welfare and prosperity of the area. Baghdad was to be the permanent seat of the organisation, which was to comprise a permanent council, secretariat, and military and economic committees; counter-subversion and scientific committees were

H

subsequently added. The United States had been represented by observers at the council meetings and has been a member of the various committees, including, since June 1957, the military committee; she has also contributed to the cost of the secretariat and maintained programmes of military, economic and technical aid to member countries. That part of the economic programme which concerns Iraq includes regional projects for roads and tele-communications, which are receiving American financial assistance, joint measures for the control of disease and pests and the establishment in Baghdad, with British assistance, of a nuclear centre for the area, a laboratory for research and training in the uses of radio isotopes.

The Pact was criticised with vehemence by those Iraqis who admitted no danger from Russia or believed that the Pact would provoke it, those who considered it responsible for division in the Arab world and those who disliked British or Turkish policy or regarded any alliance with a non-Arab State as a kind of treason; and holders of these opinions probably comprised a majority of the educated public. The Pact came particularly under attack during the Suez Crisis, when it was saved by Nuri al-Sa'id's temporary refusal to attend meetings with British representatives. This opposition to it within Iraq itself was a major weakness of the Pact, both from the fact of public opposition itself and from its possible influence on governments. The government of 'Ali Jaudat al-Ayyubi, indeed, showed a certain coolness towards it and may have been proposing to make Iraq's further adherence depend on an acceptable western attitude towards Israel; and Nuri al-Sa'id himself would seem to have decided that this alone could in the long run preserve Iraqi membership. There was in addition considerable dissatisfaction with the extent of material assistance which the Pact had procured for its members. It was apparent that any government which came to power as the representative of the new nationalism would be tempted to abandon the Pact, as a condition of rapprochement with the United Arab Republic.

Between the Muslim members of the Pact a common strategy extended the limited basis of common interest that existed. Diplomatically Iraq had already had formal links with Turkey and Persia, together with Afghanistan, in the Sa'dabad Pact of 1937, designed for mutual defence particularly against Italian pressure; but this died quickly from lack of exercise. Her practical relations with Persia have been strained by a long-drawn dispute

over the Shatt al-'Arab waterway, which was not settled until
1937, and by frequent frontier incidents which have continued diminishingly to the present day. Between Shi'i Persians
and Iraqi Sunnis there has been a certain antipathy, matched by a
warm sympathy on the part of Iraqi Shi'is. A treaty of friendship
in 1949 had no material effect on relations, and there were sharp
exchanges during the Musaddaq regime. The diminished but not
inconsiderable economic dealings between the two States have
been discussed elsewhere (p. 129).

Regard for Turkey has, as we have seen, lingered in an older
generation, where it was reinforced by admiration for the Kemalist
State. It was not inherited by younger Iraqis, who regard Turkey
as a traditional enemy of the Arabs and now an ally of the west;
they have particularly resented Turkey's absorption of Alexan-
dretta (1939) and ready acceptance of the State of Israel. The
two governments, however, once the Mosul dispute was settled
(1925–26), have maintained on the whole friendly relations,
supplemented on the part of some of the Iraqi political leaders
with personal contact. In 1941 Rashid 'Ali was prepared for
Turkish mediation in his dispute with Great Britain. In 1946
Nuri al-Sa'id, a veteran advocate of good relations, initialled a
treaty of friendship with Turkey, but in the changed political
climate it met with considerable opposition and was not ratified
until the following year. Early in 1958 the Iraqi Government gave
strong support to the Turkish case in Cyprus. Economic links
with Turkey have been slight.

With Pakistan Iraq had already a treaty of friendship (1950)
and a trade agreement—without much trade. Staunch Muslims
look with favour on Pakistan's strong Islamic character; but the
sympathies of many young nationalists are enlisted on the side of
India, with whom, and with the uncommitted nations she leads,
they are conscious of considerable fellow-feeling; Bandoengism
does not exercise the same emotional appeal as Arabism, but
nevertheless evokes a warm sense of comradeship. With India,
an antagonist of the Baghdad Pact, Iraq has a treaty of friendship
and a cultural relations agreement dating from 1952 and 1954.

Relations with the United States have been of prime importance
only since the Second War. Previously the American interest
was mainly confined to missionary activity, a share in oil production, archaeology and limited categories of trade. During the War
the connexion became closer, with assistance granted to Iraq under

lend-lease and American participation in the supply lines to Russia. After the War the United States Government, concerned with the threat of Soviet pressure, replaced British economic support to Turkey and Greece in 1947, and over the following years developed a massive programme of economic, technical and educational aid from which Iraq, as other States of the area, has benefited. Since 1954 the country has also been receiving American military equipment.

The Soviet Union and Iraq were not in diplomatic relationship before the Second War. In 1941, during the final ministry of Rashid 'Ali, the two countries agreed to establish relations; but Rashid fell from power immediately afterwards, and ministers were not exchanged until 1945. In January 1955, a month before the conclusion of her treaty with Turkey, Iraq suspended relations, having already closed her legation in Moscow; Nuri al-Sa'id subsequently stated as the reason that the Soviet Legation in Baghdad had been fomenting trouble in the country. Iraq had never recognised Communist China and in March 1958 ratified a cultural agreement with the National Chinese Government.

GOVERNMENT AND THE POLITICAL SYSTEM

UNTIL THE revolution of July 1958 the form of government in Iraq was determined by a constitution promulgated in 1924, which had been modified shortly before the revolution to accord with the federation with Jordan. By the terms of this constitution Iraq was a constitutional, representative and democratic monarchy, whose sovereignty resided in the people and had been confided by them in trust to King Faisal and his heirs after him. The royal prerogatives of a minor were to be exercised by a Regent chosen by his predecessor. In 1943 it was ordained that if there were no heir apparent to the throne an heir presumptive should be nominated from the family of King Husain of the Hijaz. On the accession of King Faisal II in 1953 his uncle, Prince 'Abdul-Ilah, became heir presumptive. The King was the supreme head of State, safeguarded and not responsible, and Commander-in-Chief of the armed forces. Legislative power was vested in the combination of King and Parliament, which consisted of a Senate and a Chamber of Deputies. The upper house was appointed by the King; the lower house was until 1953 constituted by two-stage elections, but was thereafter elected by direct secret vote of adult males. The King ordered elections to the lower house and opened, adjourned, prorogued and dissolved both houses. Before becoming law bills must be passed by both houses and confirmed by the King; if either house rejected a bill twice and the other insisted on its acceptance, it might be passed by a two-thirds majority of both houses meeting together. Should need arise, when Parliament was not in session, to take urgent measures for the maintenance of public security, to meet a public danger or extraordinary expenditure or to fulfil treaty obligations, the King was authorised, with the concurrence of the Cabinet, to issue ordinances having the force of law; these must subsequently be approved by Parliament. Executive authority resided with the Cabinet, which was responsible to the Chamber of Deputies collectively and individually for its exercise and must resign if the Chamber withheld its confidence, unless the matter in question related to one minister only, in which case the minister must resign. The Prime Minister was chosen by the King, the other ministers appointed by the King on his recommendation; since 1943 the King was empowered to dismiss the Prime Minister. Ministers must be members of Parliament or, if not, surrender office after six months; they had the right of speaking in both houses of Parliament and of voting in the house to which they belonged.

Representative constitutional government was demanded by the Iraqi Council of State which offered Faisal the throne; it had indeed become part of the creed of the politically conscious public after its adoption by the Young Turks. There was, however, no foundation of traditional practice on which to base it. Authority as exercised by Muslim rulers had been by no means without its checks, but they were neither expressed in a political constitution nor applied democratically from the bottom. With Ottoman and direct British rule removed, the indigenous political forces had to establish a balance between themselves; it was as expressing their balance that the constitution, lacking the solidarity of maturity, could be expected to maintain itself.

On paper it was ill adapted to do so, for Parliament, its very nucleus, could not directly reflect their relative strength. It represented tribal chiefs and the landlords well enough, for they influenced the votes of the majority of the electorate; and through the tribal deputies of the south it gave powerful expression to Shi'i opinion. It represented also the non-Muslim minorities, which were allotted a fixed number of seats. It could not, however,

H*

adequately represent educated townsmen as such, whose political importance was out of all proportion to their scanty numerical strength; for it was they who were the repository of political dynamism and most understood the nature of a modern State.

It was in the Cabinet that urban political consciousness rather found expression. For particular reasons it was sometimes necessary to include in it leaders of traditional social groups; but it was on the whole filled by the westernising society which was best trained for modern government. The connexion between Cabinet and Parliament was in practice less intimate than suggested by the constitution. Cabinets did not usually reflect the composition of Parliament, governmental control of elections rather making the contrary true. Ministers did not even, for a period of six months, need to be members of Parliament. Unsympathetic Parliaments were at times induced to co-operate by personal influence or the threat of dissolution. Continued friction was met by the dissolution of Parliament rather than the resignation of the Cabinet; no Cabinet has fallen on a vote of no-confidence.

The strong position of the Cabinet owed something negatively to the comparative disinterest of rural deputies in other than provincial affairs and to the decline of militant tribalism. Positively it had the advantage of education and experience, of Palace support and of the control of army, police and civil service, whose appointments it directly influenced. As important was the personal influence of its members with the different elements of society. In course of time a ministerial group crystallised within the westernising class, which, while it continued to represent the general attitude of that class, developed strong connexions outside as well as within it. Its members, by reason of their frequent tenure of office, gradually came to control circles—or pyramids— of patronage, systems of reciprocal service in a society where confidence in disinterested administration and impartial justice had still to be established. The patron might not himself be rich— and might not even exploit his influence to enrich himself—but, because ministerial office conferred the power to bestow favours, and because the minister had been often in office and was expected to return to it, he could command men's services and support, and for this reason was the more likely to retain his position. His dependants received by association some share of the numen, which they transmitted, further diluted, to their own dependants, similarly arranged in subordinate systems. In consequence of this organisation, affairs which were nominally transacted through the constitutional or administrative machinery were often settled privately within one of these communities of interest, or by negotiation between the different communities, and since the ties which bound these communities bridged the normal divisions of class, religion, locality and ideology, their patrons could together effect a balance of political forces which was beyond the capacity of Parliament. It often came about in consequence that the Cabinet not only combined effective legislative with executive power but was also the more representative body, the frequent changes of the Cabinet—whose average life has been less than a year—rather than changes of Parliament expressing the fluctuating balance of political forces. These forces at times included Shi'i sentiment and the Arab and occasionally Kurdish tribes; but until the events of 1941 the most continuous political conflict lay within the ministerial group itself. Its members had already under the Mandate established political groupings, based on political attitude—primarily towards the series of Anglo-Iraqi treaties—and personal relationship. Some of the groupings were formally constituted as political parties, for which provision had been made by law. They were designed not so much to gain support through the electoral system as to supplement it. They were usually an association of a Prime Minister and those of his coalition colleagues and the deputies who personally supported him, or else of opposition politicians who hoped by exerting pressure inside or outside Parliament to secure Cabinet representation.

The problem, given the inability of Parliament to change Cabinets, was to ensure that they did in fact change in conformity with events and the national interest. Under the Mandate the task of arbitration and mediation was undertaken by King Faisal himself. He had to a high degree the traditional qualities of a great Arab ruler: an understanding of political motives, a grasp of political essentials and a sense of political balance, and with it all a capacity to subdue strong passions in the pursuit of an end and confidence in diplomacy rather than in force to achieve lasting political decisions. Faisal had assumed personal responsibility for the nurture of the Iraqi State and perfectly appreciated the problems involved. His task demanded personal authority, which he tried at first to secure through the constitution. He wished for powers which would give him effective control of Parliament, the Cabinet and essential supplies. Overborne by political opinion, he was compelled to interpret and supplement the constitution; but his success was due even more to the wide personal ascendancy which his diplomacy, charm and integrity of purpose enabled him to establish. In his own person he united the discrete components of the nation and absorbed their stresses; and when in 1933 he died from his exertions at the early age of forty-eight the nation had lost its binding force.

King Ghazi, his young successor, had patriotism and popularity, but lacked his experience and judgment. He was in no position to curb the ambitions of political leaders and mediate in their disputes. What changes he made on the recommendation of personal advisers did not always produce tranquillity, and after the first three years his opinion was little regarded. Opposition politicians, without hope of dislodging a cabinet by peaceful means and silenced by censorship, had recourse, as we have seen, to violent action outside the constitution: to strikes, mob rioting and demonstrations, to Shi'i sectarianism and tribal rebellion and finally to the intervention of the army. The government of the final military *coup d'état* in 1941 violated the constitution to the extent of deposing the Regent, Prince 'Abdul-Ilah; its flight before British forces ended a phase of Iraqi history.

When political activity was resumed after the constraint of the war years the situation had changed in important respects. After the Rashidist collapse in 1941 the army was purged and withdrew from politics; when employed to restore order in the riots of November 1952 (p. 105) it was as a passive instrument of the régime. Tribalism, overawed by the security forces and its militancy sapped, was politically significant only in so far as successive governments required the parliamentary vote of its leaders. Politicians and shaikhs provided mutual support; the latter retained their influence by governmental indulgence and were increasingly on the defensive as a few reformist ministers and an ever larger body of public opinion turned their attention to agrarian reform.

The ministerial group, divided to some extent by personality, generation, education and policy, nevertheless maintained a unity which, in contrast with its bitter schisms of the past, appeared to its opponents discouragingly monolithic. It lost its most confirmedly Anglophobe and neutralist members in 1941, and it revolved increasingly round two centres of political power,

Nuri al-Sa'id and the Palace, whose policies, sometimes violently opposed in detail, coincided in their general trend.

Nuri al-Sa'id had during the Second War come to occupy the place left by his friend Faisal I in Iraqi and Arab politics and to gain international recognition as a statesman of magnitude. He dominated an older generation of Arabs as Gamal 'Abdul-Nasir did the new; and in the conflict of their persons the clash of the generations and their ideologies was clearly symbolised. In political experience the Pasha, as he was universally called, had no rival in Iraq; at the age of seventy he had in the summer of 1958 led fourteen of Iraq's fifty-eight cabinets and held cabinet office frequently between. He believed passionately in the progress of his country, but, distrusting rapid change on untried bases, considered that progress and stability could best be assured by firm and if necessary severe government, by political manoeuvre and above all by economic improvement, social security and gradual reform. While fighting in Faisal's Arab Revolt he had formed the conviction that the interest of the Arabs lay in close understanding with Great Britain, and to that principle he clung unwaveringly, whatever criticisms he might voice of individual British policies, notably towards Palestine. He was convinced of the menace alike of communism and of Soviet imperialism; the Baghdad Pact was largely his conception and that of Adnan Menderes. Although he was a veteran of Arab nationalism, who served the Arabs and Iraq with unsparing devotion, he was out of touch and out of sympathy with the nationalism of a later generation. He had entered political life when public opinion played a smaller part in Iraq and he made little attempt to conciliate the body of post-war opinion; indeed, he declared war on idealists whose patriotism was no less sincere than his own. To them his formidable resolution, personal integrity, quickness of decision, and political dexterity seemed the main obstacle to their cause, an obstacle with no visible term to its existence. On many of his enemies he imposed a respect compounded of fear and admiration; and part of the populace accorded him an almost affectionate regard, for he maintained connexions of familiarity and understanding with the traditional man in the Baghdad street, of whom indeed his shrewdness, toughness and humour were the perfect expression. Within the ministerial group his supremacy was only once challenged after the Second War—in the early 1950's, by the younger Shi'i statesman Salih Jabr. To Nuri's

Constitutional Union Party Salih opposed his misnamed Socialist Party of the Nation, an association of moderate conservatives which, as the rift with Nuri widened, came to depend increasingly on Shiʻi sectarian support. It was signally defeated in the elections of 1954, and Salih Jabr disappeared as a rival, to die suddenly in 1957 in the course of a senate debate.

Beside the influence of Nuri al-Saʻid stood that of the heir presumptive, Prince ʻAbdul-Ilah, who exercised sovereign powers on behalf of King Faisal II until the latter came of age in 1953, and thereafter retained his influence both in the Palace and in the general political field. A man of much personal charm, aged 45 at the time of his death in 1958, he could supplement the constitutional powers of the monarchy with wide connexions throughout the country, which recently included relationship by marriage with the influential Rabiʻa tribe. He played as active a role as Nuri al-Saʻid in political life and was considered not only an integral element but also a powerful and active maintainer of the régime; and this, together with his personal concern with details of the State machinery and State appointments, and his close association with Great Britain, incurred the suspicion of the political public. Some of the suspicion had begun to attach to the Iraqi monarchy itself, an institution with no very deep roots in popular loyalty and considered by many nationalists to separate Iraq from the body of the Arab movement. There was however considerable sympathy and indeed affection for the young King Faisal himself—aged 23 in 1958—who displayed an earnest sense of responsibility and an unassuming good will. He might, indeed, have focussed in his person that eager aspiration of young Iraqis whose enlistment behind national progress was so desirable. In fact, his public role was mainly formal, in a country where formality is apt to alienate and where his father gained popularity not only for his nationalism but also for his spontaneous contact with the people; and he was separated to some extent from his own generation of Iraqis by his English upbringing—he was educated by an English governess, at an English preparatory school and at Harrow—and by the frequent visits to England which were demanded by his health. In September 1957 his engagement was announced to the Turkish Princess Fadhila, a grand-daughter of the last Ottoman caliph ʻAbdul-Majid and great-grand-daughter of the celebrated Muhammad ʻAli Pasha of Egypt.

Dominated by an unofficial praesidium of elder statesmen and they in turn by Nuri al-Sa'id and the Palace, the ministerial group preserved their control over the country's fortunes through cabinet, parliament and individual systems of patronage. They maintained a political balance—a balance, however, in the tradition of pre-war politics, with the new trends little represented. When disorder occurred it was quelled by the security forces. The régime enjoyed the support of the landholders and a large section of the urban upper and upper-middle classes—consisting of industrialists, business men, senior officials and some of the more successful professional men—and the general acquiescence of the uneducated, most of them in any case under the influence of tribal landholders. The rapid expansion of the revenues and the institution of vast development schemes might be expected to consolidate the position of the governing group, partly by strengthening the State apparatus and subjecting more varied fields of national life to its supervision, partly by endowing the régime with wider disposal and control of employment and favours, partly by a rise in living standards, which, if it to some extent stimulated thought and criticism, might at any rate temper the violence of their practical expression.

Outwardly the post-war scene was one of greater tranquillity, but genuine stability was denied by the existence of opposition forces which were the more explosive from suppression. Their hostility to the régime rested partly on its foreign policy, partly on its monopoly and use of power. They comprised a majority of educated Iraqis, and, in particular, the students, teachers, and medium and lower levels of the civil service and professions. Some of their criticism, though not necessarily their positive proposals and active hostility, was echoed by senior officials and successful professional and business men, numbers of whom, indeed, shared their ideology. This was for the most part the socialist nationalism which has predominated in the Arab world since the Second War. Its most precise manifestation as an organised political movement has been the Ba'th Party (Arab Socialist Party of Renaissance), powerful in Syria and Jordan but with few formal members in Iraq, where it was proscribed. Its personification, for young Iraqis as for other Arabs, has come to be Gamal 'Abdul-Nasir, their nationalism having a messianic quality typical, as in the past, of Arab political aspiration.

In foreign affairs these new Iraqi nationalists demanded Arab solidarity, uncompromising rejection of the State of Israel, parity

of treatment with foreign Powers, and independence of those
Powers and their alignments. With these general principles they
usually combined suspicion or antagonism towards Great Britain
and what they termed her imperialism. This was partly a legacy
of the mandatory period, of the British intervention in 1941 to
unseat a keenly nationalist government, and of the Balfour Declaration and its consequences; it was partly the fruit of three decades
of propaganda, which had accepted Britain as a convenient scape-
goat for all manner of ills; but it arose no less from the nationalists'
interpretation of the current situation. They believed that Great
Britain intended to protect her interests in the Arab countries with
a certainty which only control could ensure, and was exercising such
control through the maintenance of Israel and of compliant Arab
governments which allowed themselves to be drawn into her defence
system; these and Israel between them might be expected to contain
Arab nationalist movements or governments which challenged
Britain's special position. Not content with this, Britain was
believed to dictate the conduct of affairs within the allied States
themselves. The intervention in 1941, as later the Suez campaign,
they considered to prove that in the last resort she was prepared
to pursue her ends by open force. The supposed subservience of
Iraq to British interests was itself reckoned an affront to national
dignity; and its material implications were equally resented, particularly the possibility that Iraq might be involved on the side of
Great Britain in war against the Soviet Union, with whom the
nationalists—quite the contrary—had no quarrel. Within Iraq
herself they believed that the assurance of British support encouraged the government to perpetuate a social, economic and
political system which they condemned. The United States came
to incur hardly less suspicion in their eyes for her part in establishing and upholding Israel and their belief that her economic and
technical aid constituted a still more insidious imperialism than the
British and an intervention no less in Iraq's internal affairs. Yet
for the two western States themselves—their democracy, social
conscience, culture and technical skill—many of the nationalists
had the profoundest admiration; many indeed had been educated
in their universities and were intellectually and culturally committed to them. They regretted only their foreign policies, which
seemed doomed to divide them from the new generation of Arabs.
With reservations about its attitude to Israel, some of them had
particular faith in the British Labour Party, should it return to
office.

If neutrality, as conceived by a majority of nationalists, implied wariness or defiance of the west, to many also it carried a predisposition towards Russia. Free, in their eyes, from the taint of imperialism, she was their self-appointed champion against the west, a juggler in attitudes towards Israel, and a flaunter of unconditional aid. Some attributed her policy to simple unselfish friendship; others, trusting in the length of their spoons, would happily fraternise with a new devil to circumvent the old. They were impressed by Soviet claims of social and political justice, which the west no doubt possessed in a more pleasing form but seemed unwilling to export to the Middle East; and as the cold war set in the Soviet dove of peace alighted pat to soothe their fears. They discounted the possibility of Soviet aggression against the Arab States, considering any suggestion of it a western ruse to distract their attention from Israel. To join with Britain in a Pact directed against Russia and certain to provoke her, they regarded as lunacy—or deliberate malice.

It was not co-operation with the west in itself that they rejected. They recognised (even if some of them resented) their need of its technical assistance and its market for oil, and could even conceive situations in which they might welcome western military support. They rejected rather what seemed to them the régime's permanent marriage with the west in preference to the Arab States, an unequal relationship, they considered, whose very constancy denied the possibility of favourable bargaining. And although they might, if in office, have had recourse in some cases to identical consultations and agreements with western governments, they condemned them when undertaken by a government in which they had no confidence.

Iraqi policy towards the Arab States they judged to have been perverted not only through predilection for the west but also through dynastic and personal rivalries which Arab nationalism, with unity as its ideal and if anything republican in spirit, could not but reprehend. When the conflict was with vociferously nationalist States and with the idol of the new nationalism himself the offence was the greater. Hashimite aspirations towards Syria and alignment with Turkey (p. 215), they argued, had created the divisions amid which Palestine was lost; and Iraq's subsequent alliance with Turkey and Great Britain had made the divisions permanent and driven the nationalist States perhaps closer to Russia than they wished. The union with Jordan was the last in a

H**

series of unpopular moves. The nationalists deprecated any consolidation of the Hashimite bloc; and this particular move was
in simple reaction to the United Arab Republic (which they
ecstatically welcomed), undertaken to prevent its extension to
Jordan. The suggestion of Iraqi military intervention against the
Jordanian or Lebanese opposition they would consider the ultimate
crime against Arabism and progress.

Their domestic judgments were, as we have seen, interwoven
with their view of foreign relationships, for they held the west
responsible to a large degree for Iraq's internal situation. In this
sphere their demands were for the free operation of democratic
machinery, including freedom of association and expression, a
competent administration uninfluenced by private interest or by
family or sectional loyalties, social reform concerned primarily
with the agrarian system, and vigorous and efficient prosecution
of development programmes; under all these heads they accused
the government of falling short.

This greater interest in democratic rights and social justice is
what mainly distinguished post- from pre-war nationalism. Before
the Second War the public, sections of it primed with the fascist
philosophy of the period, had given little support to the *Ahali*
idealists who advocated these principles. Nor had material
conditions been such as to direct attention to them; the most
depressed element of the population—the peasantry—was inert
and inarticulate, while the political classes of the towns found life
reasonably easy and government and administration reasonably
satisfactory; most cabinets moreover commanded support for their
nationalist foreign policy. The War imposed on the new State its
first serious economic stringency (p. 142) and acutely embarrassed
the still maturing administrative machine. Its efficiency and
integrity were widely questioned; shortcomings which might have
passed elsewhere were castigated mercilessly in a government
supported by British arms. Resentment crystallised round democratic and reformist ideas with which the propaganda of all the
conflicting Powers had flooded the country. Under their stimulus
there was very general criticism of post-war governments for their
conduct of internal as well as of foreign affairs, and in particular
for the manipulated elections, which had provoked far less complaint before the war, the suppression of newspapers and political
parties, the incarceration of political suspects, the expulsion of
students and the dismissal of civil servants for expressing political

opinions. The severer of these measures were applied only intermittently and were possibly magnified by the public; even so
they aroused the lively apprehension of the educated classes, in
whose eyes Iraq was no better than a police State. The primary
target of repression was communism, but the term could be
interpreted to include almost any shade of reformist opinion. At
the same time there were constant accusations of administrative
incompetence and of corruption from the top; and those who
lacked influence bitterly resented the vagaries of appointment and
promotion and the leisurely convolutions of bureaucratic procedure. Some of the shortcomings were, as we have seen, less those
of the individual politician or even of the political system than of
society as a whole, whose loyalties made nepotism—though not
peculation—something of a virtue, whose traditional outlook was
still adapting itself to a mechanical age; these obstacles would
confront any government, whatever its nature and intentions,
although some governments might strive more successfully to
overcome them. And if the régime never achieved radical social
reform—though a land-tax was at least attempted by the Jamali
Government in 1953 (p. 106) and was again under consideration
in 1958—a number of its members showed sincere enthusiasm for
national development and considerable capacity for its planning
and conduct, qualities for which they were perhaps conceded too
little credit. Yet the fact that credit was not given and that public
opinion was never enlisted behind the development programme
is perhaps in itself a condemnation. It is true that the government
began to inform the public of its projects too late and with too
little imagination, and that some of those projects—the construction of pretentious public buildings, for example—were
flagrantly tactless; but the basic truth is that it had ceased to
represent the intellectually and politically dynamic forces of the
country. In this almost complete breakdown of confidence all its
actions were suspect.

The nationalists' case rested on simple political fact or what
they honestly conceived as such. Much of the intensity, sometimes
amounting to hatred, with which they held it resulted no doubt
from fear and frustration in the face of what they interpreted as
treachery at home and vigilant malice abroad, from whose supposed alliance they despaired of deliverance. The unceasing
propaganda in newspapers, when they were permitted, and the
more violent voice of foreign radio naturally had their emotional

effect. Some of the bitterness might also be assigned to the
economic and social condition of the lower and lower-middle
educated classes in whom the new nationalism had most solidly
been represented. It was they who suffered most from the high
cost of living and white-collar under-employment of recent years,
whose drab existence conflicted most with new aspirations, who
most felt the lack of influential support; and it was they of whom,
perhaps, most of all, might be expected the psychology of the
intellectually, morally and spiritually displaced. Their education
exposed them to the siren cadences of the Arabic language, which
lure to extreme expression and convince of its truth; and it did
not always temper that conviction with the gift of objective logic.
But if some of them appeared unrealistic in their thoughts, there
existed men at the other end of the scale, many of them educated
in the west, some experienced in affairs, whose nationalism rested
less on emotion than on logic and practical appraisal; and with the
evolution of education their number was rapidly increasing. It
would remain to be seen in a time of crisis which end of the scale
would determine nationalist policy.

Frustration was inherent in the Iraqi opposition. It despaired
of winning acceptance for its policies or at times even a hearing
for its voice. The constitution offered no effective channel. However organised, the nationalists could influence the election only
of urban deputies, except in so far as the family connexions of a few
of their leaders could command rural support. The bulk of the rural
vote—decisive in any election—was controlled by the large landholders, whose tenants were only now and in limited areas becoming conscious of an independent identity; canvassing on the
estates of a powerful landholder was, governmental intervention
apart, a practical impossibility, and if a landholder should himself, for whatever reason, be won to the opposition side, he was
likely to find a more amenable kinsman elected in his place. The
opposition groups could hope no more for significant cabinet
appointment than for a parliamentary majority, for admission to
the ministerial group was by co-option or by Palace dispensation.
Their constitutional activity was consequently confined, for the
most part, to moral gestures in the form of speeches and demonstrations of solidarity—including resignation—in the Chamber.

Nor did they, even so, organise themselves to the greatest effect.
A number of opposition parties were formed after the Second War,
but, like the ministerial groups, they were mostly associations

of politicians and publicists, without machinery for wider participation; the nationalist public was not directly represented in them,
though it could feel an identity of purpose. While operating openly
they achieved only intermittent co-operation, suffering in the
intervals from the individualism which has characterised Iraqi
politics; it was only when they were finally suppressed that their
personal and doctrinal differences were compounded. Nor was
their activity, alone or united, of that patient, unspectacular kind
which might slowly have sapped the position of their adversaries,
but consisted rather of sudden incursions, with long periods of
lassitude or undirected fulmination between; it is true that governmental vigilance also impeded continuous activity. They always
spurned the possible fruits of compromise, partly from tempera-
mental aversion, partly from the fear that if they made concessions
they would be cheated of the recompense.

When political life was resumed in 1946 several opposition
parties were formed. Two of them, with fellow-travelling principles, lasted only to the following year, when they were suppressed
in a governmental drive against communism, and a third, pro-
fessing a pre-war type of nationalism, disappeared almost as
quickly. The most enduring have been the Independence (*Istiqlal*)
and National Democratic (*Watani Dimuqrati*) Parties, both of
which were openly active between 1946 and their suppression in
1954 and subsequently worked under cover. The former was
founded by dedicated nationalists of the pre-war school and
associates of Rashid 'Ali—Muhammad Mahdi Kubba, Siddiq
Shanshal and Fa'iq al-Samarra'i—who modified their philosophy
in response to the changing political atmosphere and moved into
closer relationship with the left-wing National Democratic Party.
This was led by Kamil Chadirchi, a landowner of deep reformist
conviction, who had been prominent in the *Ahali* movement of the
thirties and enjoyed the regard of much of the educated public.
He and a number of young intellectuals who associated with him
began and, despite frustration, probably continued as moderate
socialists; but the government accused the party and its influential
newspaper of communist infiltration and closed them both on
this ground. The opposition gained its greatest constitutional
success indirectly, in alliance with members of the ministerial
group. In 1951 an association called the United Popular Front was
formed by a number of senior statesmen and politicians, who
sought to combine their own prestige with the opposition dynamic

in a policy of neutrality and reform; it gained parliamentary and cabinet places but was unable to use them to effect and quickly disintegrated. In 1954 all political parties were dissolved and their promised resurrection never materialised.

Without hope of gaining influence by constitutional means, the opposition leaders sought instruments outside the constitution. Of increasing importance was the moral force of educated public opinion which, in varying degrees, they both represented and moulded with their indefatigable Press. It was a lever which could act directly upon the ruling group itself. Even the most conservative ministers found it inexpedient formally to reject the new nationalist ideas; and the group contained young men of energy and goodwill who were largely in sympathy with them. But the uncertain prospect of gradual change accorded ill with the natural impatience of the opposition, who feared, with some reason, that the process of national development would work against them.

Their only certain hope seemed to lie in the mobilisation of material forces against the régime. Economic sanctions, as we have, were denied them. Private resources were largely aligned with the government, which was coming moreover to dominate the whole economic life of the country. Labour and the civil service were never adequately organised to paralyse. Labour had still to develop enough self-conscious cohesion to withstand official discouragement, and when it did unite for positive action the object was economic rather than political. Medium and junior civil servants had much sympathy with the opposition cause, but its expression was hampered by the prohibition—applied with some vigilance—against political activity in the public services.

The most powerful blows were undoubtedly delivered through the instrument of the urban masses, whose outbursts in January 1948 and November 1952 (pp. 103, 105) brought down a cabinet and led respectively to the repudiation of the Portsmouth Treaty (p. 224) and to a quicker modification of the electoral system (from which, in practice, the opposition derived little benefit). Demonstrations were commonly started by students, not invariably for political reasons, gained political direction from the legal or underground political groups, and were quickly swollen by the people of the street. Once in motion, events were apt to pass out of the hands of the instigators, who might however use them to cover organised destruction and arson. When trouble threatened, resolute governments were quick to take preventive action and so, as in the Suez crisis, suppressed or forestalled potentially decisive movements. If, on the other hand, the police lacked timely or clear instructions, the situation might escape from their control, especially if the mob were inflamed by bloodshed; in these circumstances the army was invoked to restore order in November 1952 (p. 103).

The events of that month demonstrated what was logically inescapable, that the army was no less in the 'fifties than in the 'thirties the ultimate arbiter; the cardinal question was its obedience to the régime. Some of the officers had personal connexions with the government or the Palace, others were well content with recent improvements in pay and service. Many, however, clearly shared the views of the middle classes—were in fact the middle classes armed and in uniform—and were impressed by the military revolutions in Syria and Egypt, which recalled the political role of the Iraqi army before the Second War. There were at times rumours of disaffection among them, particularly in April 1957, at the time of the opposition putsch in Jordan. It is now known that a small but well organised officers' movement was active for several years. Not surprisingly, but at a moment that could hardly have been predicted, it became the spearhead of nationalist opposition.

Parallel with the new nationalism there has run another opposition strand, that of communism, organised in several underground groups. Sympathy with the Soviet Union apart, post-war nationalism looks on communism rather more favourably than did the fascist-influenced nationalism of the thirties, for it has itself developed a socialist ideology, and the religious voices which condemned communism before the war are now heard more faintly. The Iraqi moreover accepts the predominance of the State as natural. The Ottoman legacy of bureaucracy and centralisation has never died out and there is no deep-rooted tradition of private enterprise. Since the First War the State has further employed a majority of the educated public, has controlled the revenues from oil, has been the legal owner of most of the land, and is now playing a leading part in economic development and social security. With étatism, on the other hand, goes a sturdy feeling of personal independence, a dislike of regimentation and an individualism which has threatened to disrupt Iraqi communism itself and militates against acceptance of communist government as such. In opposition nationalist leaders might be expected to establish limited co-operation with communism, in office to regard it with considerable suspicion.

Much of what has passed for communism in Iraq has been fellow-travelling nationalism or nationalism with Soviet sympathies, born of political and general frustration, the attraction of the new and perhaps the quest for some more comprehensive system of life. There has, however, been a core of convinced communists and trained activists, in contact with larger organisations in Persia and afterwards in Syria. Although its effectiveness has been limited by internal division, it has been persistent and resilient enough to constitute a danger. Governments, indeed, have taken communism seriously. There were determined drives against it in 1947, 1949 and 1952-3, and in 1949 four of its leaders were hanged and fellow-travelling parties closed down. In 1938 communism was made a criminal offence, and in 1954 a law was passed depriving convicted communists of Iraqi nationality. Measures against the movement have in recent years been concerted with Jordan and the neighbouring members of the Baghdad Pact; and in 1957 a special security police was established to deal with subversion. Frequent arrests, followed periodically by conditional releases, were claimed to have kept communism on the defensive, but its organisation and activity have continued in being, and in the event of persistent frustration or a breakdown of government it might prove to be the ultimate beneficiary. Iraq's best defence against communism at the present time may well be a nationalist and reformist government which commands the confidence of the people and feels no necessity to seek Soviet protection.

Epilogue

At 5 a.m. on 14 July 1958 a group of officers seized control of Baghdad. The King, Crown Prince 'Abdul-Ilah and other members of the royal family were killed; Nuri al-Sa'id escaped and was killed the following day. The military stroke was accompanied in the capital by an outburst of mob violence, which accounted for the death of Ibrahim Hashim, deputy premier of the Federation, and four foreign visitors, and for severe damage to the British Embassy and the shooting of one of its staff. No other foreigners were known to be molested. The total number of dead was given as thirty. Order was eventually restored and the revolutionary government quickly extended its hold over the remainder of the country. It had overwhelming popular support.

The revolution was planned and led by Brigadiers 'Abdul-Karim Qasim and 'Abdul-Salam Muhammad 'Arif. Their aim was broadcast as being to liberate Iraq from the domination of a corrupt clique installed by imperialists in their own interest, and to entrust the conduct of affairs to a government emanating from the people. A popular republic would be formed to maintain Iraqi unity, establish fraternal ties with other Arab and Islamic countries, work in accordance with the principles of the United Nations and the Bandoeng Conference, and honour all pledges and treaties in the light of Iraqi interests.

A Sovereignty Council was formed on the morning of 14 July, consisting of General Najib al-Ruba'i as President, Muhammad Mahdi Kubba (president of the *Istiqlal* Party) and Khalid al-Naqshbandi (a former provincial governor). A cabinet was at the same time appointed under the premiership of General 'Abdul-Karim Qasim, who also held the portfolio of Defence and the position of Commander-in-Chief, with Brigadier 'Abdul-Salam 'Arif Deputy Premier and Minister of the Interior. The cabinet contained one other officer—Brigadier Naji Talib in

Social Affairs—and ten civilians: Siddiq Shanshal of the *Istiqlal* Party, Muhammad Hadid of the National Democratic Party, 'Abdul-Jabbar Jomard of the United Popular Front (pp. 105 and 241), Shaikh Baba 'Ali, the English- and American-educated son of the Kurdish leader Shaikh Mahmud (p. 209), Mustafa 'Ali, Jabr 'Umar, Ibrahim Kubba, Fu'ad al-Rikabi, Muhammad Salih Mahmud and Rashid Hajj Mahmud.

The Sovereignty Council decreed the abolition of the monarchy and establishment of a republic and declared Iraq's secession from the Arab Federation. At the end of July a provisional constitution was announced, which stated Iraq to be a sovereign independent republic and part of the Arab nation, with Islam as its official religion but legal equality and freedom of worship for all. Freedom of thought and expression were guaranteed and also private ownership, but agricultural ownership was to be defined by law. The presidency of the Republic was to be vested in a triumviral Council of State, and both legislative and executive power in the Cabinet. The people would subsequently be consulted on the permanent political system of the Republic. A large number of senior officers and officials were quickly replaced and the funds of some seventy-five ex-ministers, senior officials and other persons of influence were subsequently declared frozen. Some of these men were placed under arrest and it was announced that certain members of the previous régime would be tried for their actions; but many of those, it was said, who were deluded by the old régime had repented and become good citizens.

The new government declared its intention of pressing on with national development and raising the standard of living of the people. Agricultural expansion and reform—in which reform of land tenure was included—would have priority. Industry would be encouraged by protection and private capital would be attracted from real estate to industrial investment. Imports would be limited to goods which domestic production could not provide and the importation of luxury goods would be curtailed. Private enterprise would in general be encouraged, but not the investment of foreign capital. Continued membership of the sterling area (a matter long discussed by the previous government) would depend on the development of Iraq's foreign relations. The government meant to reduce inequalities of wealth and income. Taxation was to be reformed to ensure a more equitable grading of income tax rates and tax evasion would be stopped; indirect taxation would be reduced, agriculture would be taxed and a land tax would probably be introduced. Wholesale and retail price control was imposed; in particular the price of bread was lowered. The length of the authorised working day was reduced and committees were formed to investigate the problems of unemployment and rural labour. The tribal system of justice was abolished (p. 158).

One of the first acts of the new government was to acknowledge the United Arab Republic, and on 17 July the Soviet Union and Communist China were also recognised. All three had from the first supported the revolutionary régime. With the United Arab Republic a member of the new cabinet stated that Iraq would establish close, possibly federal relations, not however amounting to unitary Statehood. Personal contact was quickly established with President Gamal 'Abdul-Nasir and on 19 July an agreement was concluded between Iraq and the United Arab Republic which provided for mutual defence and for economic and cultural co-operation. The new government was recognised by the Muslim members of the Baghdad Pact at the end of July. It had emphasised its adherence to existing political and economic commitments, the latter specifically including current oil agreements, and expressed its anxiety to continue and increase the flow of Iraqi oil to the west. Provided that relations were based on mutual interest and respect it wished to co-operate with the west as with other friendly Powers; recognition of communist States did not mean that it was itself communist. On the strength of the government's assurances Great Britain extended recognition on 1 August and the United States on 2 August.

Appendices

LIST OF CABINETS
TABLE OF ADMINISTRATIVE UNITS
NOTE ON BOOKS

Appendix 1

LIST OF CABINETS

Oct 1920–Aug 1921 Provisional Government of 'Abdul-Rahman al-Gailani.

KING FAISAL I (Aug 1921–Sep 1933)

Sep 1921–Aug 1922 'Abdul-Rahman al-Gailani
Sep 1922–Nov 1922 'Abdul-Rahman al-Gailani
Nov 1922–Nov 1923 'Abdul-Muhsin al-Sa'dun
Nov 1923–Aug 1924 Ja'far al-'Askari
Aug 1924–Jun 1925 Yasin al-Hahimi
Jun 1925–Nov 1926 'Abdul-Muhsin al-Sa'dun
Nov 1926–Jan 1928 Ja'far al-'Askari
Jan 1928–Jan 1929 'Abdul-Muhsin al-Sa'dun
Apr 1929–Aug 1929 Taufiq al-Suwaidi
Sep 1929–Nov 1929 'Abdul-Muhsin al-Sa'dun
Nov 1929–Mar 1930 Naji al-Suwaidi
Mar 1930–Oct 1931 Nuri al-Sa'id
Oct 1931–Oct 1932 Nuri al-Sa'id
Nov 1932–Mar 1933 Naji Shaukat
Mar 1933–Sep 1933 Rashid 'Ali al-Gailani

KING GHAZI (Sep 1933–Apr 1939)

Sep 1933–Oct 1933 Rashid 'Ali al-Gailani
Nov 1933–Feb 1934 Jamil al-Midfa'i
Feb 1934–Aug 1934 Jamil al-Midfa'i
Aug 1934–Feb 1935 'Ali Jaudat al-Ayyubi
Mar 1935 Jamil al-Midfa'i
Mar 1935–Oct 1936 Yasin al-Hashimi
Oct 1936–Aug 1937 Hikmat Sulaiman
Aug 1937–Dec 1938 Jamil al-Midfa'i
Dec 1938–Apr 1939 Nuri al-Sa'id

KING FAISAL II (Apr 1939–Jul 1958: Regency of Prince
'Abdul-Ilah Apr 1939–May 1953)

Apr 1939–Feb 1940	Nuri al-Sa'id
Feb 1940–Mar 1940	Nuri al-Sa'id
Mar 1940–Jan 1941	Rashid 'Ali al-Gailani
Feb 1941–Apr 1941	General Taha al-Hashimi
Apr 1941	Government of National Defence
Apr 1941–May 1941	Rashid 'Ali al-Gailani
Jun 1941–Oct 1941	Jamil al-Midfa'i
Oct 1941–Oct 1942	Nuri al-Sa'id
Oct 1942–Dec 1943	Nuri al-Sa'id
Dec 1943–Jun 1944	Nuri al-Sa'id
Jun 1944–Aug 1944	Hamdi al-Pachachi
Aug 1944–Jan 1946	Hamdi al-Pachachi
Feb 1946–May 1946	Taufiq al-Suwaidi
Jun 1946–Nov 1946	Arshad al-'Umari
Nov 1946–Mar 1947	Nuri al-Sa'id
Mar 1947–Jan 1948	Salih Jabr
Jan 1948–Jun 1948	Muhammad al-Sadr
Jun 1948–Jan 1949	Muzahim al-Pachachi
Jan 1949–Dec 1949	Nuri al-Sa'id
Dec 1949–Feb 1950	'Ali Jaudat al-Ayyubi
Feb 1950–Sep 1950	Taufiq al-Suwaidi
Sep 1950–Jul 1952	Nuri al-Sa'id
Jul 1952–Nov 1952	Mustafa al-'Umari
Nov 1952–Jan 1953	General Nur al-Din Mahmud
Jan 1953–May 1953	Jamil al-Midfa'i
May 1953–Sep 1953	Jamil al-Midfa'i
Sep 1953–Mar 1954	Fadhil al-Jamali
Mar 1954–Apr 1954	Fadhil al-Jamali
Apr 1954–Jul 1954	Arshad al-'Umari
Aug 1954–Dec 1955	Nuri al-Sa'id
Dec 1955–Jun 1957	Nuri al-Sa'id
Jun 1957–Dec 1957	'Ali Jaudat al-Ayyubi
Dec 1957–Mar 1958	'Abdul-Wahhab Mirjan
Mar 1958–May 1958	Nuri al-Sa'id
May 1958–Jul 1958	Ahmad Muktar Baban

Appendix 2

TABLE OF ADMINISTRATIVE UNITS

LIWA	AREA IN SQ. KM.	POPU-LATION*	COMPONENT QADHAS WITH AREA IN SQ. KM.
Baghdad .	12,800	1,307,000	Baghdad (2,000); Kadhimiya (1,600); Samarra (6,700); Tikrit (1,200); Mahmudiya (1,300).
Mosul . .	29,600	718,000	Shora (8,000); 'Amadiya (3,000); Zakho (2,200); Dohuk (2,200); 'Aqra (3,200); Sinjar (4,800); Shaikhan (1,500); Tall 'Afar (4,700).
Basra . .	12,300	503,000	Basra (4,500); Abu al-Khasib (3,900); Qurna (4,000).
Kirkuk . .	20,400	389,000	Kirkuk (5,700); Kifri (5,200); Chamchamal (2,500); Tuz Khurmatu (7,000).
Arbil . .	15,700	273,000	Arbil (3,000); Shaqlawa (1,100); Makhmur (4,100); Koi Sanjaq (2,000); Rowanduz (4,700); Zibar (800).
Sulaimaniya .	11,800	300,000	Sulaimaniya (3,100); Halabja (3,100); Shahrbazher (2,000); Pizhdar (1,200); Raniya (2,300).
Dulaim . . (H.Q. Ramadi)	40,800	234,000	Ramadi (15,500); Faluja (4,400); 'Ana (20,900).
Hilla . .	5,400	354,000	Hilla (1,200); Hashimiya (1,800); Hindiya (1,100); Musaiyib (1,400).
Kut . .	16,600	290,000	Kut (5,100); Hai (2,500); Badra (3,800); Suwaira (5,200).
Karbala . .	6,100	217,000	Karbala (5,700); Najaf (400).
Diwaniya .	15,100	508,000	Diwaniya (2,300); 'Afaq (4,400); Samawa (4,500); Shamiya (2,400); Abu Sukhair (1,500).
Muntafiq (H.Q. Nasiriya)	14,800	456,000	Nasiriya (5,500); Suq al-Shuyukh (4,300); Rifa'i (3,200); Shatra (1,800).
Diyala . . (H.Q. Ba'quba)	16,100	330,000	Ba'quba (1,300); Khalis (3,600); Khanaqin (3,500); Mandali (6,600); Miqdadiya (1,100).
'Amara .	18,400	330,000	'Amara (8,500) ; 'Ali al-Gharbi (5,500); Qal'at Salih (4,500).
Northern Desert	101,300 ⎫		
Southern Desert	76,100 ⎬ 69,000		
Al-Jazira Desert	31,200 ⎭		
TOTAL .	444,500	6,496,000	

*Preliminary figures for 1957 census; the total includes an estimate for persons not yet registered at time of publication.

253

Appendix 3

NOTE ON BOOKS

THE GENERAL reader may find the following selection of books helpful; they are all readily accessible in libraries, if not all in print. For a more detailed study of the pre-1914 period the easily available French bibliography of J. Sauvaget is recommended, entitled 'Introduction à l'histoire de l'Orient musulman' (Paris 1942); and for modern Iraq (to 1950) bibliographies are to be found as appendices in the books listed below under LONGRIGG, S. H.

1] ANTIQUITY

Cambridge Ancient History, vols I-III (Camb., 1923–5)

Lloyd, Seton F. H.	*Mesopotamia* (London, 1936)
	Ruined Cities of Iraq (Oxford, 1943)
	Twin Rivers (Oxford, 1943)
	Foundations in the Dust (Oxford, 1949)
Mackay, D.	*Ancient Cities of Iraq* (Baghdad, 1929)
Smith, Sydney	*Early History of Assyria* (London, 1928)
Speiser, E. A.	*Mesopotamian Origins* (Philadelphia, 1930)
Woolley, Sir C. L.	*The Sumerians* (London, 1936)

2] ISLAMIC PERIOD (*to 1914*)

Alexander, C. M.	*Baghdad in Bygone Days* (London, 1928)
Bowen, H.	*The Life and Times of 'Ali Ibn 'Isa, the Good Vizier* (Cambridge, 1928)
Gibb, H. A. R. and Bowen, H.	*Islamic Society and the West*, vol I parts i and ii (Oxford, 1950, 1957)
Hitti, P.	*History of the Arabs* (London, 1940)
Huart, C.	*Histoire des Arabes* (Paris, 1912)
Le Strange, G.	*Lands of the Eastern Caliphate* (Cambridge, 1905)
	Baghdad during the Abbassid Caliphate (Oxford, reprinted 1924)
Levy, R.	*The Social Structure of Islam* (Cambridge, 1957)
Lewis, B.	*The Arabs in History* (London, 1950)
Longrigg, S. H.	*Four Centuries of Modern Iraq* (Oxford, 1925)
Mez, A.	*The Renaissance of Islam* (London, 1933)
Muir, Sir W.	*The Caliphate* (4th ed., Edinburgh, 1915)

Some interesting travel books (period 1550–1914) are those of R. Fitch (1583), P. Teixeira (1604), P. della Valle (1615), J. B. Tavernier (1638 ff), A. Hamilton (1721 f.), E. Ives (1758), C. Niebuhr (1765), J. S. Buckingham (1816), C. J. Rich (1820), J. R. Wellsted (1830 f.), A. N. Groves (1830 f.), J. B. Fraser (1834), W. F. Ainsworth (1836 ff.), Sir A. H. Layard (1840 ff.), Lady A. Blunt (1878), Sir M. Sykes (1899 ff.), E. B. Sloane (1908), G. L. Bell (1909). (Dates are those of the travels: for bibliographical details, see Longrigg, op. cit.).

3] *Since 1914*

Antonius, G.	*The Arab Awakening* (London, 1938)
Bell, Miss G. L.	*Letters* (London, 1927)
Bonné, A.	*The Economic Development of the Middle East* (London, 1945)
	State and Economics in the Middle East (London, 1955)
Central Office of Information.	*Paiforce* (London, 1948)
Damluji, F.	*Some Aspects of Modern Iraq* (London, 1950)
Edmonds, C. J.	*Kurds, Turks and Arabs* (London, 1957)
Fisher, W. B.	*The Middle East* (London, 1950)
Foster, H. A.	*The Making of Modern Iraq* (Oklahoma, 1935)
'Fulanain'	*Hajji Rikkan* (London, 1927)
Graves, P.	*The Life of Sir Percy Cox* (London 1941)
Hourani, A. H.	*Minorities in the Arab World* (Oxford, 1947)
International Bank.	*Economic Development of Iraq* (Washington, 1952)
Ireland, P. W.	*Iraq* (London, 1937)
Kedourie, E.	*England and the Middle East, the Destruction of the Ottoman Empire 1914–21* (London, 1956)
Khadduri, M.	*Independent Iraq* (London, 1950)
Kirk, G.	*The Middle East in the War* (London, 1952)
	The Middle East: 1945–50 (London, 1954)
Laqueur, W. Z.	*Communism and Nationalism in the Middle East* (London, 1956)
Longrigg, S. H.	*Iraq 1900 to 1950* (London, 1953)
	Oil in the Middle East (London, 1954)
Luke, Sir H.	*Mosul and its Minorities* (London, 1925)
Main, E.	*Iraq from Mandate to Independence* (London, 1935)
Maxwell, G.	*A Reed shaken by the Wind* (London, 1957)
Moberly, F. J.	*The Campaign in Mesopotamia* (London, 1923)
Philby, H. St J. B.	*Arabian Days* (London, 1948)
Salter, Lord	*The Development of Iraq: a Plan of Action* (Iraq Development Board 1955)

Stark, Miss F.   *Baghdad Sketches* (London, 1937)
                        East is West (London, 1945)
                        Beyond Euphrates (London, 1951)
Stewart, D. and   *New Babylon* (London, 1956)
  Haylock, J.
Temperley, H. W. V.   *The Peace Conference of Paris* (vol VI London,
                        1921)
Toynbee, A. J.   *Survey of International Affairs* for 1925, '28, '30,
                        '34, '36 (London)
Warriner, Miss D.   *Land Reform and Development in the Middle East*
                        (London, 1957)
Wilson, Sir A. T.   *Loyalties, Mesopotamia: 1914–17* (London, 1930)
                        Mesopotamia, 1917–20: a Clash of Loyalties
                        (London, 1931)